W9-CDF-830

**Keep this book. You will
need it and use it throughout
your career.**

About the American Hotel & Lodging Association (AH&LA)

Founded in 1910, AH&LA is the trade association representing the lodging industry in the United States. AH&LA is a federation of state lodging associations throughout the United States with 11,000 lodging properties worldwide as members. The association offers its members assistance with governmental affairs representation, communications, marketing, hospitality operations, training and education, technology issues, and more. For information, call 202-289-3100.

LODGING, the management magazine of AH&LA, is a "living textbook" for hospitality students that provides timely features, industry news, and vital lodging information.

About the Educational Institute of AH&LA (EI)

An affiliate of AH&LA, the Educational Institute is the world's largest source of quality training and educational materials for the lodging industry. EI develops textbooks and courses that are used in more than 1,200 colleges and universities worldwide, and also offers courses to individuals through its Distance Learning program. Hotels worldwide rely on EI for training resources that focus on every aspect of lodging operations. Industry-tested videos, CD-ROMs, seminars, and skills guides prepare employees at every skill level. EI also offers professional certification for the industry's top performers. For information about EI's products and services, call 800-349-0299 or 407-999-8100.

About the American Hotel & Lodging Educational Foundation (AH&LEF)

An affiliate of AH&LA, the American Hotel & Lodging Educational Foundation provides financial support that enhances the stability, prosperity, and growth of the lodging industry through educational and research programs. AH&LEF has awarded hundreds of thousands of dollars in scholarship funds for students pursuing higher education in hospitality management. AH&LEF has also funded research projects on topics important to the industry, including occupational safety and health, turnover and diversity, and best practices in the U.S. lodging industry. For information, call 202-289-3180.

MARKETING
in the
HOSPITALITY
INDUSTRY

Educational Institute Books

UNIFORM SYSTEM OF ACCOUNTS FOR THE LODGING INDUSTRY
Tenth Revised Edition

RESORT DEVELOPMENT AND MANAGEMENT
Second Edition
Chuck Y. Gee

PLANNING AND CONTROL FOR FOOD AND BEVERAGE OPERATIONS
Sixth Edition
Jack D. Ninemeier

UNDERSTANDING HOSPITALITY LAW
Fourth Edition
Jack P. Jefferies/Banks Brown

SUPERVISION IN THE HOSPITALITY INDUSTRY
Third Edition
Raphael R. Kavanaugh/Jack D. Ninemeier

MANAGEMENT OF FOOD AND BEVERAGE OPERATIONS
Fourth Edition
Jack D. Ninemeier

MANAGING FRONT OFFICE OPERATIONS
Seventh Edition
Michael L. Kasavana/Richard M. Brooks

MANAGING SERVICE IN FOOD AND BEVERAGE OPERATIONS
Third Edition
Ronald F. Cichy/Philip J. Hickey, Jr.

THE LODGING AND FOOD SERVICE INDUSTRY
Sixth Edition
Gerald W. Lattin

SECURITY AND LOSS PREVENTION MANAGEMENT
Second Edition
Raymond C. Ellis, Jr./David M. Stipanuk

HOSPITALITY INDUSTRY MANAGERIAL ACCOUNTING
Sixth Edition
Raymond S. Schmidgall

PURCHASING FOR HOSPITALITY OPERATIONS
William B. Virts

MANAGING TECHNOLOGY IN THE HOSPITALITY INDUSTRY
Fourth Edition
Michael L. Kasavana/John J. Cahill

BASIC HOTEL AND RESTAURANT ACCOUNTING
Sixth Edition
Raymond Cote

ACCOUNTING FOR HOSPITALITY MANAGERS
Fourth Edition
Raymond Cote

CONVENTION MANAGEMENT AND SERVICE
Seventh Edition
Milton T. Astroff/James R. Abbey

HOSPITALITY SALES AND MARKETING
Fourth Edition
James R. Abbey

MANAGING HOUSEKEEPING OPERATIONS
Second Edition
Margaret M. Kappa/Aleta Nitschke/Patricia B. Schappert

DIMENSIONS OF TOURISM
Joseph D. Fridgen

HOSPITALITY TODAY: AN INTRODUCTION
Fifth Edition
Rocco M. Angelo/Andrew N. Vladimir

MANAGING BAR AND BEVERAGE OPERATIONS
Lendal H. Kotschevar/Mary L. Tanke

ETHICS IN HOSPITALITY MANAGEMENT: A BOOK OF READINGS
Edited by Stephen S. J. Hall

HOSPITALITY FACILITIES MANAGEMENT AND DESIGN
Third Edition
David M. Stipanuk

MANAGING HOSPITALITY HUMAN RESOURCES
Fourth Edition
Robert H. Woods

FINANCIAL MANAGEMENT FOR THE HOSPITALITY INDUSTRY
William P. Andrew/Raymond S. Schmidgall

HOSPITALITY INDUSTRY FINANCIAL ACCOUNTING
Third Edition
Raymond S. Schmidgall/James W. Damitio

INTERNATIONAL HOTEL MANAGEMENT
Chuck Y. Gee

QUALITY SANITATION MANAGEMENT
Ronald F. Cichy

HOTEL INVESTMENTS: ISSUES & PERSPECTIVES
Fourth Edition
Edited by Lori E. Raleigh and Rachel J. Roginsky

LEADERSHIP AND MANAGEMENT IN THE HOSPITALITY INDUSTRY
Second Edition
Robert H. Woods/Judy Z. King

MARKETING IN THE HOSPITALITY INDUSTRY
Fourth Edition
Ronald A. Nykiel

CONTEMPORARY HOSPITALITY MARKETING
William Lazer/Roger Layton

UNIFORM SYSTEM OF ACCOUNTS FOR THE HEALTH, RACQUET AND SPORTSCLUB INDUSTRY

CONTEMPORARY CLUB MANAGEMENT
Second Edition
Edited by Joe Perdue for the Club Managers Association of America

RESORT CONDOMINIUM AND VACATION OWNERSHIP MANAGEMENT: A HOSPITALITY PERSPECTIVE
Robert A. Gentry/Pedro Mandoki/Jack Rush

ACCOUNTING FOR CLUB OPERATIONS
Raymond S. Schmidgall/James W. Damitio

TRAINING AND DEVELOPMENT FOR THE HOSPITALITY INDUSTRY
Debra F. Cannon/Catherine M. Gustafson

UNIFORM SYSTEM OF FINANCIAL REPORTING FOR CLUBS
Sixth Revised Edition

HOTEL ASSET MANAGEMENT: PRINCIPLES & PRACTICES
Edited by Paul Beals and Greg Denton

MANAGING BEVERAGE SERVICE
Lendal H. Kotschevar/Ronald F. Cichy

FOOD SAFETY: MANAGING THE HACCP PROCESS
Ronald F. Cichy

UNIFORM SYSTEM OF FINANCIAL REPORTING FOR SPAS

FUNDAMENTALS OF DESTINATION MANAGEMENT AND MARKETING
Edited by Rich Harrill

ETHICS IN THE HOSPITALITY AND TOURISM INDUSTRY
Karen Lieberman/Bruce Nissen

HOSPITALITY AND TOURISM MARKETING
William Lazer/Melissa Dallas/Carl Riegel

MARKETING
in the
HOSPITALITY
INDUSTRY

Fourth Edition

Ronald A. Nykiel, Ph.D., CHA, CHE

EDUCATIONAL INSTITUTE
American Hotel & Lodging Association

Disclaimer

This publication is designed to provide accurate and authoritative information in regard to the subject matter covered. It is sold with the understanding that the publisher is not engaged in rendering legal, accounting, or other professional service. If legal advice or other expert assistance is required, the services of a competent professional person should be sought.
  —*From the Declaration of Principles jointly adopted by the American Bar Association and a Committee of Publishers and Associations*

The author, Ronald A. Nykiel, Ph.D., CHA, CHE, is solely responsible for the contents of this publication. All views expressed herein are solely those of the authors and do not necessarily reflect the views of the Educational Institute of the American Hotel & Lodging Association (the Institute) or the American Hotel & Lodging Association (AH&LA).

Nothing contained in this publication shall constitute a standard, an endorsement, or a recommendation of the Institute or AH&LA. The Institute and AH&LA disclaim any liability with respect to the use of any information, procedure, or product, or reliance thereon by any member of the hospitality industry.

Cover photo: The Regent Singapore. Courtesy of Carlson Companies.

To my wife, Karen, our son, Ron, and my friends in the hospitality industry. A special thanks to Trish and Pete for all their help in this endeavor.

Contents

Preface

IN ORDER TO UNDERSTAND MARKETING in the hospitality industry today, one must have a thorough understanding of the marketplace. The consumers of lodging, food and beverage, and other travel-related products and services have changed. A look at the demographics, psychographics, user characteristics, or any other measure of the market will demonstrate that marketing hospitality products and services no longer consists of a simple sales call or a good advertising message. The key to marketing in the hospitality industry today is understanding that there is no *one* consumer; there are many, even within the same individual, as defined by a particular set of needs. Comprehending this concept, understanding the needs of consumers, knowing the segmentations of the market, and selecting the best marketing tool to reach your consumers are what this book is all about.

Let's think about the consumer for a moment. When this individual travels or makes use of the products and services offered by the hospitality industry, there is a response to a marketing message that can trigger a decision to purchase from you. This purchase translates into market share, sales, occupancy, average check, rate, profit, passenger miles, or whatever your measure of success is for your marketing program. The key to marketing today is to find the right marketing messages. When this individual travels for business purposes and dines out with clients, his or her needs may be very different than when he or she is traveling or dining out with family or friends.

The hospitality industry has responded to consumers and their changing wants and needs. In the food and beverage sector of the industry we have seen the all-purpose, all-occasion restaurant come and go—and come again. We have seen numerous fast-food concepts, theme restaurants, and even new dining environments emerge. In air travel, deregulation has led to everything from the specialized segmentation of carriers offering all one type or class of service to a plethora of discount and advance-purchase fares. In air travel the response has also included frequent-flyer programs, consolidations, the "hub" concept, and new automated technologies. In lodging, many segmented product specialties have emerged, ranging from budget to all-suite concepts. Major downtown mega-hotels arrived, departed, and returned. The motor inn replaced the motel and the motel returned. Concepts such as club/concierge floors, high-tech rooms, and contracted services emerged. While new chains popped up weekly in the mid-1980s, the result of the overbuilding of the 1980s and the recessions during that decade resulted in massive financial losses and property turnover. By the mid-1990s, demand for lodging was strong again, and occupancies, rates, and profits hit new heights. In the early 2000s the industry again experienced a downturn and a recession. Pressure was placed both on rate and occupancy.

This dynamic environment caused many changes in the hospitality products and services offered and in the marketing methodologies marketers used to address the needs of different market segments. Where is hospitality marketing now? More importantly, where should it be and what should it be doing? These questions will surface throughout this book. We will examine and dissect many marketing ideas and techniques—some that have succeeded and some that have failed.

Acknowledgements

Working in the hospitality industry is perhaps one of the greatest learning experiences an individual can have. Over the years I have learned from every travel experience and from each person I have met and worked with or for. The contents of this book were influenced by the exposure I have had to a number of people within the industry and in other professions.

I would like to thank the following individuals: Dr. Jim Myers, author of *Marketing Structure Analysis;* Peter F. Drucker, Professor of Marketing Emeritus at The Claremont Graduate School, for sharing his knowledge on market positioning and brand preference; and Dr. Robert Buzzell, former Sabastian S. Kresge Professor of Marketing at the Harvard University Graduate School of Business, for helping me remain academically active in the field. To my good friend, Bob Aronin, thanks for the discussions on travel market intermediaries. To Eric Orkin, a sincere thanks for the healthy discussions on setting rates and managing revenue. My special appreciation goes to Bill Marriott, Chairman of the Marriott Corporation; Kemmons Wilson, founder of Holiday Inn and Chairman of the Wilson Companies; Mike Rose, retired Chairman of the Promus Companies; Juergen Bartels, Chairman of Meridien Hotels and Resorts; Bill Hulett, former President of Stouffer Hotels and Resorts; and Jim Biggar, former Chairman and CEO of Nestlé Enterprises, Inc., for the opportunities they gave me to learn more about the industry and the knowledge I gained from exposure to their leadership.

Some of my greatest marketing successes were due to the receptivity of my friends in the media, so special thanks to *USA TODAY*'s former president Cathy Black and former publisher Carolyn Vesper. Thanks to Steve Forbes, CEO of *Forbes* magazine and Martin Deutch, former publisher of *Frequent Flyer Magazine.*

A deep appreciation goes to my colleagues in academia and to The Conrad N. Hilton Foundation. Thank you, Ray Swan, former president of the Educational Institute of the American Hotel & Lodging Association, for your persistence and help in making this book possible.

Finally, a special acknowledgment to my father for sharing with me his wisdom learned during 40 years in sales and marketing at Colgate Palmolive Company, and to my son, Ron for helping me master the computer, teaching me some new marketing tricks of his own, and listening to both my good and bad promotional ideas during the course of my career.

Ronald A. Nykiel

About the Author

Author, business executive, lecturer, professor, and founder are all appropriate descriptions for Dr. Ronald A. Nykiel.

He began his business career with IBM in human resources. With Xerox and Marriott Corporation he held managerial positions in market research and strategic and operational planning. He has been a senior officer of Holiday Corporation, serving in a development and strategic planning capacity. As a senior officer of Ramada Incorporated, Nestlé's Stouffer Hotel Company, and Grand Met's Pearle Incorporated, he was responsible for all brand management and marketing functions on a worldwide basis.

Dr. Nykiel has served on the boards of associations, corporations, public television stations, and universities. He has consulted with two United States Presidential Commissions, various other federal and state entities, and numerous corporations. He founded and is chairman of World Institute Associates, a global business strategy and marketing consulting firm.

He has addressed many corporate and association groups and has lectured at the Harvard Graduate School of business and other prestigious universities on subjects such as corporate strategy, marketing, consumer behavior, brand management, service excellence, and executive development topics. He is recognized as an international authority in the field of hospitality, travel, and tourism marketing, and is the author of a leading hospitality industry marketing text. He has also authored a number of books on business strategy, non-hospitality marketing, consumer behavior, and service excellence. He has appeared on national television and radio broadcasts and has contributed to a variety of journals, magazines, and other publications.

Dr. Nykiel received his Bachelor of Arts degree in Liberal Arts from the State University of New York, his Master of Arts degree in Spanish from the Pennsylvania State University, and his Ph.D. in Management and Administration from Walden University. He also holds the Certified Hotel Administrator (CHA) and Certified Hospitality Educator (CHE) designations from the Educational Institute of the American Hotel & Lodging Association. Dr. Nykiel is currently the Conrad N. Hilton Distinguished Chair and Professor of Hotel and Restaurant Management at the University of Houston's Conrad N. Hilton College. He is also the chairman of the Hospitality Industry Hall of Honor and publisher of the *Hospitality Business Review*. Dr. Nykiel is a member of the Board of Directors of the Travel Industry Association of America and Examiner for the Hotel Sales and Marketing Association International CHME program. He is also a member of the American Hotel & Lodging Association Sales and Marketing committee.

Chapter 1 Outline

A Historical Perspective—The Growth of
  Industry Brands
A Marketing Perspective of the Industry
A Consumer Perspective of the Industry

Competencies

1. Identify the major sectors of the
   hospitality industry. (p. 3)

2. Describe the rise of brands within the
   hospitality industry. (pp. 3–6)

3. Identify the many different audiences
   marketing must address and explain
   how marketing activities in the
   hospitality industry address the needs
   of many different types of buyers.
   (pp. 6–7)

4. Explain why a consumer's perspective
   of the hospitality industry changes in
   relation to the purpose for venturing
   away from home. (p. 7)

1

Understanding the Hospitality Industry

A CONCISE DEFINITION for an industry that has experienced rapid development, like the hospitality industry, is virtually impossible. Moreover, definitions of the hospitality industry are often limited by the unique viewpoints of sectors within the industry. A hotelier might see the industry defined as rooms with food and beverage. A restaurateur might picture the industry as a quality dining experience with the focus on menu offerings and good service. An airline executive might believe that providing travel to people for business or pleasure defines the industry best. All of these viewpoints fit under a wider perspective that defines the hospitality industry in terms of products and services offered to consumers away from home. As shown in Exhibit 1, the industry, in its broadest perspective, encompasses travel, lodging, food and beverage, clubs, gaming, attractions, entertainment, and recreation.

This chapter provides a brief historical overview of the hospitality industry in terms of the emergence and growth of brands within some of the major sectors of the industry. The chapter also examines the multiple purposes of hospitality industry marketing and how marketing activities must address many different types of buyers—from consumers of products and services to owners and investors of the business. Finally, the chapter looks at how consumers' perspectives of the industry and of its product and service offerings change in relation to the reason or purpose for the consumers' ventures away from home.

A Historical Perspective—The Growth of Industry Brands

Restaurants with white tablecloths, hotels with grand ballrooms, business executives pampered by their favorite airlines with personalized matches and reserved seats—these are traditional and, to some extent, obsolete images of the hospitality industry. Today, more than just the personalized matches are gone. New images of the industry abound, created by the way in which airlines, hotels, and restaurants have developed and marketed products and services to meet the changing needs of consumers. Exhibit 2 briefly identifies some milestones of industry development prompted by the changing needs of consumers.

Historically, the consumer's perception of the industry centered on full-service independent hotels, business travelers, and the "glory" of travel. Conrad

3

Exhibit 1   Sectors of the Hospitality Industry

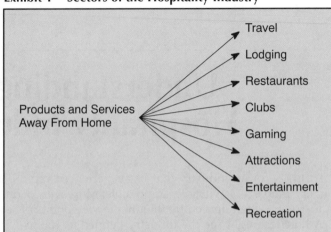

Hilton changed the image that consumers had of the lodging industry by creating one of the first powerful hotel **brands.** The chain of hotels and the name "Hilton" positioned the concept of a brand (Hilton) as synonymous with the word "hotel" in the minds of consumers across the country and eventually around the globe.

New concepts in lodging evolved as other great entrepreneurs conceived new products and services. Kemmons Wilson founded what would become the world's largest single lodging chain, Holiday Inn. In the 1950s, Holiday Inn developed a lodging product that met the needs of a rapidly growing consumer segment—the interstate auto traveler. The adventure of family vacations replaced the traditional image of the glory of travel. Across the market, the brand name "Holiday Inn" became synonymous with the word "motel." The continued success of Holiday Inn Worldwide can be attributed to its ability to change its product and associated levels of service to reach many market segments and fulfill many different consumer segment needs.

The hospitality industry grew rapidly due to the genius and hard work of other founders who built great hospitality companies. Willard and Alice Marriott developed food service concepts (such as the Hot Shoppe Cafeteria and in-flight catering) that met the needs of particular market segments. Their son, Bill Marriott, continued their work in the hospitality industry and made the "Marriott" brand known around the world.

New food concepts became globally recognized brands as companies targeted the ever-changing needs of consumers. McDonald's, KFC, and other companies went beyond being just food concepts; they became delivery systems as well that specifically addressed the needs of consumers.

Today, Hilton, Holiday Inn (now part of InterContinental Hotels Group), and Marriott are multi-billion-dollar companies and are very different from what they were even just twenty years ago. For that matter, most of the growth firms in the hospitality industry today are very different from what they were ten or even five years ago. Their products and services evolved from consumers' needs, their

Exhibit 2   Some Milestones of Industry Development

1800s	Private rooms become the norm in hotels.
1859	First hotel elevator is installed in New York's Fifth Avenue Hotel.
1860-1900	The Manhattan cocktail is invented.
	The Tremont House in Boston becomes the first hotel to have indoor plumbing, free soap, and guestroom doors with locks.
	The Waiters and Bartenders National Union is formed.
1900	The American Hotel Association is formed.
1920	More new hotels are built (1920-1930) than during any other ten-year period before or since, resulting in a record low occupancy rate of 51% in 1933.
1929	The first airport hotel opens in Oakland, California.
1935	Howard Johnson initiates the first hospitality industry franchise.
1940	The first hotel management contract is signed by Inter-Continental Hotels.
1946	The hotel industry experiences its highest occupancy rate ever—95%.
1950s	Holiday Inns' roadside properties begin the era of the motel.
1960s	Market segmentation and product segmentation begin in earnest in the hotel industry.
	Motor hotels and roadside inns develop along the interstate highway system.
1970s	Spectacular design and architecture (exemplified by the Hyatt Hotel in Atlanta) establish a new era of the hotel.
1980s	Major developments in computers, telecommunications, and other technological areas result in sophisticated reservation systems.
	Industry deregulation arrives.
	Full product segmentation occurs in lodging with brands ranging from economy/budget lines to full-service hotels, all-suite properties, resorts, and mega-hotels.
1990s	Travel-related companies emerge as multi-billion-dollar forces in lodging and air transportation.
	Travel purchasing systems emerge, as the marketing giants step in on the purchasing process.
2000s	Consumer-driven technology results in paperless airline tickets, keyless doors, at-home purchasing and delivery systems.
	Supersonic mass passenger aircraft coupled with computer-directed ground transport usher in a new age of travel.

creativity resulted in new forms of businesses, and their profits from sales of products and services have grown substantially.

Just as the lodging and restaurant sectors of the industry saw their "founders'" names become household words representing globally recognized brands, the same occurred in other sectors of the industry as well. The name "Walt Disney" became a brand in the entertainment and attractions sectors, and the name "Curt

Exhibit 3   The Audience for Marketing

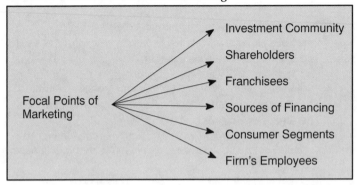

Carlson" became associated with the travel management and services sectors of hospitality. These individuals conceived products and services that turned into brands that not only fulfilled the needs of consumers but also stimulated others to develop more industry products and services and more brands.

Millions of consumers around the globe developed sets of expectations associated with the logos and signs of hospitality brands. The same development and growth of brands held true for airlines (American, Delta, United, etc.) and car rental firms (Avis, Hertz, etc.). Consumers responded to products and services that met their needs, and marketing quickly developed the "brand" names associated with those products and services.

A Marketing Perspective of the Industry

As products and services offered by the hospitality industry have evolved, so has the **marketing** of these products and services. Marketing focuses on the needs of the buyer. In today's hospitality industry, the **audience** of buyers has become complex. Not only do the firms' products or services have buyers, but so do the hospitality firms themselves. As shown in Exhibit 3, marketing must be aware of and relate to the total audience, including the firm's buyers (such as shareholders, the investment community, individual investors, and franchisees).

To explain the importance of these multiple purposes of marketing, it is necessary to briefly touch upon how the hospitality industry functions to achieve its growth and vitality. In order for a firm to function, sources of capital are required for investment. These sources come from internal profits generated by the firm and from a variety of outside investors. A hotel executive was asked who owned the most hotels in the United States today. His response was quick—the insurance companies who hold the mortgages. In the food sector, owners would be the banks, groups of local investors, and so on. The importance of the firm's buyers explains why hospitality industry firms spend marketing dollars on everything from image and awareness advertising to producing the firm's annual report to shareholders. The annual report represents a principal marketing vehicle to those who purchase pieces of the firm. Even more illustrative is the next tier of marketing to the franchise section of the audience of buyers. Annual franchise conferences often rival the best Broadway productions. The reason is simple. Hospitality firms are marketing to a very important audience—those who make the company grow.

To summarize, the hospitality industry marketing perspective is multi-purpose and must relate to many different audiences. The overall goal is not only the sale of the product or service, but the sale of the firm's image to its total audience.

A Consumer Perspective of the Industry

Marketers create a marketing message that sells products and services by understanding the **consumer's perspective.** As a matter of fact, if the marketing process is thorough in its research and analysis of the consumer, then it can perform yet another service for the hospitality firm. This is to influence product development or to recommend changes to services offered so they are more in line with what consumers express as their needs. Marketing cannot succeed if the product or service offering is not in line with its consumers' needs.

The consumer's perspective centers on the needs fulfilled by a product or service. The marketing challenge is that not all consumers have the same needs. In fact, the same consumer can have very different sets of needs. Much depends on the consumer's purpose or reason for using the product or service. For example, when an executive travels for business purposes, his or her needs may well relate to a nonstop air route, a full-service hotel with meeting facilities, and a gourmet restaurant. The executive, therefore, may have a set of needs that is best served by a specific airline and a specific upscale hotel. This same executive, when traveling with his or her family for purposes of pleasure, may have a set of needs that corresponds to economy multiple-stop air travel and a budget lodging facility with a nearby fast-food restaurant. The point to remember is that a consumer's perspective of the industry and of its products and services changes in relation to the reason or purpose for his or her venture away from home.

When planning trips, the executive in our example may well identify specific airlines, lodging facilities, or restaurants by their brand names because the executive perceives that their product and service offerings will best meet his or her specific needs. The executive's expectation is that the brand will fulfill the needs.

The nature, care, and conveying of what the brand stands for and how it meets the needs of the consumer are what marketing is all about. The nature and care of the brand creates a perception by the consumer. This perception translates into a value. Investors pay a premium for this value, a sum of money beyond what they would be willing to invest in the same property or business unit if it were *not* associated with that brand. The perception created by packaging the brand helps to dictate the price consumers are willing to pay for the brand. Conveying how the brand meets the specific needs of buyers is the role of the various marketing methods and techniques.

Key Terms

audience—The collective term for buyers of products and services. Audiences are the focal points of marketing.

brand—The name associated with products or services that conveys a specific perception related to the needs of consumers.

consumer's perspective—The consumer's attitude toward a product or service that centers on the needs that it satisfies.

marketing—Selling a service or product by focusing on the needs of the buyer.

Chapter 2 Outline

Geographic Segmentation
    Regions, Zones, and Districts
    Metropolitan Statistical Areas
    Cities
    Zip Codes
    Other Geographic Segmentation Tools
Demographic Segmentation
Benefit and Need Segmentation
Psychographic Segmentation
Combining Segmentation Techniques
The Pendulum Swings Toward Value

Competencies

1. Describe the value of geographic segmentation for marketing in the hospitality industry. (p. 11)

2. Explain how feeder cities and city pairs may help focus a company's marketing efforts. (pp. 11–13)

3. Distinguish destination cities from destination markets. (pp. 13–15)

4. Describe the value of demographic customer profiles for marketing in the hospitality industry. (p. 15)

5. Explain how the knowledge gained from benefit and need segmentation can bring hospitality marketers and operations managers into close working relationships. (pp. 15–16)

6. Describe the value of psychographic segmentation for marketing in the hospitality industry. (pp. 16–18)

7. Explain how combining different market segmentation techniques provide valuable research tools for marketing in today's hospitality industry. (pp. 18–19)

2

Market Segmentation and the Hospitality Industry

MARKETS CAN BE SEGMENTED or subdivided in many different ways. This chapter briefly describes the traditional territorial concepts, as well as contemporary segmentation methods, and how each can be applied to the hospitality industry.

Geographic Segmentation

Geographic segmentation is the division of a market generally by region, zone, state, district, metropolitan statistical area, and postal zip code zones. There are many purposes and applications of this type of segmentation within the hospitality industry today. Establishing geographic market segments enables marketers to focus sales, advertising, public relations, and promotional activities in the most appropriate areas of the country.

Regions, Zones, and Districts

Regions are used primarily to establish geographic subdivisions of a country. Natural borders often define a region. For example, the area of the United States west of the Rocky Mountains is known as the western region. Regional subdivisions are useful to marketing in the hospitality industry because the bulk of travel by corporate sales forces is within a region. In fact, travel between cities within regions accounts for two-thirds of all travel in the United States. Regional advertising, sales efforts, public relations, and promotions can concentrate on where the business comes from and where it goes to in terms of geographic markets.

Feeder cities are principal cities within a region that tend to "feed" travel to each other. For example, in the western region of the United States, travel from Los Angeles feeds such cities as Palm Springs, Las Vegas, Phoenix, and San Francisco, all of which in turn feed Los Angeles. Marketing efforts within a region may, therefore, concentrate on both the primary feeder market—say, Los Angeles—as well as the markets that feed Los Angeles.

Some hospitality organizations with international operations may designate zones as sections of the world, such as the Southeast Asian Zone or the Northern European Zone. However, for most domestic marketing purposes, a **zone** is a geographic area smaller than a region. The area in the state of New York from Albany to Syracuse to Rochester might be classified as a zone.

A district is a geographic area, generally smaller than a zone, with a concentration of customers. For example, a hotel chain's midwest regional office may have, for marketing purposes, an Illinois-Wisconsin zone. This zone would have subdivisions called districts, such as Chicago, Milwaukee, La Crosse, etc.

Metropolitan Statistical Areas

The U.S. Census Bureau for many years gathered, compiled, and presented census data by what it defined as Standard Metropolitan Statistical Areas, or SMSAs. In 1990, the Census Bureau refined its definitions and terminology, eliminating the SMSA category by dividing it into Primary Metropolitan Statistical Areas (PMSAs) and Consolidated Metropolitan Statistical Areas (CMSAs). (The bureau also presents data according to two smaller classifications, Metropolitan Areas and Metropolitan Statistical Areas.) The precise definitions of these terms as used by the Census Bureau are beyond our scope here, but two points should be made. First, although the Census Bureau no longer uses the SMSA category, it had become so widely used and accepted that many people outside the government continue to use it; references to SMSAs remain common. Second, in the following discussion, we will refer generically to CMSAs and PMSAs (that is, those areas that used to be SMSAs) simply as **metropolitan statistical areas.**

Metropolitan statistical areas tend to be the population within a large county or within a number of small counties. However, the core of a metropolitan statistical area is usually a major city. For example, the New York City metropolitan statistical area, which is a huge market in terms of population, encompasses counties in three states and Long Island. Approximately 50 percent of the overnight travel in the United States is generated from 24 metropolitan statistical areas, some of which are listed below:

Los Angeles	Denver	Atlanta
Dallas	Chicago	Minneapolis-St. Paul
New York	Boston	Washington, D.C.
San Francisco	Houston	Seattle
Detroit	Pittsburgh	Miami/Dade County
Phoenix	Cleveland	

These areas become key strategic markets in which to sell travel products or services.

Metropolitan statistical areas play an important role in marketing for the travel sectors of the hospitality industry, such as airlines, bus companies, rail service, and lodging. Frequently, both print and broadcast media exposure are defined in terms of geographic areas related to metropolitan statistical areas. Also, there are direct correlations between the size of metropolitan statistical areas and the number and type of food service outlets such areas can absorb.

Counties are also important geographic areas because laws concerning business operations vary by county in relation to liquor license requirements, hours of restaurant operations, food service regulations, and so on.

City pairs such as Boston and New York City, or Washington, D.C., and New York City are cities between which a heavy travel pattern exists. Knowing major city pairs and understanding relationships between metropolitan statistical areas is essential for assessing the best use of marketing expenditures on a geographic

Exhibit 1   Map of Major Traffic Flows in the United States

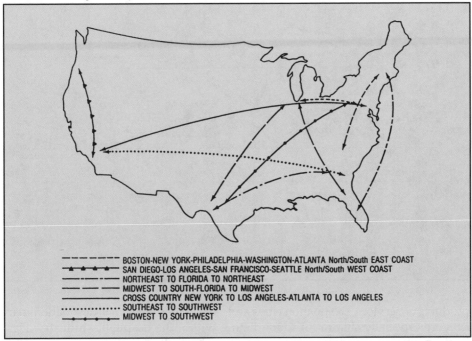

—————— BOSTON-NEW YORK-PHILADELPHIA-WASHINGTON-ATLANTA North/South EAST COAST
▲—▲—▲—▲ SAN DIEGO-LOS ANGELES-SAN FRANCISCO-SEATTLE North/South WEST COAST
————·— NORTHEAST TO FLORIDA TO NORTHEAST
———— MIDWEST TO SOUTH-FLORIDA TO MIDWEST
———— CROSS COUNTRY NEW YORK TO LOS ANGELES-ATLANTA TO LOS ANGELES
·············· SOUTHEAST TO SOUTHWEST
—·—·—·— MIDWEST TO SOUTHWEST

basis. Marketing expenditures can concentrate on the city pairs that generate the largest number of consumers for travel products or services.

The travel between key strategic markets and city pairs is referred to as traffic flow. Exhibit 1 maps some of the major traffic flows in the United States. Exhibit 2 maps major world traffic flows. Examples of major world traffic flows are:

- East Coast of North America to Europe.
- Europe to East Coast of North America.
- Northern Europe to Southern Europe and the Mediterranean.
- West Coast of United States to Japan and Asia.
- Far East to West Coast of United States.
- North and South United States to Mexico and Latin America.
- Japan to Hawaii and West Coast of United States.
- Japan to Asia and South Pacific.
- United Kingdom to Germany, France, and Spain.

Cities

Cities are often ranked in order of size of population, degree of affluence, type of industry base, or other criteria useful for the purposes of marketing specific

Exhibit 2 Map of Major World Traffic Flows

products or services. Destination cities and major cities viewed as destination markets are especially significant to marketing within the hospitality industry. Destination cities have unique attractions unto themselves that create demand for travel. For example, in the last 50 years, such major destination cities as Orlando, Las Vegas, Acapulco, West Palm Beach, Lake Tahoe, and Atlantic City have emerged (or re-emerged) as significant travel markets. While Las Vegas and Acapulco represent examples of pure destination cities, many major cities such as New York City and Los Angeles are viewed as destination markets. These cities create demand for travel not only from the unique attractions they offer, but also from their many centers of business and commerce.

Zip Codes

Zip codes—five-digit United States Postal Service designations with four-digit suffixes—correspond to some extent with cities and metropolitan statistical areas. However, zip codes further define an area into smaller sections, even to square blocks of a city. Zip codes and the first three digits of a zip code (known as the sectional center) have special significance for direct mail marketing. This significance has been greatly enhanced through the correlation of zip codes and demographic data from the U.S. Census Bureau reports.

Other Geographic Segmentation Tools

Other geographic segmentation tools that relate to metropolitan statistical area and zip code segmentation include Designated Market Areas (DMAs) and Areas of Dominant Influence (ADIs).

Designated Market Areas, conceived by the A. C. Nielsen Company, are composed of areas based on the dominance of clusters of television stations. DMAs are useful marketing tools in relation to media planning and for researching TV audiences.

Areas of Dominant Influence are geographic market designations developed by the Arbitron audience research firm. An ADI is a geographic area in which the majority of households are served by a given city's cluster of media. ADI boundaries are typically defined by the circulation patterns of magazines, newspapers, and other publications. ADIs can also be defined by zip code sectional centers and have excellent application for media planning in hospitality marketing.

Demographic Segmentation

Demographic segmentation is the categorization of consumers by like characteristics such as sex, age, income, home ownership, marital status, occupation, and education. Demographically different consumers reside within each region, state, district, zone, metropolitan statistical area, city, and even zip code. As a result of the comprehensive demographic data available through the U.S. Census Bureau reports and private research firms specializing in demographic market data, there are virtually hundreds of ways by which to demographically segment the market.

For years, direct mail operators, publishers, retailers of consumer goods, and others have developed **demographic profiles** of their consumers. These profiles vary in relation to the type of product or service marketed. To demonstrate how cost effective a good demographic profile and purchase pattern correlation can be, consider the example of the effective direct mail marketer. For some products, less than 35 percent of the zip codes generate more than 80 percent of the sales. A good mailing list correlates zip codes with demographic customer profiles and eliminates 65 percent of non-respondent market areas.

In the hospitality industry, there are direct correlations between income and the likelihood of using travel services. To a point, the higher the income, the greater the frequency of travel. In today's food service industry, fast-food restaurants, bars, and full-service restaurants develop demographic profiles of their customers.

Benefit and Need Segmentation

Benefit and need segmentation divides a market into groups of consumers on the basis of the benefits they seek, the needs they expect to satisfy, and, in some instances, the factors they hope to avoid. For years, the consumer-products industry has applied this market segmentation tool to determine what consumers look for in a product and what they avoid. This research is applied to everything from the color, smell, size, shape, and appearance of the product and package to the advertising message. Granted, a hotel, restaurant, or airline does not lend itself to this same level of refinement as far as the physical product is concerned, but each can be packaged and marketed using the same principles of benefit and need segmentation.

In the 1980s, a number of hospitality industry firms began to make use of benefits and needs research. For example, the airline shuttles between New York City, Boston, and Washington, D.C., now serve a large group of consumers whose single greatest need is the convenience of no-reservation, multiple-departure-time transportation. Scheduling shuttles on the hour or on the half hour from early morning to late night fulfills the primary need of these consumers. Likewise, a fast-food restaurant may satisfy a number of needs or provide various benefits in terms of offering low prices, convenient location, and fast service.

Consider the situation of couples escaping for a weekend to a hotel. They seek a memorable experience in a relaxed atmosphere. Further, they try to avoid a child-oriented facility or one full of business meetings. If a lodging facility wants to successfully attract this market, it must recognize what these couples wish to avoid, as well as the benefits they seek. It is in this area of segmentation that marketing and product research must closely relate to operations and product development.

Marketing and operations work together to maximize the sale of products or services while satisfying the different needs of guests. Consider the hotel that promoted two types of "escape weekend" programs. One program was a "second honeymoon" escape, the other a family weekend escape. The second honeymooners were escaping from the children for peace, relaxation, and a memorable experience. The family escapees were out to have fun with their children and were looking for activities, excitement, and a very different kind of experience from that sought by the second honeymooners. The hotel's marketing and operations team came up with the solution. All families on an escape weekend were roomed in the wings of the property surrounding the pool, game room, and coffee shop. The hotel lodged all second honeymooners in rooms high up in the tower section of the hotel or near the indoor pool and bar. Also, the second honeymooners were served breakfast in bed and their dining reservations were made in the hotel's upscale restaurant, which was far removed from the coffee shop where the family escapees generally ate their meals.

Since each market segment frequently seeks different benefits or has different needs to satisfy, benefit and need segmentation presents a challenge to the hospitality industry. The business executive trying to impress a client and close a major contract needs an atmosphere conducive to a business discussion that will impress the client. An upscale hotel with a special table in the dining room might fulfill these needs. But the same environment that meets the executive's need while negotiating a business deal may be exactly what he or she wants to avoid when traveling for pleasure.

Psychographic Segmentation

Psychographic segmentation is a method of subdividing a market based on like needs and psychological motivations of consumer groups. Psychographic segmentation along with benefit and need segmentation provides insight into the psychological aspects of buyer behavior.

The firm of Yankelovich, Clancy, and Shulman (formerly Yankelovich, Skelly and White) pioneered the development and use of psychographic segmentation through its research tool called MONITOR. MONITOR profiled the U.S. population by regularly measuring over 60 trends such as:

- Economizing on food purchases.

- Dining out more or less often.

- Planning more or fewer vacations.

- Planning shorter or longer vacations.

- Postponing major purchases.

- Concern or lack of concern about credit usage.

- Desire for more or fewer materialistic purchases.

For participating clients, MONITOR psychographically segmented the population based on groups holding common values. For example, the MONITOR program measured the percentage of the U.S. population holding traditional values of a Protestant work ethic. It also identified other population groups holding common values and profiled them in categories of value segments with names like forerunners, new conformists, conservatives, and others. Each of these value segments was profiled demographically and geographically.

Many industries have applied the output from MONITOR to guide such marketing activities as product development, advertising, promotions, and the creation of brand images. The travel-related elements of MONITOR were sufficient to merit a separate study. In the early 1990s, the firm of Yesawich, Pepperdine, and Brown acquired the administration of the MONITOR studies that relate to travel.

Psychographic segmentation tends to focus trends into key areas such as activities, interests, and opinions (AIO). In programs like MONITOR, social attitudes help predict the propensity to travel, likely future rates of growth, willingness to pay, redefining the parameters of value, etc. Activity-related factors are also included, such as leisure-travel preferences and desired leisure activities. The degree and rank of interests are reviewed from year to year to determine attitudinal changes. Also, opinions on current issues and events influencing consumer behavior are identified.

While MONITOR looks at a comprehensive list of factors over a broad travel-related definition, other psychographic research programs focus on specific areas of the hospitality industry. *Values And LifeStyles* (VALS), developed by SRI International, focuses on the food service area. VALS categorizes the population (market) into different types (segments) with distinctive food preferences. VALS looks at attitudes and lifestyles as well as current and emerging trends to project potential buying habits and media preferences. VALS is used to assist food service companies in conceiving new restaurant concepts, food and beverage themes, menus, facilities, etc. VALS is also extensively used in media selection and planning and in the creative process connected with developing advertising and promotional campaigns.

Exhibit 3   Sample Frequent Traveler Profile

Age:	25 to 44 years old
Income:	$45,000 plus
Education:	College degree plus
Occupations:	Administration, Sales, Marketing, Engineers, Technicians, Business Executives, Buyers, Consultants
Industry Origins:	Electronics, Pharmaceuticals, Chemicals, Service, Manufacturing, Publishing, Banking, and Finance
Travel Habits:	Ten business trips plus, per year Heavy air travel Intra- and inter-regional travel Two pleasure trips plus, per year
Location:	Suburban and center city Corresponding sectional centers/Zips to above High income geodemographic census tracks

Another attitudinal segmentation applied in food service marketing comes from CREST studies. CREST looks at QSC issues (quality, service, and cleanliness) as well as other issues like nutrition. CREST studies segment consumers into groups with distinctive attitudes. The studies then categorize groups with names such as nutritionally fit, conventional taste, restrictive dieters, busy urbanites, etc., that are helpful to the marketing efforts of quick-service, casual, and upscale dining operations.

Combining Segmentation Techniques

Geographic, demographic, benefit/need, and psychographic segmentation techniques by themselves and in combination with each other are valuable marketing research tools in today's hospitality industry. For example, the **heavy user** is a recurrent consumer of a product or service who can be identified through demographics and other market segmentation techniques. To the fast-food industry, the heavy user is the regular at McDonald's, Burger King, KFC, and Wendy's. To airlines and lodging companies, the heavy user is the frequent traveler who could well become their repeat customer. Exhibit 3 presents a sample frequent traveler profile that incorporates demographic, geographic, and some psychographic data. Effective marketing tools for reaching the recurrent business traveler are mailing lists from major credit card companies and advertising media such as in-flight magazines.

Combining segmentation techniques helps to identify and monitor quantitative and qualitative trends. Also, hospitality organizations and market research firms work together to cut the market into increasingly finer segments, both in terms of its psychographic components (attitudes, opinions, interests, etc.) and its **geodemographic** nature (classifying how many people have characteristics of a like nature and where they reside). Since lifestyles change and new values and beliefs continue to evolve, understanding how consumers think and why consumers buy presents never-ending challenges for marketing in the hospitality industry.

The Pendulum Swings Toward Value

Price segmentation identifies groups of consumers within a market whose purchase of products or services is within the limits of certain dollar amounts. Such identification has always been important to the hospitality industry. In times of high inflation, business recessions, and economic turmoil, price segmentation becomes even more significant.

Groups of consumers are often segmented by price as a result of per diem allowances for travel, lodging, and meals. For example, government employees, salespeople, and military personnel are usually price-sensitive market segments because they have limited per diem allowances. Price sensitivity and related segmentation extends to virtually every area of the hospitality industry, ranging from the family who goes out for an inexpensive meal at the local fast-food restaurant, to the salesperson who wants a comfortable but inexpensive room within the per diem allowance of his or her firm, to the executive whose need to impress a client supersedes any interest in economizing.

While price sensitivity is always important, the overriding objective of marketing in the hospitality industry is to ensure customer satisfaction by providing *value.* Regardless of the market segment, hospitality organizations provide value by offering a quality product or service at a fair price.

One very interesting response to a research question demonstrates how the emphasis on value cuts across every segment of the market. The same question was asked to buyers of two automobiles, Volvo and Mercedes-Benz: "Why did you buy this car?" The response was the same: "Its quality and value." The same type of question was posed to a family eating at McDonald's: "Why do you buy your family dinner at McDonald's?" Although the family was from entirely different geographic, demographic, and psychographic segments than the Volvo/Mercedes customers, the response was the same: "Because of its value—good quality at a fair price." Every demographic, psychographic, and economic indicator points to *value* as the key need that marketing must fulfill in the decade ahead.

⚷ Key Terms

benefit and need segmentation—Divides a market into groups of consumers on the basis of the benefits they see, the needs they expect to satisfy, and—in some instances—the factors they hope to avoid.

city pairs—Cities (such as Boston and New York, or Washington, D.C. and New York) between which a heavy travel pattern exists; knowing major city pairs and understanding relationships between metropolitan statistical areas are essential for assessing the best use of marketing expenditures on a geographic basis.

demographic profile—Demographic data describing characteristics of consumers related to specific products and services.

demographic segmentation—The division of a market by like characteristics such as sex, age, income, home ownership, marital status, occupation, and education.

feeder cities—Principal cities within a geographic region that tend to "feed" travel to each other. For example, in the western region of the United States, travel from Los Angeles feeds Palm Springs, Las Vegas, Phoenix, and San Francisco, and vice versa.

geodemographic segmentation—The division of a market along geographic and demographic dimensions; for example, linking the number of people with similar characteristics (age, income, etc.) with specific geographic locations.

geographic segmentation—The division of a market generally by region, zone, state, district, metropolitan statistical area, or postal zip codes.

heavy user—A recurrent consumer of a product or service who can be identified through demographics and other market segmentation techniques.

metropolitan statistical areas—A geographic segmentation technique that divides a market into areas within a large county or within a number of small counties; the core of such an area is usually a major city.

price segmentation—Identifies groups of consumers within a market whose purchase of products or services is within the limits of certain dollar amounts.

psychographic segmentation—A method of subdividing a market based on like needs and psychological motivations of consumer groups.

region—A geographic subdivision within a country, often defined by natural borders such as mountains, major rivers, etc.

zone—A geographic subdivision within a country useful for domestic marketing purposes; also, geographic subdivisions of the world useful for international marketing purposes.

Chapter 3 Outline

End Users
    Business Travelers
    Pleasure Travelers
Travel Intermediaries
Food Service Market Segmentation
    Desired Dining Experience
    Price Sensitivity
    Convenience and Location

Competencies

1. Distinguish end users from intermediaries in the travel and hospitality market. (p. 23)

2. Describe characteristics of business travel market segments. (pp. 23–25)

3. Describe characteristics of pleasure travel market segments. (p. 25)

4. Identify travel intermediaries for business and pleasure travel market segments.(pp. 25–27)

5. Describe user characteristics of consumer segments in the food service market. (pp. 27–29)

3

Positioning in Line with Consumer Preferences

THERE ARE MANY KEYS to successful marketing in the hospitality industry. Most begin with an understanding of consumer preferences. Marketing's function is to target these preferences when communicating product and service offerings to specific consumer segments.

The first part of this chapter examines two broad consumer categories for the hospitality industry's products and services: end users and intermediaries. An **end user** is the ultimate consumer of the product or service offered. An **intermediary** is a person or company who influences the buying decisions of end users. Sections that follow focus on the needs of different types of end users and identify the major intermediaries specific to the hospitality industry.

The second part of the chapter looks more closely at segmentation in the food service industry. General consumer preferences are described in relation to desired dining experiences or purposes for eating away from home. Price segmentation of the food service market is also addressed, as well as the importance of convenience and location of food service operations to consumers who choose to eat away from home. Understanding consumer preferences is essential for properly positioning product and service offerings.

End Users

End users can be segmented in relation to their overall purpose for traveling—for business or for pleasure. Exhibit 1 identifies some major types of end users of lodging products and services. Each of these market segments is dynamic. Variations in the amount and type of travel are subject to internal factors such as a company's travel policy or an individual's tastes and habits. Variations are also caused by external factors such as the current economic situation as well as social and political events.

Business Travelers

In the business travel segment, there are three major sub-segments of travelers:

- Meeting, conference, or convention attendees
- Travelers with relatively unrestricted expense accounts
- Price-conscious business travelers

Exhibit 1   End Users

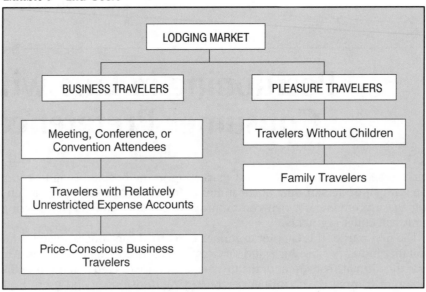

Meeting, Conference, or Convention Attendees. The individual business traveler attending a meeting, conference, or convention usually has little control over the selection of accommodations or the room rates he or she will pay. In some cases, the only choice the attendee may really have is whether to attend the function at all (although, in some instances, even attendance may be mandatory). Business travelers attending functions planned by associations tend to be more price conscious than those who attend corporate meetings or conferences. Almost always, the individuals in this sub-segment make a reservation before arrival or are pre-registered by their respective group, organization, or company.

The primary needs of this sub-segment of the business travel market include not only comfortable meeting environments but also ample telephones and other communication devices to help them remain in touch with their businesses before sessions, during breaks, and after sessions. Attendees also need entertainment and other sorts of opportunities to relax after a day's intense round of meetings and functions.

Travelers with Relatively Unrestricted Expense Accounts. These individuals generally seek comfortable, dependable, full-service accommodations and are usually less price-sensitive than other types of business travelers. Individuals in this sub-segment are likely to be business executives, international travelers, and high-income independent travelers. These end users are likely to prefer specific hotel locations or individual hotel brands. Their room reservations are likely to be guaranteed and placed through the services of a travel agent or secretary. Major needs and concerns of these travelers include security, convenient locations, and business related services such as fax machines, message services, and guestrooms equipped to facilitate the operation of portable computers.

Price-Conscious Business Travelers. As corporations and government departments become more cost conscious, price-sensitive travelers are becoming a rapidly growing sub-segment of the business market. These individuals may travel on a per diem basis. A **per diem** sets upper limits to the amount of money that individuals can recover from their organizations for expenses such as travel, lodging, and meals. While these travelers are sensitive to how much travel products and services cost, they still want as much comfort and service as their money can buy. Usually, a travel department, contracted travel agency, or department secretary makes their travel arrangements and room reservations, although these business travelers sometimes arrive at their destinations without room reservations.

Pleasure Travelers

In the pleasure travel segment, there are two broad sub-segments of travelers: travelers without children and family travelers (travelers with children).

Travelers Without Children. Travelers without children include individuals, couples, and groups traveling for pleasure. They are not restricted by child-related responsibilities and may be interested in "living it up," enjoying various restaurant and entertainment facilities. These travelers are generally interested in comfort and service, but may also be price-conscious.

Family Travelers. Adults traveling with children are more restricted in their pleasure travel than are travelers without children. Family travelers are often more focused on the essential daily routines of feeding, caring for, and lodging their children than on "living it up." Important accommodation benefits include economical and casual restaurant facilities, in-room interactive television games, swimming pools, and other features that make the job of caring for the family away from home convenient and uncomplicated.

A sub-segment of family travelers includes those vacationers who are extremely price-conscious and are not interested in paying for amenities or extras of any kind. They simply seek a place to eat and sleep that serves as a home base for their excursions. Another sub-segment seeks simplicity, outdoor recreation, and freedom in their pleasure travel experience. These families are not interested in hotel services and seek unstructured, do-it-yourself vacations. They look to avoid the service, tipping, and costs of hotels and resorts, preferring instead to stay at campgrounds, beach cottages, mountain cabins, or condominiums.

Travel Intermediaries

Intermediaries are generally not end users of products or services, but they are important to marketing efforts because they assist and influence end users in their selections of travel and hospitality options. Exhibit 2 identifies some of the intermediaries for both the business and pleasure market segments.

Meeting planners are generally association executives, corporate executives, or training company executives whose major goal is to plan and execute successful conventions, conferences, or meetings. Meeting room facilities, meeting-related services, and banquet operations are usually more important concerns than are the

Exhibit 2   Lodging Market Intermediaries

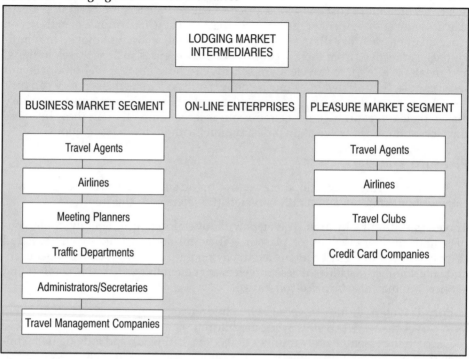

types of room accommodations or the variety of restaurant and food service outlets. Meeting planners are typically price-sensitive, but this may vary with the policies of their associations or corporations.

A number of major corporations have set up **traffic departments** to manage and schedule their high volume of company travel.

Administrators/secretaries are one of the largest groups of intermediaries in relation to business travel. However, the influence of this group on travel purchase decisions can vary tremendously, even within the same organization. In some cases, an administrative assistant or secretary may be the decision-maker in booking travel arrangements, car rentals, and hotel accommodations. In other cases, he or she may simply execute the travel decisions made by individual company managers and executives.

Travel management companies provide travel management services on a contractual or fee basis to corporations, government agencies, associations, and other organizations with business-related travel needs. American Express Travel Services, Carlson-Wagonlits, and Rosenbluth Travel are examples of large travel management companies.

Travel agents arrange air, cruise, and rail travel and place reservations for car rentals and lodging accommodations for both business and pleasure travelers. They are interested in booking their clients with hospitality companies that are dependable in honoring reservations and that offer consistent levels of service.

Travel agents prefer to work with hospitality companies that offer uncomplicated reservation processes and ensure prompt payment of commissions for booking business with them.

Capitalizing on the sophistication of their reservation systems, *airlines* may perform the role of a travel intermediary by handling requests for hotel and car rental reservations. Most airlines also sell to the pleasure travel market segment through other intermediaries such as travel and tour wholesalers, retail travel agents, travel clubs, and others. The airlines assist other intermediaries in selling to consumers and also offer flights and seat capacities that are sold as part of travel packages.

Travel clubs influence the travel purchase decisions of their members. As the pleasure travel market became more sophisticated, travel clubs emerged to meet both general and specific consumer needs. These travel clubs, such as Club Universe and Club Med, target the frequent pleasure traveler and offer club members special packages to desirable destinations. In addition, these packages are frequently tailored to specific interests, such as golf, tennis, visiting historic sites, or simply getting away from civilization.

Many **credit card companies** influence purchase decisions by promoting and selling consumer travel packages put together by other intermediaries, such as tour wholesalers. In addition, the larger credit card companies, banks, and even major department stores often have in-house divisions to promote travel and travel packages to their customers.

With the wide acceptance of booking on-line, a number of significant **on-line enterprises** are now successfully offering their services as on-line travel intermediaries—firms such as Travelocity exemplify this type of intermediary.

Food Service Market Segmentation

The food service or eating-away-from-home market can be segmented along many dimensions useful for the purposes of marketing. Exhibit 3 identifies some types of food service establishments that market to specific consumer segments. The sections that follow look briefly at user characteristics of consumers in the food service market in terms of desired dining experience, price sensitivity, and convenience and location.

Desired Dining Experience

Segmenting the food service market in relation to the overall desired dining experience subdivides the market into groups of consumers with specific purposes for eating away from home. For example, businesspeople may seek to impress clients, couples may seek romance, families may just want to get out of the house, and so on. Desired menu offerings and expected levels of service vary with the consumer's purpose for eating away from home. Marketing messages to food service segments are tailored to the consumer's desired dining experience and focus on the consumer's purpose for eating away from home.

The desired dining experience may also center on individual consumer tastes and types of food. Our culturally diverse society can be segmented by preferred

Exhibit 3   Food Service Establishments with Specific Consumer Segments

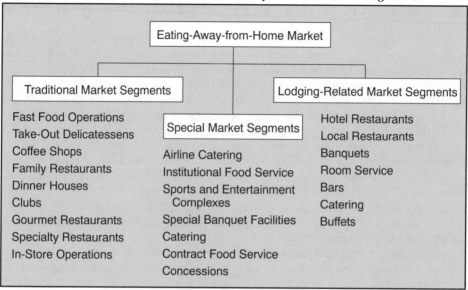

cuisine (Mexican, Italian, Chinese, and so on) or even by taste preferences (from bland to spicy). A few of the numerous other ways to segment the market are: nutrition or health segments, diet-conscious segments, and segments based on preferred type of food such as meat and potatoes, home cooking, pizza, pasta, beef, chicken, fish, and so on.

Price Sensitivity

Market segmentation by price and related demographic consumer characteristics has been the topic of many food service industry studies. Usually, the higher the income (up to a certain point), the greater the propensity for consumers to dine out and spend. An exception to this tendency is the fast food or convenience-food market segment, which includes customers of McDonald's, Burger King, Wendy's, as well as customers of pizza chains and locally owned and operated convenience-food operations. Within this segment, consumers not only seek convenience, they are also price conscious.

Exhibit 4 diagrams a three-tiered segmentation of the food service market based on price sensitivity. The first tier represents the fast food or convenience food consumer. The second tier identifies the medium-priced segment. These consumers seek a step up and a change of pace from fast food and look for a dining "experience." Consumers within this tier are also value-oriented and expect quality at a fair price. The type of food service operations for the medium-priced segment might range from a prime rib house to a lobster barn to a specialty restaurant. Again, the consumer's purpose for eating away from home and preferences for different types of food are the key factors determining the buyer's behavior. The third tier is the least sensitive to price. This tier or sub-segment includes two groups

Exhibit 4   Food Service Market—Price Segmentation

	Price Sensitivity		
	Low	Medium	High
Tier 1 Convenience			Fast food chains Pizza shops Delicatessens In-store operations
Tier 2 Value and Experience		Steak houses Seafood restaurants Specialty restaurants	
Tier 3 Special Occasion	Gourmet restaurants Upscale theme restaurants		

with different needs. The first is the special occasion group, exemplified by a couple celebrating a wedding anniversary by going to the "best" restaurant in town. Here, purpose overrides sensitivity to price. The second group is categorized by a need to impress others. Conveying the impression of affluence often becomes the primary motive for selecting the "best" restaurant (which may equate to the most expensive restaurant, or the restaurant with the "best chef," etc.). This second group looks for gourmet menu items, upscale service, and unique ambience—all appealing to the dining experience they wish to have for themselves and helping to create the impression of affluence that they wish to give others.

Convenience and Location

When time is a critical factor determining where consumers choose to eat away from home, convenience and location become overriding consumer needs. This does not simply mean geographic location or proximity to a specific type of food service operation. In fact, convenience more often implies quickness of service. This is often the single most important factor for any food service sub-segment when time plays into the decision to eat away from home. Convenience and location also contribute to the healthy growth of in-store operations, such as dining areas within supermarkets, food franchises in mega stores such as a Wal-Mart, and kiosk operations.

Key Terms

administrators/secretaries—Business travel intermediaries who generally are employed by the organization requesting travel services.

credit card companies—travel intermediaries that can influence purchase decisions by promoting and selling consumer travel packages put together by other intermediaries.

end user—The ultimate consumer of a travel product or service.

intermediary—An individual or firm that facilitates transactions between travel consumers and travel suppliers. There are two types: commercial (those earning commissions) and captive—those who make travel plans for others as part of their regular jobs (for example, secretaries) and do not earn commissions.

meeting planners—Usually association, corporate, or training company executives whose major goal is to plan and execute successful conventions, conferences, or meetings.

on-line enterprises—Companies created to offer search, comparison, booking, and other services via the Internet.

per diem—The amount of money that individuals can recover from their organizations for travel expenses.

traffic department—An area within a company that manages and schedules business travel for company employees.

travel agents—Firms or individuals that arrange air, cruise, and rail travel and place reservations for car rentals and lodging accommodations for both business and pleasure travelers.

travel club—An organization that targets frequent pleasure travelers and offers club members special travel packages to travel destinations.

travel management company—An organization that provides travel management services on a contractual or fee basis to corporations, government agencies, associations, and other organizations with business-related travel needs.

Chapter 4 Outline

Channels of Distribution
    Travel Intermediaries
    Electronic Travel Distribution Systems
    Ground Operators
    Air Carriers
    Channels of Distribution in Europe
       and Japan
Government Regulation of Travel
    United States
    Foreign Governments
Vertical, Horizontal, Backward, and
    Forward Integration

Competencies

1. Describe channels of distribution within the hospitality industry. (pp. 33–40)

2. List and briefly describe U.S. and international governmental entities that regulate or influence travel. (pp. 40–42)

3. Describe vertical and horizontal integration in the hospitality industry. (pp. 42–43)

4

The Channels of Distribution

BECAUSE THE HOSPITALITY INDUSTRY serves many consumer segments, it has established channels of distribution through which it markets its products and services. A **channel of distribution** is an entity through which the consumer may purchase all or parts of a travel product or service directly or indirectly. Advances in technology have created a dynamic environment within existing distribution channels, as well as adding new systems to the purchase process. The industry is also becoming increasingly complex, in that often a variety of travel products and services is offered by the same firm or interrelated firms. The purpose of this chapter is to describe the hospitality industry's channels of distribution, touch on governmental regulation of travel, and discuss the evolution of integrated hospitality industry firms and their relationship to marketing.

Channels of Distribution

Channels of distribution within the hospitality industry include travel intermediaries (such as travel agents and tour operators), electronic travel distribution systems, ground operators, and air carriers. We will discuss each of these channels of distribution in the following sections.

Travel Intermediaries

In order to understand the complexity of how travel products can be purchased and marketed, let's return briefly to the consumer. Consumers may travel to visit friends and relatives, for business, for recreation, for sightseeing and entertainment, for personal or family reasons, to gamble, or to visit a specific destination or attraction (see Exhibit 1). A travel product or service, be it for business or pleasure, can be purchased directly and usually in its entirety (from flight to lodging to meals) by individual consumers. However, today there is a much greater inclination among consumers to seek and use the services of either a captive or commercial **travel intermediary**.

A *captive intermediary* is an individual who does not receive a commission for handling travel arrangements for others. Examples of captive intermediaries include secretaries, office managers, and employees in company travel departments. A *commercial intermediary* is an individual (or entity) who works for a commission from a supplier of travel for handling the travel arrangements of individual or group consumers. Whether captive or commercial, the intermediary obtains the travel product and service through specific channels of distribution.

Examples of commercial intermediaries include the following:

Exhibit 1   The Purpose of Travel

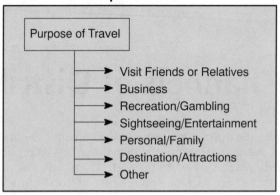

- *Retail travel agents (RTAs).* Retail travel agents sell tours, hotel rooms, airline tickets, steamship tickets, and so forth for wholesalers and tour operators. Retail travel agents earn all or most of their gross revenue from commissions. Travel agent commissions from travel suppliers vary by supplier and by country, but usually range from 10 to 40 percent.

- *Travel management companies.* Travel management companies provide a variety of travel management services, from financial management and credit card services to completely managing a firm's entire travel operation. Travel management companies are growing rapidly as travel becomes a focal point of cost management in corporations and government. Many large travel management companies also own or operate groups of retail travel agencies.

- *Tour operators-retailers.* **Tour operators-retailers** create "packages" for tourists that may include air, lodging, and ground services, and then offer them to consumers through a variety of such marketing tools as print and broadcast media, storefront operations, travel agents, and direct mail. In some countries (Germany and the United Kingdom, for example), these travel packages are sold through retail outlets directly to consumers on a large-scale basis.

- *Tour operators-wholesalers.* **Tour operators-wholesalers** create tour packages by buying the transportation, accommodations, and attraction components, then retail the packages through travel agents. Tour wholesalers service retail travel agents by preparing tour packages, ordering brochures and posters, and advertising. The difference between a tour operator-wholesaler and a tour operator-retailer is that the tour operator-wholesaler never sells directly to consumers, whereas a tour operator-retailer may.

- *Packagers/retailers.* Some packagers of tour products and services have now integrated vertically into retailing through their own outlets, after having moved into ownership of their own accommodations or transportation. One example of a packager/retailer is Club Med, which owns its resorts, charters transportation to them, and even markets/retails direct to individual consumers.

- *Incentive travel company.* Incentive travel companies specialize in putting together and selling travel awards, prizes, gifts, premiums, and so forth for individuals, groups, companies, and associations. The **incentive travel** trip or tour is usually sold to the user organization as part of a complete motivational package. Incentive travel is often used in a sales or marketing area to raise money for a group such as a church or other association, or to stimulate interest in a new product. In addition to the tour, incentive travel companies may also supply other administrative and creative capabilities to buyers.

- *Convention movers.* Convention movers specialize in moving people to and from conventions, usually using the major airlines and their regularly scheduled flights. Convention movers may also offer pre- or post-convention tours.

- *Travel clubs.* A relatively new merchandising method in group travel is the travel club. A travel club usually offers a group travel plan whereby membership in the club makes travel opportunities and vacation destination facilities available to members at discounted prices. The accommodations offered by travel clubs range from deluxe to very modest. Usually travel clubs offer a wide choice of locations, climate, terrain, and other vacation features. Unique atmospheres and sometimes-specialized areas, events, and activities are often selling points of travel clubs.

- *Charter travel company.* A charter travel company specializes in putting together groups of people with common interests. The individuals are then eligible for charter flights, which are governed by specific regulations. A charter travel company also helps groups pay for and operate tours.

- *Electronic/on-line travel service providers.* Electronic/on-line travel service providers have emerged as informational sources as well as direct booking services. Examples range from American Express Travel Services on-line to Travelocity and other discounters. Most Internet service providers such as AOL and MSN have agreements with one or more on-line travel intermediaries.

Electronic Travel Distribution Systems

Electronic travel distribution systems were conceived in the 1960s when the airlines created their first computerized reservation systems. In the 1970s, airline reservation computer terminals were installed in travel agencies, and both car-rental and hotel reservations capabilities were added to the airlines' reservation systems. Thus, wherever an airline reservation terminal was installed, a new distribution location for booking travel emerged. As airline reservation systems expanded throughout the world, they created automated travel booking capabilities on a global basis.

In the 1980s, deregulation of U.S. airlines allowed for these now global electronic travel distribution systems to be developed as businesses unto themselves. Further dramatic expansion, combined with enhanced technologies, resulted in the majority of major travel agencies and corporate travel offices being automated and tied directly into the electronic travel distribution system of their choice. The U.S. systems were Apollo (also referred to as COVIA), Sabre, System One, and

Worldspan. The Canadian system is Gemini; European systems were Amadeus and Galileo; and Asian systems included AXESS, Fantasia, and Abacus. Apollo, originally a United Airlines reservations product, and Sabre, originally an American Airlines product, each had approximately 30 percent of worldwide market share.

During the 1990s the global electronic travel distribution systems improved their hotel reservation capabilities, allowing for multiple room types, rate codes, negotiated rates, and other pertinent lodging information to be included in their programs. Today and in the future more "seamless" links and "mirroring" of hotel reservation, property management, central reservation, and yield management systems within the global electronic travel distribution systems are emerging as new networks are developed. Enhancements in product displays, pictures, voice, video, and other capabilities are being introduced daily into these global systems.

The four major **global distribution systems (GDS)** today are Amadeus, Galileo, Sabre, and Worldspan.

Amadeus is a global distribution system providing on-line distribution, marketing, and sales tools to travel professionals around the globe. Amadeus was founded in 1987 by Air France, Iberia, Lufthansa, and SAS. Shortly after its formation, SAS sold its shares to Amadeus Data Processing. As of today, three founder airline shareholders hold 59.92 percent of the company: Air France (23.36 percent), Iberia (18.28 percent), and Lufthansa (18.28 percent). Remaining shares are held publicly.

Even though Amadeus is the youngest of the four GDS companies, it has done remarkably well during its short life span. Amadeus' comprehensive data network and database, among the largest of their kind in Europe, serve more than 57,000 travel agency locations and more than 10,500 airline sales offices in some 200 markets worldwide. The system can also provide access to approximately 58,000 hotels and 50 rental companies serving some 24,000 locations, as well as other provider groups, including ferry, rail, cruise, insurance, and tour operators. Over 174,000 travel agency terminals are connected to Amadeus.

While the company is number one in locations worldwide, serving the greatest number of countries, it provides the fewest U.S. destinations of the top four GDSs. As with its competitors, the future for Amadeus will continue to be linked to the technological and structural changes that are revolutionizing the travel industry. Amadeus appears to be adapting well to the shift of business to the Internet. With its strong company infrastructure worldwide, impressive product set, and growing customer base, Amadeus is one of the most significant players in shaping the future of the GDS.

Galileo International is one of the world's leading providers of electronic global distribution services. Its business expands throughout 116 countries in North America, Europe, the Middle East, Africa, and the Asia/Pacific region. Galileo International was founded in 1993 by 11 major North American and European airlines: Aer Lingus, Air Canada, Alitalia, Austrian Airlines, British Airways, KLM Royal Dutch Airlines, Olympic Airlines, Swissair, TAP Air Portugal, United Airlines, and US Airways. In 1997, Galileo International became a publicly traded company, listed on the New York and Chicago Stock Exchanges. In October of

2001, Cendant Corporation acquired Galileo International for approximately $1.8 billion in common stock and cash.

Galileo's global distribution system has a state-of-the-art development center supplying information and system support to travel agencies operating more than 178,000 computer terminals, all of which are linked to the Galileo's Data Center. Galileo provides subscribers with the ability to access schedule and fare information, book reservations, and issue tickets. Galileo also provides subscribers with information and booking capabilities covering 51,000 hotel properties, 34 car rental companies, 431 tour operators, 47 travel agency locations, 503 airlines, and all major cruise lines throughout the world.

Galileo is pursuing a strategy that includes expanding its global distribution, strengthening customer loyalty, leveraging technology, and capitalizing on opportunities created by increasing Internet use. Galileo sees the GDS industry as having the ability and potential to provide electronic distribution and many components of e-commerce to other industries, and is utilizing its strengths to provide expanding services to its growing customer base.

Sabre is a global leader in information technology for the travel and transportation industries. Headquartered in Texas for more than 40 years, Sabre has been developing innovations and transforming the business of travel. From the original Sabre computer reservations system in the 1960s, to advanced airline yield management systems in the 1980s, to leading travel web sites (Travelocity, Virtually There) today, Sabre technology has traveled through time. In July of 1996, Sabre became a separate legal entity of AMR (parent company of American Airlines). Sabre, represented in 45 countries, is a leading provider of technology for the travel industry and provides innovative products that enable travel commerce and services and enhance airline/supplier operations.

Sabre has its presence in 45 countries, connecting more than 60,000 travel agencies to more than 400 airlines, 55,000 hotel properties, 52 car rental companies, 9 cruise lines, 33 railroads, and 229 tour operators.

Sabre's competitive strengths include market position, global reach, stable product line, diversification of revenue streams, and intellectual capital. The Sabre business model is a strong one, and continues to make significant progress in advancing both its electronic travel distribution and its information technology solutions businesses.

Worldspan provides global electronic distribution of travel information, Internet products and connectivity, and electronic commerce capabilities for travel agencies, travel service providers, and corporations worldwide. The company's three lines of business are travel suppliers services, e-commerce, and global distribution systems for the worldwide travel industry.

Founded February 7, 1990, Worldspan is currently owned by affiliates of Delta Air Lines, (40 percent), Northwest Airlines (34 percent), and American Airlines, Inc. (26 percent). Since its 1995 advance into the world of Internet technology for the travel industry, Worldspan has successfully developed the strategies, solutions, and services to ensure the company's long-term success in web-based travel distribution. Worldspan currently serves 21,000 travel agencies in nearly 90 countries and territories. Headquartered in Atlanta, Georgia, Worldspan connects approximately 421 airlines, 210 hotel companies, 40 car rental companies, 39 tour and vacation operators, and 44 special travel service suppliers.

Worldspan has a legacy of industry firsts that are not well known. The company therefore has an opportunity to raise the industry's awareness of its accomplishments and, more importantly, its future strategies. Worldspan continues to look at the benefits of creating its own consumer brand and has been partnering with different companies to expand the services that it can provide to its customer base.

Ground Operators

Ground operators are those businesses that provide ground services related to a tour (rooms, meals, and so on) at destinations. A ground operator may be independent, part of a larger tour operator, or have some other direct or indirect relationship with a tour operator. In the case of large and some specialized (by destination) tour operators, a tour conductor—an individual who personally escorts a group of passengers for all or part of an itinerary—may have the expertise to provide most of these ground-operator services.

Air Carriers

The airline industry has helped to develop the entire hospitality industry. There are two types of air carriers that transport people: scheduled carriers and supplemental carriers.

Scheduled carriers provide air transportation at specified times over specified routes and have published schedules. Until the mid-1980s the fares and routes of U.S. scheduled carriers were regulated by the Civil Aeronautics Board (CAB). In an effort to streamline government, the president and Congress eliminated CAB. While some jurisdictional functions were transferred to the Department of Transportation and the Department of Justice, most were reduced to allow for what was referred to as *deregulation.* Under deregulation, mergers and acquisitions have prevailed, as the combined pressures of fare wars, lack of capitalization, and extensive route competition have weeded out the weaker airline companies.

Under deregulation, the Federal Aviation Administration (FAA), the Department of Transportation (DOT), and—in cases of mergers and acquisitions—the Department of Justice are the major government entities involved in regulating the carriers. The FAA and DOT still closely monitor routes, safety, air traffic control, airport development, and other aspects of the industry. Deregulation's impact was, and is, primarily felt in the rate area.

DOT must approve the participation of U.S.-flagged carriers serving international routes. (U.S.-flagged carriers are airlines based in the United States that are owned by U.S. corporations.) In addition, agreement must be reached with the International Air Transport Association (IATA). IATA is the trade and service organization for most of the world's scheduled airlines serving international routes. The Air Transport Association of America is the trade and service organization representing U.S. scheduled carriers.

Supplemental carriers are a class of nonscheduled air carriers that hold certificates to supplement the regular service provided by scheduled carriers. Supplemental carriers are authorized to operate over broad areas. The National Air Carrier Association (NACA) is the trade and service organization that represents the U.S. supplemental carriers.

Channels of Distribution in Europe and Japan

While the channels of distribution or travel intermediaries just described represent methods of marketing travel products in the United States, they also exist in other parts of the world. The European and Japanese approaches to selling travel (including marketing and distribution services) are geared to a mature mass market. In Europe and Japan there is usually a more defined "holiday" period, which means that large portions of the population take their vacations at the same time of the year. The travel industry in Europe and Japan markets to these masses in every imaginable way—both through the media and directly through sales outlets. Tourism retains a high level of recognition in European countries. In addition to the operations of the national tourist offices, travel is marketed by the following techniques:

- Mass media (through catalogs, newspapers, magazines, direct mail promotion, radio, and TV)

- Merchandising (through travel and recreational clubs)

- Direct sales outlets (through storefront operations, tour operators, wholesalers selling directly to the public, banks, and—in Germany and Switzerland—sales in department stores)

Travel is marketed by airlines, travel companies (retail and wholesale), banks, tour organizers, tour operators, hotels, tourist ministries and departments, local tourist authorities, and other travel organizations. Low-cost holidays are made available to the public through the use of charter airlines and through tour operators or wholesalers who purchase seats, rooms, beds, food, and so on in bulk.

Travel marketers in the United States are starting to adopt some of the travel-marketing tactics that have proved successful in Europe and Japan. These tactics include innovations in promotion and advertising, pricing, packaging, and selling. In the area of promotion and advertising, U.S. airlines are making greater use of direct mail and special promotions aimed directly at consumers. The U.S. travel industry has become much more aggressive about luring consumers with attractive prices, using special promotional fares, excursion tours, and discount rates. Travel-industry advertising is putting more emphasis on travel packages, which include airfare, lodging, meals, car rental, and other services. There are also many new developments in merchandising, such as selling travel more directly to consumers through travel clubs, department stores, and bank credit card companies. In addition, there is a movement toward consolidation in the retail and wholesale areas that is resulting in changes in the traditional roles of wholesalers and retailers.

In addition to these outlets for travel products, there are many others through which a consumer may purchase travel. These include, but are not limited to, auto clubs, vacation clubs, time-sharing resort condominiums, and holiday club plans.

Government Regulation of Travel

There are numerous U.S. and international governmental entities that regulate or influence travel.

United States

A number of U.S. government organizations play a role in regulating the travel industry in the United States, including the following:

- Interstate Commerce Commission (ICC), which has jurisdiction over railroads and motorcoaches
- Federal Maritime Commission (FMC), which has jurisdiction over U.S.-flagged ships
- Department of Transportation (DOT), which has jurisdiction over the Federal Aviation Administration (FAA)
- Department of State, which negotiates bilateral agreements with other nations and handles matters of diplomatic concern
- Department of Justice (DOJ), which enforces antitrust laws and whose antitrust division sometimes participates in cases involving mergers, acquisitions, and expansion efforts
- Department of Commerce, whose United States Travel Service (USTS) is designed to promote travel to and within the United States
- Department of the Treasury, which concerns itself with the balance of payments
- Congress, whose Senate Commerce Committee's Subcommittee on Aviation and Subcommittee on Foreign Commerce and Tourism have jurisdiction over legislation related to international travel

Foreign Governments

Virtually all foreign governments play a major role in shaping policy on internal and external tourism. The degree of foreign-government involvement, which is substantially greater than in the United States, flows from several factors. One is that most foreign governments have a higher appreciation for the importance of tourism, particularly in an economic sense, than does the United States. Also, with very few exceptions, the flagged carriers of foreign countries are owned and controlled by their governments.

The ministries of tourism in foreign countries exert a great deal of influence on government policy. Most foreign governments, particularly in Europe, tend to be more involved than the U.S. government in guiding or dictating the direction of their tourism industries. European governments also tend to participate more in intergovernmental organizations, such as the International Civil Aviation Organization (ICAO), the European Civil Aviation Conference (ECAC), and the International Union of Official Travel Organizations (IUOTO).

In addition, many areas of the world support large influential associations that have travel at the forefront of their interests. For example, PATA—the Pacific Area Travel Association—is a large group promoting travel and tourism in the Pacific.

Most of the countries that are prominent in the tourism field encourage travel to their countries, particularly from the United States, but discourage travel by their own citizens to other countries. This attitude is prompted by economic and financial motives. The two major organizations in the United States and globally today are the Travel Industry Association of America (TIA) and the World Tourism Organization (WTO).

The Travel Industry Association of America, in existence since 1941, is the Washington, D.C.-based, non-profit association that represents and speaks for the common interests and concerns of all components of the U.S. travel industry. It is the recognized leader in promoting and facilitating increased travel to and within the United States in order to make America the world's number one tourism destination. It is also the authoritative and recognized source of research, analysis, and forecasting for the entire industry and the industry's primary focal point for the domestic and international media.

TIA seeks to increase understanding of tourism's impact and the immense importance of tourism to the economic, social, and cultural life of the United States. TIA accomplishes its objectives by providing an array of marketing programs, forums, and marketing and research publications that provide opportunities for all components of the industry, both large and small. TIA seeks to protect the industry from governmental initiatives that would impede travel by discriminating against the traveler or the travel industry. TIA does not seek to duplicate the objectives or efforts of other travel industry associations or organizations, which represent the specific interests of individual industry components. TIA focuses on five major objectives:

- To promote a wider understanding of travel and tourism as a major U.S. industry that contributes substantially to the economic well-being of the nation

- To bring cohesion to the travel industry and provide communications forums for industry leaders

- To serve as the authoritative source for travel industry research, analysis, and forecasting

- To initiate and to cooperate with government entities in the development and implementation of programs, policies, and legislation that are responsive to the needs of the industry and to intervene in those issues and initiatives that would directly affect the facilitation and promotion of travel to and within the United States

*   To develop and implement programs beneficial to the travel supplier and consumer

The World Tourism Organization is the leading international organization in the field of travel and tourism. It serves as a global forum for tourism policy issues and a practical source of tourism know-how and statistics. Its membership includes 139 countries, seven territories, and some 350 affiliate members representing regional and local promotion boards, tourism trade associations, educational institutions, and private sector companies, including airlines, hotel groups, and tour operators.

With its headquarters in Madrid and an international staff of 90 tourism specialists, WTO is an intergovernmental organization vested by the United Nations with a central and decisive role in promoting the development of responsible, sustainable, and universally accessible tourism. Through tourism, WTO aims to stimulate economic growth and job creation, provide incentives for protecting the environment and cultural heritage, and promote peace, prosperity, and respect for human rights.

The World Tourism Organization believes that governments have a vital role to play in tourism. WTO exists to help nations throughout the world maximize the positive impacts of tourism, such as job creation, new infrastructure, and foreign exchange earnings, while at the same time minimizing negative environmental or social impacts.

Vertical, Horizontal, Backward, and Forward Integration

The hospitality industry provides multiple examples of **integration**. These various types of integration often play a vital role in marketing strategy. Let's briefly look at each form of integration.

Vertical integration occurs when a firm is involved in more than one element of the purchasing and distribution process. An example would be Carlson Companies, which has the hotel and resort element, the travel agency network, the incentive travel operations, etc.

Horizontal integration occurs when a company gains increasing market share of a given segment of the industry. An example of horizontal integration would be Marriott International which has numerous lodging brands under its roof such as Courtyard, Marriott Hotels and Resorts, Renaissance, Ritz-Carlton, etc.

Backward integration occurs when a firm takes over operations previously the responsibility of suppliers. An example would be a fast food chain owning the potato supplier or airline owning the food service supplier.

Forward integration occurs when a hospitality firm begins to control the outlets for its products or services. An example would be a company like Pleasant Holidays, a major "packager" that owns its own hotels at some of its destinations.

A general definition of integration is the ownership, control, or joint venture involving two or more hospitality industry products or services by the same firm. The hospitality industry is perhaps unique in this regard in that a large number of firms within the industry engage in more than one function from a product, service, distribution, and marketing perspective. One only needs to think of such brands as Cendant, Carlson Companies, Marriott International, Hilton, Six Continents, or United Airlines to understand the depth and breadth of integration in the hospitality industry.

Key Terms

channels of distribution—Vehicles through which travel-related products and services may be marketed by suppliers or purchased by consumers.

global distribution system (GDS)—The computer systems that travel agents use to book airline seats, rental cars, hotel rooms, and other travel reservations and services.

incentive travel—A trip offered as a reward.

integration—The ownership, control, or joint venture involving two or more hospitality industry products or services by the same firm.

tour operator-retailer—A company that specializes in the planning and operation of prepaid, preplanned vacations, and makes these available to the public through travel agents.

tour operator-wholesaler—A company that services retail travel agents in the preparation of tour packages, ordering, billing, and advertising.

travel intermediary—An individual or firm that facilitates transactions between travel consumers and travel suppliers. There are two types: commercial (those earning commissions) and captive—those who make travel plans for others as part of their regular jobs (for example, secretaries) and do not earn commissions.

Chapter 5 Outline

Planning Resources for the Marketing
    Effort
Targeting Profitable Consumer Segments
Reaching the Market

Competencies

1. Explain why hospitality companies need flexible marketing strategies. (p. 45)

2. Describe how marketing efforts benefit from a zero-base budgeting process. (pp. 45–46)

3. Explain the function of internal and external analyses in determining company needs that marketing can fulfill. (pp. 46–47)

4. Describe how the concept of segment profitability applies to the marketing of hospitality products and services. (p. 47)

5. Identify some of the key motivational factors of travel retailers and wholesalers that could help shape a hospitality company's marketing efforts. (pp. 48–49)

5

Marketing in Perspective

TODAY MORE THAN EVER BEFORE, marketing strategies must be flexible. In a crowded and highly competitive marketplace, "change" is the key word in marketing. Marketers must have the flexibility to alter strategies and respond quickly to challenges arising either from changes in market conditions or from actions taken by aggressive competitors. This is why, over the last several years, we have seen a variety of hospitality marketing strategies such as frequent traveler programs and incentives for repeat customers, as well as price wars and discount advertising campaigns.

This chapter places marketing in perspective by examining the needs of hospitality companies for specific marketing efforts and how those efforts are funded through an effective budgeting process. While marketing activities focus on the needs of consumers, the budget funding those activities must focus on the specific marketing needs of the company. The chapter also explores marketing by showing how companies determine the best uses for marketing resources by targeting the most profitable market segments. The final section of the chapter briefly looks at how the most effective marketing techniques are selected for reaching appropriate market segments.

Planning Resources for the Marketing Effort

Hotels, restaurants, and other hospitality businesses face the same challenge: how to plan marketing activities that make the best use of the limited resources budgeted for the company's marketing effort.

This challenge is often complicated by poor budgeting practices. Time and time again, dollars for marketing are determined on the basis of amounts set by the previous year's budget—which, in turn, were based on the budget for the year before that. This kind of budgeting process fails to respond to the current and future marketing needs of a company. The hospitality marketplace is dynamic. The needs of consumers are constantly changing. A company's competitors are also constantly changing as they adapt their marketing messages and activities to address new consumer needs. A marketing budget formed on the basis of prior years' expenses often stagnates the marketing activities of a company in the ruts and routines of the past.

Resources for marketing efforts should be based on specific company goals that identify the kind of business that the company needs and when it needs that business. This approach to funding the marketing efforts of a company is part of a zero-base budgeting process. **Zero-base budgeting** requires the justification of all expenses. This approach assumes that each department, including marketing, starts with zero dollars and must justify all budgeted amounts. No expenditure is justified just because it was spent last year. Every expense is re-analyzed and justified each year on the basis that its expenditure this year will yield more favorable results than spending the same amount in another way.

Marketing planning begins with defining the products and services to be marketed and identifying the "core" dollars needed by marketing to maintain a desired level of business. For example, consider a casual-dining restaurant that serves lunch and dinner seven days a week. If the volume of business during weekday lunch periods is currently at or over capacity, then the restaurant may not need to allocate additional marketing dollars to increasing customer counts at lunch. The current level of marketing activity and expense may be sufficient to maintain the desired level of business. Similarly, consider a 1,000-room hotel that achieves near 100 percent occupancy during Monday and Tuesday nights, mainly from business off its reservations system. This hotel may not need to spend any marketing dollars for building business on these nights, other than the fee paid for accessing the reservations system. In both of these cases, an analysis of business activity shows where *not* to concentrate new marketing activities and identifies the "core" dollars needed to maintain a desired level of business. These amounts become justified under a zero-base approach to budgeting and are set as part of the overall marketing budget. The next step is to identify areas in which the company wishes to increase business and justify the marketing expenses that will be necessary to make the increases happen.

Targeting Profitable Consumer Segments

Planning resources for the marketing effort (beyond allocating core dollars needed to maintain current levels of business) begins with identifying specific company needs and targeting consumer segments that can most profitably meet those company needs.

Consider again the 1,000-room hotel that sells out nearly every Monday and Tuesday night. Let's assume that further analysis of the hotel's current pattern of business shows that, on average, only 330 rooms are sold on Friday nights and only 250 rooms are sold on Saturday nights. With 33-percent and 25-percent occupancy rates respectively, Friday and Saturday nights are clearly areas of company need for building more business. Marketing's task is to target specific consumer segments that could provide the most profitable business for the hotel on these nights.

Most of the business market segments can be eliminated; individuals from these segments do not travel much on weekends. In fact, this is probably why the hotel's occupancy rate is so low on Friday and Saturday nights in the first place. What's called for here is an internal and external analysis of pleasure market segments. The internal analysis identifies current customers—the pleasure travel segments that the hotel currently attracts with minimal marketing expense. Internal analysis also seeks to understand the needs of these customers and explain why they stay at the hotel on weekend nights. An external analysis studies the hotel's competitors. The objectives here are to determine which market segments the competition attracts and understand their customers' needs for weekend accommodations.

Based on the results of internal and external analysis, targeted pleasure market segments can be ranked in order of potential business volume. For example, a partial listing might include:

- Second honeymooners.

- Families escaping for the weekend.

- Sight-seeing groups.

- Regional sports teams.

Before allocating resources for marketing to any one of these segments, the profitability of each segment should be analyzed.

Segment profitability is determined by analyzing the revenue and profit generated through the sale of products and services to a particular type of consumer or market segment. As in all businesses, some customers are more profitable to serve than others. A hotel can determine the profitability of market segments by reviewing purchasing patterns of past customers. Historical information from guest folios shows the number and types of purchases made by customers grouped into the market segments under analysis. Although the profitability of market segments varies from property to property, the segment profitability ranking that follows could apply to many hotels:

1. International executives on unrestricted expense accounts with multiple-night stays

2. Executives on relatively unrestricted expense accounts

3. Individuals attending a corporate group meeting, conference, or convention

4. Individuals attending an association group meeting, conference, or convention

5. Second honeymooners

6. Regional sports clubs and teams

7. Families with children

8. Individuals on restricted expense accounts

Given the need of the hotel in our example to build weekend business, the first reaction might be to focus resources on attracting business from second honeymooners. However, before spending precious marketing dollars, it's important to examine if it's possible to get a multiple sale for the same cost involved in securing a single sale. That is, can the marketing effort attract a group—such as family reunions—that will fill many rooms instead of filling rooms one at a time with marketing activities directed at individual second honeymooners? Perhaps the marketing effort should focus on attracting the local or state chapter of the Jaguar or Corvette Owners Club of America. Failing this, perhaps booking weekend business from sports clubs and teams would prove more profitable in terms of the return on investment of marketing dollars than promoting weekend stays to individual second honeymooners.

Exhibit 1   Marketing Within Distribution Channels

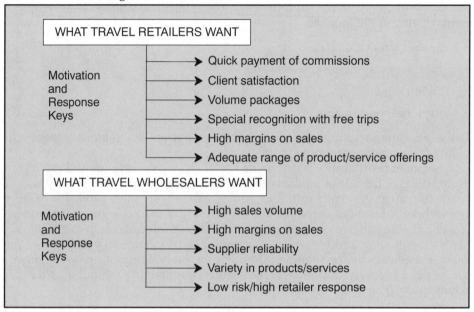

Reaching the Market ———————————————————————————————

After identifying the business needs of the company and the most profitable market segments that could achieve the desired results, the next step is to determine the marketing resources needed to effectively reach the targeted audiences. Different consumer segments respond to different marketing approaches. The wrong method or the wrong message can be counterproductive.

The most effective marketing methods or techniques are defined in terms of unique characteristics of the targeted market segments. Each market segment is motivated by a specific set of needs to purchase hospitality products and services. Lists of market segments, distribution channels, and marketing techniques are useless without understanding what is important to the consumer—what needs motivate market segments to seek hospitality products and services.

Let's assume that the marketing strategy of the hotel in our example is to build weekend business by attracting sightseeing groups as well as sports clubs and teams. One of the marketing methods used to activate this strategy would be to reach travel retailers and wholesalers who book accommodations for these market segments. The intermediaries, however, are motivated by a very different set of needs than the clients they serve. Understanding their unique needs will help create the most effective marketing messages for them. Exhibit 1 lists motivational factors that are keys to eliciting effective responses to marketing efforts directed to travel retailers and wholesalers. This is only one example of how two different groups in the distribution chain are motivated by unique needs. Similar sets of motivation factors and response keys can be developed for other distribution

Exhibit 2   Marketing in Perspective

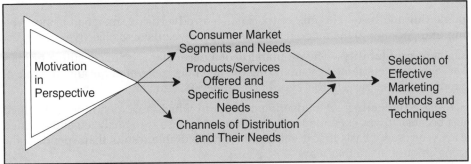

Exhibit 3   The Marketing Toolbox

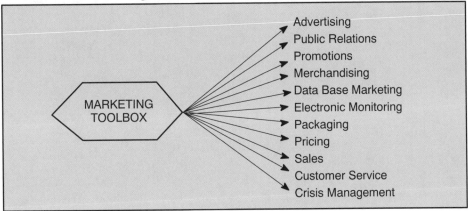

channels as well as for each end user and market segment. The motivation factors and response keys direct the marketing effort toward the most effective method for marketing.

Exhibit 2 puts hospitality marketing in perspective by showing how the most effective marketing methods are selected only after developing a thorough understanding of three important areas:

1. The consumer market segments and their needs

2. The products and services offered by the hospitality company and its specific business needs

3. The motivation factors and response keys of the various distribution channels for hospitality products and services

For any business, product/service, or brand, understanding what each tool in your **marketing toolbox** is capable of doing and how and when to use it is yet another key component for marketing strategy (see Exhibit 3).

Key Terms

marketing toolbox—The mix of tools (such as advertising, merchandising, pricing, and packaging) the marketer can use to achieve business objectives.

segment profitability—The profitability of a particular type of consumer or market segment, determined by analyzing the revenues generated through the sale of products and services to that type of consumer or segment.

zero-base budgeting—A budgeting concept in which no expenditure is justified just because it was expended last year. Every expense is re-analyzed and justified each year on the basis that it will yield more favorable results than spending the same amount in another way.

Chapter 6 Outline

Competencies

1. Explain the purpose of marketing research, and describe types of marketing research. (pp. 53–55)

2. Describe three basic marketing research techniques. (pp. 55–57)

3. Delineate five essential "marketing intelligence" tools. (pp. 57–58)

4. Describe marketing research presentation tools. (pp. 58–67)

6

Applying Key Marketing Methodologies: Marketing Research

BEFORE YOU DEVELOP a marketing strategy and select a marketing tool to execute that strategy, you have to know your product/service, your target markets and their needs, and your competition. Your marketing strategies should be based on sound research, employ appropriate marketing tools, and be aimed directly at your target markets. The purpose of this chapter is to provide you with tools and techniques to research and analyze your product/service and the marketplace.

Marketing Research

One of the most difficult and important tasks in developing a marketing strategy is understanding objectively what your product or service really is in relation to your competition and the marketplace. The purpose of marketing research is to provide facts to help you make the proper judgments about your products, prices, and marketing strategies. Generally speaking, the more objective facts you have available to you, the sounder will be your selection of a marketing strategy.

There are many ways to classify, conduct, and categorize marketing research. In the following sections we will focus on the major types of marketing research, identify selected research techniques, and examine some tools for presenting marketing research data.

Types of Marketing Research

Broadly speaking, marketing research can be either quantitative or qualitative. Quantitative marketing research seeks to quantify data using numbers, projections, forecasts, etc. Qualitative marketing research seeks to identify, analyze, or profile consumers, working with consumer attitudes, behaviors, etc. Both quantitative and qualitative marketing research can be either primary or secondary. Primary research is research you conduct yourself; secondary research is research that someone else has conducted.

Marketing research can also be categorized with respect to:

- Markets.
- Products or services.

- Consumers.

- The competition.

- The environment.

- Trends.

Let's briefly examine each of these marketing research categories.

Market Research. Also referred to as area demand analysis when dealing with lodging facilities, **market research** seeks to quantify and segment demand. The standard guest segments in the lodging industry are transient, group, business, and leisure. Demand also is usually classified with respect to weekdays, weekends, rate categories, and sources. Common sources of demand include local sources (areas near the hotel/motel), retail sources, service and manufacturing concerns, tourist attractions, convention facilities, cultural events, and sources related to traffic flow and transportation arteries.

Product or Service Research. Product or service research usually focuses on your product's/service's strengths and weaknesses in relation to the products/services of competitors. In the lodging industry, this is often referred to as property research. Typically, a hotel's tangible features (physical assets) are profiled, such as number of guestrooms, square footage and layout of meeting space, recreational facilities, property amenities, etc. Likewise, intangibles (qualitative assets) are also profiled, such as guest perceptions, quality and customer service ratings, reputation, ratings by travel organizations (such as the American Automobile Association), and relative competitive positioning within the marketplace. Product or service research also takes into consideration factors such as substitutability—alternatives to the property of equal or similar rating; proximity—the advantages and disadvantages of the hotel's location; and rate data—rate surveys of similar properties. Some hotels include only rate surveys of those properties within a fixed percentage (e.g., 15 percent) of their rates, while others profile the entire market.

Consumer Research. Consumer research takes many different forms in the hospitality industry. One of the most common with respect to hotels and resorts is referred to as **prospect research.** This research provides a profile of present and future guests. Sources of information include reservations data, registration input, check-out information, and origin- and destination-market data.

The origin market is where the traveler has come from. Origin-market data can be classified in a number of ways. The most widely used classifications are geographic, such as country, region, state, city, etc. Origin markets can also be classified by MSA (metropolitan statistical areas) and postal zip codes.

Since marketing frequently relies on the media as one method to reach prospective customers, present and future guests can be categorized by DMAs (Designated Market Areas—geographic areas reached by clusters of television stations, as defined by the A. C. Nielson Co.) or ADIs (Areas of Dominant Influence—geographic areas defined by the circulation zones of major newspapers, as categorized by Arbitron, an audience research firm).

Consumer research seeks to identify the usage patterns of consumers, such as general travel habits and hotel or motel preferences. Consumer research also seeks to classify consumers by age, income, education, etc. (demographics), as well as discover their habits (psychographics) with respect to likes, dislikes, etc., always seeking to quantify where possible. Consumer research today explores everything from the purchasing habits to the attitudes and behaviors of consumers.

Competitive Research. One of the keys to successful marketing is understanding how your product or service compares to your top competitors' products or services. **Competitive research** compares your product or service to the products or services of competitors and tries to discover how consumers perceive and experience your product/service offering in relation to the competitors' products/services. Research questions are usually developed with respect to price/rates, quality of facility, service levels, convenience to purchase, etc. Competitive research reveals how your competitors are positioned—in relation to your product or service—to meet the needs of your key market segments, now and in the future.

Environmental Research. Marketing must take into account not only what consumers and competitors are doing, but also what is occurring within and to the total industry environment. **Environmental research** focuses on external forces (economic, social, political, technological, etc.) that are having or will have an impact on your product or service in some manner.

One key focus of environmental research is to look ahead at what form and shape opportunities and threats may take and how they will affect your activities. Frequently, competitive research and environmental research are linked. The output of these research assessments is often referred to with the acronym **SWOT**, which stands for Strengths, Weaknesses, Opportunities, and Threats. These strengths, weaknesses, opportunities, and threats can then be analyzed to provide support rationale for developing marketing action plans.

Trend Research. Trend research focuses on both quantitative and qualitative trends. Quantitative trend research seeks to identify significant increases or declines in customer preferences, methods of purchase, usage/frequency, and other factors affecting future demand. Qualitative trend research seeks to identify changes in consumer attitudes, interests, tastes, benefits sought, and so on. Trend research findings help marketers make strategic marketing decisions.

Marketing Research Techniques

Many types of marketing research techniques can be used to help you make sound marketing decisions. Which technique works best depends on many factors, such as the product/service offering, nature of the problem or opportunity, amount of resources available, time or urgency, budget, etc. Basic marketing research techniques widely used in the hospitality industry today include surveys, questionnaires, and focus groups. Of course, there are many other quantitative and qualitative research techniques employed in the industry, but the purpose of this section is to familiarize you with these three basic techniques. Regardless of the research technique selected, the goal remains the same—to gain information and apply the findings to improve the marketing and/or marketability of a product or service.

Surveys. A **survey** seeks to elicit consumer opinion, uncover facts, and gain insights on potential trends. Surveys may be conducted in a variety of ways, at various locations, among customers or potential customers, or even among competitors' customers. Surveys may be conducted in person, by phone, electronically, or by mail.

A survey is a structured document, usually seeking to quantify its findings in terms of percentages of those who agree or disagree with particular statements. It also seeks to measure the depth of agreement or disagreement, often employing a point scale—for example, "Circle 1 if you strongly agree, 5 if you strongly disagree." Five-, seven-, and ten-point scales are commonly used. Surveys are also used to seek qualitative information, especially when open-ended questions are asked—e.g., "What else would you like to see or have," etc. Surveys may be conducted only once or periodically scheduled, such as an annual frequent-flyer-program-preference survey. Multiple-period (semi-annual, monthly, etc.) surveys often seek to spot improvements or declines in such areas as property service levels or consumer preferences, thus providing a rationale for a marketing, operational, or development decision.

Questionnaires. Perhaps the most widely used research technique, **questionnaires** come in all types of forms and are used for multiple purposes. As data collection vehicles, questionnaires seek both factual information and opinion. Data that questionnaires are designed to collect include guest comments, customer profiles, product and service information, demographic and psychographic data, attitudinal information, consumer usage patterns and preferences, etc. The data collected may be used to measure property performance, improve products or services, qualify prospects, build leads, create mailing lists, determine consumer price sensitivity, analyze menus, and so on.

Like surveys, questionnaires can be conducted in person, by phone, by mail, or electronically. Questionnaires often are ongoing, such as guest-comment questionnaires, new customer/purchaser questionnaires, etc. Also like surveys, questionnaires can use scales or point systems to yield quantifiable data or rank items in order of importance.

Frequently, the terms "survey" and "questionnaire" are used interchangeably. However, questionnaires tend to be briefer than surveys and are usually less complex in content.

Focus Groups. A **focus group** is a marketing research technique that combines personal-opinion solicitation in the form of group discussion with a structured set of questions. During a focus group session, a "moderator" conducts or facilitates the discussion using a script designed to elicit opinions from focus group members on predetermined subjects. In some cases, time for more free-flowing discussion is built into a session. For additional analysis, focus groups may be recorded or observed via one-way mirrors. Focus group members may volunteer their time or be compensated.

There are a number of types of focus groups, ranging from single-area focus groups to regional/market-area focus groups to multiple focus groups. Single-area focus groups are focus groups drawn from one market; regional/market-area focus groups are single focus groups held in one or more regions of the country; multiple focus groups are more than one focus group held in multiple regions of the country. Also, there are product/service-user focus groups and non-user focus groups. Focus groups may be made up of your customers, your competitors' customers, prospective customers, or any combination thereof.

Focus groups by nature are more time-consuming for marketers to conduct and follow through on than surveys or questionnaires. Focus groups involve script writing, hiring a professional group leader, holding the focus group session itself, and then analyzing the focus group and its responses. In general, focus groups provide more in-depth qualitative findings related to attitudes and behavior than do questionnaires or surveys. Sometimes focus groups come up with useful questions that can be placed on subsequent questionnaires or surveys.

Five Essential Marketing Intelligence Tools

Before developing your strategic marketing plan, you need to "look within," "look around," and "look ahead." The following five **marketing intelligence tools** provide for key research findings or a "failsafe" for any business:

1. *SWOT Analysis.* Recording and analyzing your capabilities or resources can improve your competitive position and performance. You develop this intelligence by looking within at your internal company data. SWOT analysis helps you identify any capability or resource that may cause your organization to underperform or lose market share. Your external focus—looking around at competition and looking ahead at environmental trends—provides you with the marketing intelligence to spot opportunities, to justify new marketing strategy, and to identify trends that require changes to marketing strategy.

2. *Customer Satisfaction Index (CSI).* Consistently measuring customer satisfaction is essential to marketing strategy. Developing a methodical marketing intelligence tool such as a **Customer Satisfaction Index** can provide you with an on-going periodic scorecard on how your business is performing. Wherever possible, your CSI should be closely linked to performance evaluation and reward systems throughout every level of your organization.

3. *Customer Perceptions Audits (CPA).* **Customer Perceptions Audits** are marketing intelligence tools that provide objective (external) evaluation of how your business is performing and delivering throughout the entire pre-purchase to post-purchase experience. A CPA is a step-by-step walkthrough of all "points of encounters" with the customer from the customer's perspective—pre- through post-purchase. Often, mystery shoppers or external firms are used to perform the audit.

4. *GAP Analysis.* A **GAP analysis** as a marketing intelligence tool seeks to identify the difference between management's perspective of how the business is performing with respect to customer satisfaction and how the customer evaluates that performance. The difference is referred to as the GAP. A good GAP

analysis can be quantified/measured using an index. For example, on a 100-point index, management rates unit customer satisfaction at 85 percent and customers rate their experience at 65 percent—thus a 20 percent GAP between management's perspective and the customers'.

5. *Other People's Data (OPD).* Not every business can afford to conduct extensive marketing research with their limited resources. One solution is to employ the marketing intelligence tool called **Other People's Data**. OPD is secondary research that is conducted or compiled by someone other than yourself. It may be industry or product category information. Many people (agencies, competitors, the U.S. government, etc.) are constantly conducting research (primary research) and reporting or sharing the findings with the public. Take advantage of this free or very inexpensive marketing intelligence tool.

Marketing Research Presentation Tools

There are many presentation tools that marketers can use to help individuals understand and analyze research findings. Some of these presentation tools are simple graphics such as triangles and pyramids, circles or maps, linear diagrams, boxes or rectangles, and grids or matrices. Granted, some may view this as an oversimplification of the presentation process. However, the majority of research findings and models are visually presented using these simple forms. Let's look at a few research presentation tools that you will probably encounter during your career in the hospitality industry.

Pyramids. Pyramids are often used to depict size of markets, service levels, rates/prices, and product/brand positioning. Exhibit 1 presents a pyramid that profiles brands in the lodging industry by service levels and rates. This same presentation tool can be used to structure rates or profile market and price strategies.

Circles. Circles are frequently used for "mapping" purposes, wherein you are comparing your product/service to the expressed needs and wants of consumers and/or in relation to the products/services of competitors (see Exhibit 2). A "perceptual map" will help you focus on how well your product or service is doing in comparison to others in terms of quality and value, as perceived by your customers. In Exhibit 2, "quality" is plotted along the horizontal axis, "value" along the vertical axis. How your product/service is perceived by consumers is what locates you on the map. A perceptual map can help identify your problems and opportunities in relation to the market and your competition. A perceptual map can also be of great value in creating advertising or pricing strategies, or determining the necessity for product or service-level enhancements.

Linear Diagrams. Linear diagrams are frequently used to show "pathways" to targets, look at alternative strategies, develop networks and alliances, and aid in the decision-making process. One of the most popular linear diagrams is the "decision tree" (see Exhibit 3), most often used to view product/service extensions and expansions, market segment alternatives, product/service hybrids, etc. Decision trees show various possible "branches" that you might take to reach an objective or

Exhibit 1   Sample Pyramid

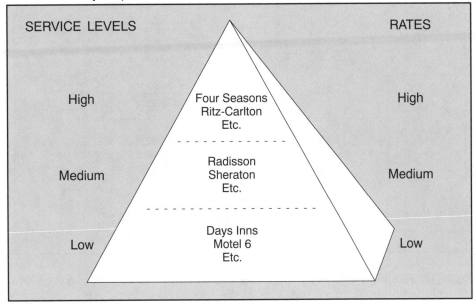

Exhibit 2   Sample Circle—Perceptual Map

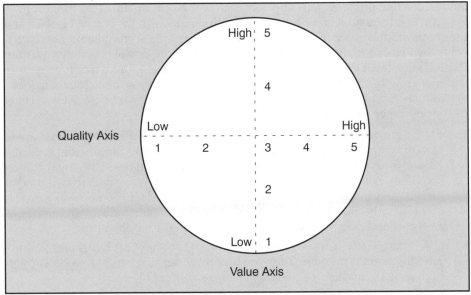

outcome. Decision trees have applicability in the product or service development process, operations, and marketing. Their benefit is to clearly show alternate or multiple routes to achieve goals and objectives.

Exhibit 3   Sample Linear Diagram—Decision Tree

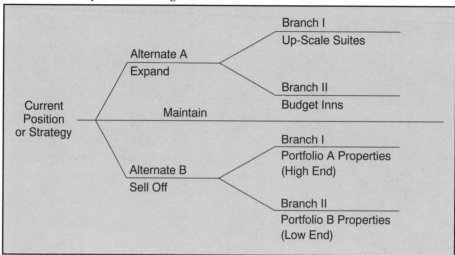

Boxes/Rectangles. For many years, boxes and rectangles have proved to be useful presentation tools for marketers. One of the most well-known "box" creations is attributed to the Boston Consulting Group and is referred to as the "portfolio approach to strategy formulation." This leading management consulting firm recommended that organizations appraise each of their products on the basis of market growth rate (annual growth rate of the market in which the product is sold) and the organization's share of the market relative to its largest competitor. Each product is then placed in the corresponding quadrant of the Boston Consulting Group Portfolio Box (see Exhibit 4). By dividing product-market growth into high growth and low growth, and **market share** into high share and low share, four categories of products can be identified: stars, cash cows, question marks, and dogs. These categories can be summarized as follows:

*   *Stars.* Stars are those products in which an organization enjoys a high share of fast-growing (new) markets. Star products are growing rapidly and typically require heavy investment of resources. In such instances, the organization should mobilize its resources to develop stars in such a way that their market growth and market-share leadership is maintained. If the necessary investment is made and the growth proves enduring, a star product will turn into a cash cow and generate income in excess of expenses in the future.

*   *Cash cows.* Cash cows are those products that enjoy a high share of slow-growth (mature) markets. They produce revenues that can be used to support high-growth products or underwrite those with problems.

*   *Question marks.* Question marks are those products that have only a small share of a fast growing market. Organizations face the question of whether to increase investment in question mark products, hoping to make them stars, or to reduce or terminate investment, on the grounds that funds could be better spent elsewhere.

Exhibit 4   The Boston Consulting Group Portfolio Box

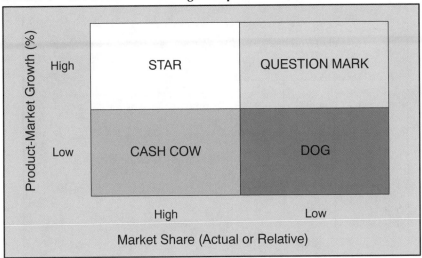

* *Dogs.* Dogs are those products that have a small market share of slow-growth or declining markets. Since dogs usually make little money or even lose money, a decision may be made to drop them. Sometimes a business, for a variety of reasons, continues to sell dogs even though they are unprofitable. However, managers must remember that the resources that go into maintaining dogs are resources that business can't use for other opportunities.

The Boston Consulting Group Portfolio Box can also be used to analyze companies, brands, or markets.

Another box/rectangle tool is the G. E. Portfolio approach, which expands the Boston Consulting Group concept by adding the dimensions of market attractiveness and organizational strengths to the design. Both the Boston Consulting Group Portfolio Box and the G. E. Portfolio, as well as other boxes/rectangles, provide visual mechanisms that can help marketers understand data and formulate or select marketing strategies.

Grids. An extension of the box concept is the grid concept. Grids are excellent tools to help a business formulate marketing strategies and plans. The **marketing strategy grid,** for example, is a dynamic tool that usually views both present and future market and competitive conditions (see Exhibit 5). It allows you to gain perspective on your own product or service through an honest and frank evaluation. In order to objectively select the appropriate marketing strategies, you must understand the conditions (present and future) of the market you are in, where the market is going, and how your product relates to both the current and future conditions as well as the competition's products.

The marketing strategy grid profiles the success of your product or service. A product's or service's position on the grid is a function of both the potential of the market and the competitive position within the market of the product or service.

Exhibit 5   Marketing Strategy Grid

Present Time
(Market Potential)

Strong Moderate Weak

1	2	3	Strong
4	5	6	Moderate (Competitive Position)
7	8	9	Weak

Future Time
(Market Potential)

Strong Moderate Weak

1	2	3	Strong
4	5	6	Moderate (Competitive Position)
7	8	9	Weak

The horizontal axis of the grid denotes the potential of the market sector, while the vertical axis represents the competitive position of the product or service within the market sector. The possible rankings on both axes range from strong to weak. If you are ranking your property as a whole, your property's competitive position is a function of both quantitative and qualitative considerations, such as the amount and quality of competition; your property's competitive advantages as to location, access, image, facilities, size, rate, and so on; and your property's ability to meet the needs of available market segments. It is a good practice to develop two grids—one on your present competitive position, the second on your projected competitive position two to five years into the future. This will help you focus on the dynamics of your marketplace and competition.

Obviously, there is meaning to the position on the grid in which a particular product or service is placed:

- Boxes 1, 2, and 4 denote a favorable, advantageous, or "go" situation. This situation occurs when both factors—market potential and competitive position—are either strong or moderate.

- Boxes 3, 5, and 7 denote a less favorable, less advantageous, or "caution" situation. A "caution" situation occurs when one factor is weak and one is strong, or both factors are moderate.

- Boxes 6, 8, and 9 denote an unfavorable, disadvantageous, or "no go" situation. This situation occurs when one or both factors are weak and neither factor is above the moderate level.

Given these definitions, the optimum position on the grid is the upper-left corner (the "1" box), where a strong market potential combines with a strong competitive position within the market. The worst position on the grid is the bottom-right corner (the "9" box), where a weak market potential combines with a weak competitive position within the market.

Since both factors being evaluated (market potential and competitive position) are dynamic, movement can take place within the grid framework—that is, the position of a particular product or service can vary over time. Horizontal movement involves changes in the potential of a market. Such changes are due to pressures in both the overall and local external economic and social forces. Vertical movement on the grid is possible from the lower six positions. These positions can be considered "action squares," because anyone with a product or service in these squares would want to take action to move up. Such vertical movement denotes changes in the product's/service's competitive position within the market and can be accomplished through the upgrading of management, marketing, products, facilities, or services.

The use of the grid concept is based on two key assumptions:

1. In order to best meet the needs of each market segment as well as maintain a strong image and market share, we can assume that properties will seek the 1, 2, and 4 positions (favorable positions) on the grid whenever possible.

2. The position on the grid in which you place your property assumes that no major improvement programs or other strategy changes to the property will be undertaken soon, and few, if any, major changes will be made in marketing. As previously stated, you may wish to use two grids—one for the present and one for the future (usually within the next five years).

Let's review one example of how to apply the marketing strategy grid to a hospitality industry property. The first step is to objectively evaluate your property and locate it within the grid. Let's assume you own a restaurant and its position on the grid is in box #1. This means your restaurant is in a strong market and is a strong restaurant, maybe even the best restaurant in that market. So, what are some marketing strategies you should employ?

One plan of action is to do everything possible to protect your position by maintaining not only the quality of your food and operation but also the core clientele who put you in that position. Special recognition programs for this core clientele could be developed. Another strategy that could be considered in view of a very solid #1 position would be to raise your prices to take advantage of your market position and maximize profits.

Not everyone is situated in the #1 position on the marketing strategy grid. Let's look at a hotel that is in the #4 position on the grid. This hotel is an average hotel located in San Francisco—a strong market. The competition across the street is in the #1 position—a strong product in this strong market. What can this average San Francisco property do to maximize its profitability? Let's say that right now the market is running at 80-percent average occupancy, which is a very strong market. Demand is projected to continue strong, with a minimal amount of new guestrooms coming into the market. The hotel in position #1 on the grid is charging $170 to $195 per night and enjoys an average rate of $181.75. Our average hotel across the street in the #4 position is charging $140 to $148 per night and has an average rate of $144.85. Both properties are running at 80-percent occupancy.

The ingenious hotel marketing department in our average hotel came up with the following strategies: (1) change the hotel's image by adding a canopy and doorperson and refurbishing the hotel's public space, and (2) raise the rate structure to $161 to $175 per night. The result? No loss in occupancy (because of the strength of the market) and a bulge in profitability.

There are many different marketing strategies you can use. Which ones you choose depends on your property's position on the marketing strategy grid. Upgrading (refurbishing) and raising prices represent two marketing strategies that worked in the preceding example; there are many other strategies to consider, based on your position on the grid. The following nine grids show the nine possible grid positions and accompanying marketing strategies appropriate to the positions.

Marketing Strategy Grids
(and Possible Marketing Steps)
Position #1: Strong Market—Strong/Best Product or Service

(Market Potential)

Strong	Moderate	Weak	
1	2	3	Strong
4	5	6	Moderate
7	8	9	Weak

(Competitive Position)

1. Maintain position.
2. Cultivate core customers.
3. Maximize profits through pricing.
4. Keep competitively ahead by adding services or upgrading product.
5. Expand your product or service (for example, more rooms, more restaurant seats, more flights, more gaming devices, etc.).

Position #2: Moderate Market—Strong Product or Service

(Market Potential)

Strong	Moderate	Weak		(Competitive Position)
1	2	3	Strong	
4	5	6	Moderate	
7	8	9	Weak	

1. Go for market share via competitive pricing.

2. If the market movement tends to be strong in future years, improve to a #1 position.

3. If the market movement tends to be weak, go after additional marketing segments (for example, build core market, consider alternate pricing strategy, etc.).

4. Become the "only" place in town to stay or eat, become the "only" airline to take.

Position #3: Strong Product—Weak Market

(Market Potential)

Strong	Moderate	Weak		(Competitive Position)
1	2	3	Strong	
4	5	6	Moderate	
7	8	9	Weak	

1. If the market is moving toward becoming moderate or strong, build market core now and retain loyalty of consumers.

2. Go after all market segments with multiple pricing strategies and/or product and service offerings.

3. Strongly emphasize cost control and targeted promotions.

Position #4: Strong Market—Moderate/Average Product or Service

(Market Potential)

Strong	Moderate	Weak		(Competitive Position)
1	2	3	Strong	
4	5	6	Moderate	
7	8	9	Weak	

1. Maximize profits through pricing slightly below the #1 competitor.

2. Consider upgrading your product or service to move closer to or into the #1 position if the future markets look strong.

3. Go after the "value-oriented" market segments.

4. Distinguish your product or service as an acceptable replacement for the #1 competitor.

Position #5: Moderate Market—Moderate/Average Product or Service

(Market Potential)

Strong Moderate Weak

1	2	3
4	5	6
7	8	9

Strong

Moderate

Weak

(Competitive Position)

1. If the direction is toward a stronger market, put the product or service in a stronger position with upgrading.

2. Expand the number of market segments you are attracting with specialized promotions.

3. Go after market share through competitive pricing.

Position #6: Weak Market—Moderate/Average Product or Service

(Market Potential)

Strong Moderate Weak

1	2	3
4	5	6
7	8	9

Strong

Moderate

Weak

(Competitive Position)

1. If the market is moving toward becoming moderate or strong in the future, maintain your core market through recognition programs and go after your weakest competitors with special pricing to gain share.

2. If the market is stagnant, and it appears that it will remain weak in the foreseeable future, gear your marketing programs to capture as many segments as possible.

3. Create your own markets via specialized promotions and programs.

Position #7: Strong Market—Weak Product or Service

(Market Potential)

Strong Moderate Weak

1	2	3
4	5	6
7	8	9

Strong

Moderate

Weak

(Competitive Position)

1. Upgrade the most visible aspects of your product or service.

2. Once the upgrading is completed, increase your rates or prices to take advantage of overflow or strong sell-out times or periods.

3. Become the best at servicing the market segments your stronger competitors are not paying attention to.

4. Theme your promotions toward special functions and go for volume.

Position #8: Moderate Market—Weak Product or Service

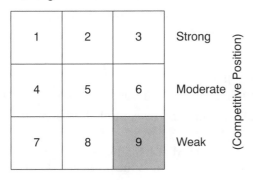

(Market Potential)

Strong   Moderate   Weak

1	2	3	Strong
4	5	6	Moderate
7	8	9	Weak

(Competitive Position)

1. If the market is not moving toward being strong, look at special rate or price schemes to build share.

2. If the market is moving toward strong, make every effort to upgrade the product or service offering to move along with the market.

3. If the above is true, work promotions, sales, and advertising to convey your product's or service's availability and value orientation.

4. Consider marketing your product or service around a theme such that you serve segments but obtain greater volume from competition by this specialization.

Position #9: Weak Market—Weak Product or Service

(Market Potential)

Strong   Moderate   Weak

1	2	3	Strong
4	5	6	Moderate
7	8	9	Weak

(Competitive Position)

1. It is time to dispose of your product or service.

2. Consider alternate uses for your product or service that make sense in this poor environment.

The marketing strategies accompanying these nine sample grids are only suggestions. There are many variables to consider, and each product or service may have a uniqueness unto itself that needs to be taken into consideration prior to selecting a strategy. The marketing strategy grid is a tool designed to help you think about how to maximize your marketing strategies for the most productive results. In the final analysis, it is management's judgment that will dictate the strategy selected; the marketing strategy grid only helps sharpen that judgment.

🔑 Key Terms ————————————————————————————

competitive research—Marketing research that compares your product to the products or services of competitors and tries to discover how consumers perceive and experience your product/service offering in relation to the competitors' products/services.

Customer Perceptions Audit (CPA)—A marketing intelligence tool that provides objective (external) evaluation of how your business is performing and delivering throughout the entire pre-purchase experience. Often, mystery shoppers are used to conduct a CPA.

Customer Satisfaction Index (CSI)—A marketing intelligence tool designed to measure customer satisfaction with your product or service. Such an index provides an on-going periodic scorecard on how your business is performing.

environmental research—The study of external forces (economic, social, political, technological, etc.) that are having or will have an impact on your product or service.

focus group—A marketing research technique that combines personal-opinion solicitation in the form of group discussion with a structured set of questions.

GAP Analysis—A marketing intelligence tool that seeks to identify the difference between management's perspective of how the business is performing with respect to customer satisfaction and how the customer evaluates that performance.

market research—Research that seeks to quantify and segment market demand.

market share—A product's or service's piece of the total market for that product or service, usually expressed as a percentage or on a point scale.

marketing intelligence tools—Any of several marketing tools (such as SWOT Analysis, CSI, and CPA) that provide for key research findings or a "failsafe" for a business.

marketing strategy grid—A dynamic tool that usually views both present and future market and competitive conditions. It allows the market researcher to gain perspective on products or services through an honest and frank evaluation.

Other People's Data—Secondary research conducted or compiled by someone other than yourself.

product or service research—Marketing research that usually focuses on your product's/service's strengths and weaknesses in relation to the products/services of competitors.

prospect research—Marketing research aimed at providing a profile of present and future guests.

questionnaire—A data collection vehicle similar to a survey, but usually briefer and less complex in content.

survey—A structured research document designed to elicit consumer opinion, uncover facts, and gain insights on potential trends.

SWOT—An acronym for strengths, weaknesses, opportunities, and threats.

trend research—Identification of quantitative and qualitative preferences and attitudinal and behavioral directions in which the market or segments thereof are moving.

Chapter 7 Outline

Organizing the Sales Effort
Personal Sales
Telephone Sales
The Importance of Interdepartmental
    Communication

Competencies

1. Describe common sales tools and
   procedures used in hotel sales
   departments. (pp. 71–81)

2. Summarize three keys to personal
   selling. (pp. 81–85)

3. Summarize keys to telephone sales.
   (pp. 85–86)

4. Describe the importance of
   interdepartmental communication to
   the sales process. (p. 86)

7

Applying Key Marketing Methodologies: Sales

THE PURPOSE OF THIS CHAPTER is to examine the sales function. We will discuss organizing the sales effort, personal sales, telephone sales, and the importance of communication to the sales process. We will concentrate on the hotel sector of the hospitality industry because it encompasses more sales functions than most other sectors.

At the outset it should be noted that the sales forms shown in the chapter are examples only. Similar forms are available from many vendors. Computerized forms are also available that can be tailored to meet the unique needs of individual hotels or hotel chains. This chapter discusses the basic sales methods and forms with which a hotel sales department should work, but keep in mind that hotels and hotel chains modify these methods and forms to suit their own needs.

Organizing the Sales Effort

This section discusses the basic tools and procedures that a hotel sales department works with to sell meetings, conventions, and other group events. The following is a sales-tool checklist for hotels:

_____ **Sales Brochures.** Do you have a brochure that includes the following: a description of the hotel's meeting rooms, including seating charts showing different arrangements (theater style, U-shaped, schoolroom, etc.) and room capacities; a list of the property's amenities; property services available; directions to the hotel and a map; transportation services; the hotel's phone number and address; and sales personnel to contact?
   Comment: There are many examples today of beautiful four-color hotel brochures. Look them over and you may find nice pictures, but if any of the above elements are missing, they are not good *sales* brochures.

_____ **Activities and Amenities Guidebook or Brochure.** Do you have a guidebook or brochure for guests that describes what activities are available at or near the property? Does it address entertainment options for the spouse and children? The guidebook/brochure should contain a list of shops, recreational offerings, nearby attractions, and so on.

Exhibit 1   Sample VIP Reservation Request Form

Name:_____	Arrival Date:_____
Title:_____	Time:_____
Organization:_____	Departure Date:_____
Address:_____	Time:_____
Phone:_____	No. in Party:_____

Purpose of Visit: Personal
                               Inspection
                               Other (State):_____

Accommodations Requested: Single   Queen
                           Double   King
                           Double/Double   Jr. Suite
                           View   Suite

Rate Instructions: Comp.
                           Special (State):_____
                           Billing Instructions:_____

Instructions: Wine & Cheese   Std. Fruit
                           Std. Liquor Tray   Wine Only
                           Champagne   Other (State) _____
                                                                   _____

Requested by:_____   Date:_____
Approved by:_____   Date:_____

Comment: No one wants to meet in or bring his or her family to a hotel surrounded by an entertainment and cultural wasteland. Telling what is offered—not only at your facility, but also nearby—can help you *maximize* your market.

_____ **VIP Reservation Request Form.** This important sales tool is designed to record a VIP's name, title, organization, address, and phone number; arrival and departure dates and times; the number of people in the VIP's party; the reason for the visit; accommodation instructions; rate instructions; special requests, such as wine, flowers, etc.; the name of the person who will make sure all of the above occurs; and the appropriate approval. (See Exhibit 1 for a sample VIP reservation request form.)

Comment: Take your time to ensure that this form is filled out entirely and correctly. If at all possible, personally review all VIP requirements with the manager on duty at the projected time of arrival of your VIP guests.

_____ **Tentative Confirmation Letter.** Do you have a model tentative confirmation letter, and does it include the following: date(s) of proposed meeting; arrival and departure dates; clearly stated rates;

number of rooms and type being held; and an outline of the meeting requirements, including set-up of the room, meal functions, equipment reserved, and coffee-break information? (See Exhibit 2 for a sample tentative confirmation letter.) This letter is important because it is the basis for your eventual "contract" with the customer. A brochure about the property and its amenities can be sent along with the letter.

    Comment: Cover all the facts, and say "thank you."

Sales Checklist. A sales checklist is a working document that should be stapled to the client's file folder. It provides room for recording (and changing, if necessary) all arrangements, so that anyone in the sales department can see exactly what the customer wants, with whom the customer has spoken, and what has been said to date. The sales checklist should have space for recording a salesperson's name; the dates the tentative confirmation letter and reminder/final confirmation letter were mailed; dates for the meeting, and whether those dates are confirmed; room data, including rates agreed to, front office instructions (copies of the tentative confirmation letter and reminder/final confirmation letter should be attached), special housing procedures, and complimentary room information; billing instructions; catering department instructions, including dates, rates, and liquor/beverage special arrangements; exhibit requirements; research data on arrival/departure times, flights, and van/limo transportation requirements; and miscellaneous comments such as special rooms, amenities, anticipated problems, etc. (See Exhibit 3 for a sample sales checklist.)

    Comment: Leave no stone unturned. Make sure personal contact is made by a salesperson with every other area in the hotel so that all the details are covered.

Contact Report. This is a simple chronological listing of the contacts made with an organization. It should contain the following: organization name; key contact's name, title, address, and phone number; secretary's name; and a chronological list of contacts in the form of brief sentence recaps. (See Exhibit 4 for a sample contact report.)

    Comment: This report not only helps salespeople avoid overkill (contacting a prospect too often), it can also serve as a "tickler file" because you can use it not only to record the last contact made, but also to record the date by which you want to make the next one.

Reminder/Final Confirmation Letter. This letter should contain all the final details and include all items listed in the original tentative confirmation letter. It serves both as a reminder to the customer and as another opportunity for the salesperson to ensure that all details and customer requests/requirements are in order. It also helps to prevent the surprise of a late cancellation or no-show. The reminder/final confirmation letter should be signed by both parties; it serves as a "contract" or binding letter of agreement.

Exhibit 2   Sample Tentative Confirmation Letter

October 11, 20____

Mr. Phil Jackson
Vice President of Marketing
Michigan Insurance Co.
811 Anchor Way
Lansing, Michigan

Dear Phil:

It certainly was a pleasure speaking with you yesterday concerning the possibility of the Grand Plaza Park Hotel hosting the Michigan Insurance Company in February of 20____.

I'm now holding 120 rooms on a tentative basis for arrival on Wednesday, February 4th, and departure on Saturday, February 7th, 20____.

The following rates will be in effect for your meeting:

Singles:	$95.00
Doubles or Twins:	$105.00
Junior Suites:	$125.00
Parkside Suites:	$150.00
Skyline Suites:	$175.00

The following is my understanding of your meeting requirements. On February 4th you will need a reception/dinner for 120 guests. On February 5th, 6th, and 7th you will need a meeting room set for 120 guests, from 8:00 A.M. until 3:00 P.M.

Bill Robinson, our Director of Banquets and Convention Services, will be in touch with you to further finalize all details such as coffee breaks, audiovisual equipment, etc.

It is my understanding that all room, tax, and incidental charges will be charged directly to the Master Account.

Phil, it is my further understanding that you will be forwarding a rooming list; we need to be in receipt of this rooming list no later than January 6, 20____ to ensure proper confirmation. After that time, rooms will be on a space-available basis.

I've enclosed detailed brochures on both the meeting facilities and property amenities that we have available, and we will make every effort to make your meeting a success.

Phil, enclosed is an additional copy of this letter that can be signed and returned as definite confirmation.

Again, thank you for calling and we look forward to working with you and the Michigan Insurance Company in 20____.

Sincerely,

Paul J. Winslow
Director of Marketing

PJW:ms
#432

APPROVED BY:

_____
Phil Jackson, V.P. Marketing

_____
Date

Exhibit 3   Sample Sales Checklist

Salesperson Responsible _____   Date _____

Confirmation Letter Sent _____   Date _____

Key Dates: CONFIRMED ___ YES ___ NO If Yes, when _____ To _____

    If No, Tentative _____   To _____

                Logged in Master Book ____ Yes ____ No

Room Data: _____   To Front Office with Confirmation Letter

        _____   To Front Office with type, number, and special requirements

        _____   Specified rates for all room types to Front Office and Book-keeping

        _____   Special Housing Procedures—list, VIPs, etc.

        _____   Complimentary rooms—numbers, location, list match

        _____   Final confirmation _____ date _____ initials

        _____   Final log in Master Book

        _____   Reservation cards _____ reply required

Billing Instructions: _____   Individual

                _____   Master Account number _____

                _____   Other (Specify) _____

Catering: _____   Program listing confirmed with client

                Date confirmed _____   Copy sent _____

      _____   Rates per person or meal confirmed

      _____   Liquor/Beverage special arrangements

Exhibit Requirements:

      _____   Yes _____   No (If Yes, dates and schedule recorded)

      _____   Rates _____   Move in _____   Move out

      _____   Special needs list _____

                _____

Key Data: _____   Arrival time/flights recorded

      _____   Departure time/flights recorded

      _____   Van/limo pick-up/drop required

Comments: _____   Special people requirements, e.g., disabled, children, etc.

                Specify _____

                _____

          _____   Anticipated problems (if any, identify problem and who is responsible to pre-resolve) _____

                _____

Exhibit 4   Sample Contact Report

Date: _____	Organization _____
	Key Contact _____
	Title _____
	Address _____
	Phone No. _____
	Sect'y Name _____

Interview and Comments: _____

Date: _____

Date: _____

Date: _____

Date: _____

Date: _____

Do's _____   Don'ts _____

_____ **Telephone Assurance Procedures.** These procedures help sales-people make follow-up telephone calls to clients to make sure that the reminder/final confirmation letter the clients received is accurate and mutually agreed upon. This is one final chance for the salesperson to change items or even sell up.

_____ **Meeting/Convention Definite Booking Form.** This form is designed to provide a permanent record of a definite booking of a meeting or convention. It should be cross-referenced with the organization's file number. The following items should be on the meeting/convention definite booking form: the salesperson's name; group name and address; key contact person's name, title, address, and phone number; attendance anticipated; rooms promised; main arrival date; main departure date; room blocks identified and cut-off date for holding; final decision date; single and double rates; suite rates; billing instructions; complimentary rooms; and special instructions, if any. (See Exhibit 5 for a sample meeting/convention definite booking form.)

Exhibit 5   Sample Meeting/Convention Definite Booking Form

File # _____   Salesperson's name _____

Definite _____   Date _____   Approval _____

Booking group name and   _____
address   _____
_____
_____
_____

Key contact name, title,   _____
address, and phone   _____
_____
_____

Key Data:
    Attendance   _____
    Rooms Committed   _____
    Main Arrival Date   _____   Time _____
    Main Departure Date   _____   Time _____
    Hold Rooms Until   _____   Contact _____

    Rates Promised: $_____ Singles $_____ Doubles
                 $_____ Jr. Suites $_____ Suites

    Billing: _____ Individual _____ Master Account
                 Special Instructions—Detail_____
_____

    Reservation Process: _____ List by sales office
                 _____ Other

    Comps: _____ # _____ Names
                 _____ Approved

Sun.	Mon.	Tues.	Weds.	Thurs.	Fri.	Sat.	Auth. Sign. _____
							Room Req.	Date:
Check In _____ .							
Check Out _____ .							

_____ **Key-Contact Assignment.** For the duration of the meeting or convention, one person—preferably the salesperson who made the sale and handled the arrangements—should be available to the customer at all times to take care of any problems. This is perhaps the single greatest key to a successful customer experience.

Comment: When something goes wrong, make sure you are there to personally handle it. Don't tell the customer to "call maintenance" or "call catering." *Do it yourself.* Remember, you work for the customers, they don't work for the property!

_____ **Events Timetable/Workplan Form.** This document should be posted and reviewed by everyone involved in serving the group. It should contain the group's name; key contact persons and telephone numbers; signing officers for billing and approval purposes; billing instructions; event name; room block information; audiovisual and other equipment requirements; special instructions; billing policy on the meeting room (comp or charge); and a listing of key events, in chronological order, with specific descriptions on set-up, cocktails, bar service, menu, and other details, along with the person responsible for each event. (See Exhibit 6 for a sample events timetable/workplan form.)

Comment: Having a completely filled-out events timetable/workplan form to which the entire hotel will march can help make for successful meetings and satisfied customers.

_____ **Billing Procedures.** Does the sales department have clear billing procedures for everyone to follow? Billing should be concise, accurate, and to the letter of the agreement—with no variations or surprises. Clear and accurate billing ensures not only a satisfied customer but quick payment.

_____ **Post-Meeting/Convention Report.** This report is filled out after the event to make sure the billing was accurate and the customer was satisfied. This report contains a reference file number; the name of the organization; arrival and departure dates; the contact's name, title, address, and phone number; a brief history of the account/event; action steps for follow-up regarding future business, including dates and the people responsible for the follow-up; guestrooms booked and actually used, including complimentary rooms; early arrivals and late check-outs; rate history; meeting room charges; history of catering functions; and special remarks, such as customer comments, complaints, and important non-routine requests that occurred. (See Exhibit 7 for a sample post-meeting/convention report.)

_____ **Thank-You Process.** The thank-you process should consist of two specific actions. One, it should include a personal letter from the salesperson who actually booked and handled the business. And two, the salesperson should call the client to express thanks. This also gives the salesperson an opportunity to clear up any complaints on a one-on-one basis.

_____ **"Please-Come-Back" Letter.** This is the letter that closes the sales loop and just may bring you valuable repeat business. This is an opportunity to thank the client again and ask for the chance to satisfy the client's meeting needs in the future.

Exhibit 6   Sample Events Timetable/Workplan Form

Group/Party Name: _____

Key Person(s): _____   _____

Telephone Number(s): _____

    ☐ Do above have signature authorization for account?

    ☐ Master Account/Billing Ref. #   _____

    ☐ Individual Account/Instructions   _____

    _____

Event: _____

Rooms Assigned: _____

A-V Requirements: _____

Special Instructions: _____ ☐ _____ ☐ _____ ☐ _____ ☐ _____

Comp. on Meeting Room: ☐

Charge on Meeting Room: ☐ If Yes, state agreement _____

Day	Time	Event	Description (All details specified)	Person Resp.

If you have all of these checklist items in place and believe you are organized to sell, you're wrong! What happens when you are not at your desk and Mr. VIP calls? Are your department secretaries trained? You should make sure that they are. Just as the department's salespeople need a manual or workplan, so do its secretaries.

A desk manual should be part of every sales secretary's office equipment. Included in this manual should be telephone answering instructions, greeting procedures for walk-in customers, and instructions on how to fill out various sales-department forms:

Exhibit 7   Sample Post-Meeting/Convention Report

File #_____

Organization_____

Arrival_____   Departure_____

Contact_____   Title_____

Address_____   Phone_____

History_____

_____

Action Steps   1._____   Person Resp._____

　　　　　　　 2._____   Person Resp._____

　　　　　　　 3._____   Person Resp._____

Follow-Up: Dates:_____   Steps:_____   Call_____

　　　　　　　　 _____   _____   Letter_____

　　　　　　　　 _____   _____   Visit_____

Rooms Booked_____   Rooms Used_____   _____Comps.

Early Arrivals_____   Late Check-Outs_____

Rate History_____ S_____ D_____ JS_____ S_____Other

Meeting Room_____Charge_____Set-Up

Catering Functions _____No.

　　　　　　　　　_____Menu Ref. # for File

Special Remarks_____

_____

Booked By_____

- *Telephone answering instructions.* Answering the telephone properly is perhaps the most important, yet often mishandled, activity in any sales department. Secretaries should be provided with a form on which they can record a caller's name, address, title, company, and phone number, along with the caller's meeting dates and general requirements. Also on this form should be a clear statement on rates—either giving secretaries a very broad range of rates to quote, or simply advising them to tell callers that rates are negotiable. This form should also contain the general property brochure's descriptive data about the hotel, and a salesperson's name that the secretary can give to the caller, along with a time at which this salesperson will get back to the caller.

  Hotels lose untold amounts of business because telephone answering instructions do not exist or are not used. It should be made clear to all sales department secretaries that such instructions are part of the job and should be followed.

- *Greeting procedures for walk-in customers.* A warm, friendly, but businesslike greeting procedure should be outlined for all personnel who greet walk-in guests. If no salesperson is immediately available, a sales secretary should provide the walk-in with coffee and a brochure or other collateral material about the hotel. The goal is to keep the walk-in "warm"!

- *Form instructions.* All secretarial personnel (as well as the sales staff) should be trained and provided with an instructions guide on how to fill out sales-department forms such as requisition and purchase order forms, brochure request forms, tentative convention booking forms, cancellation forms, and VIP reservation request forms. They should also know how to make, trace, and kill a file.

Organizing for the sales effort is an important and essential step. The checklist presented in this section lists basic tools and procedures salespeople can use to do the sales job properly and book business. The results of using these tools and procedures consistently will be an organized, efficient sales department—and satisfied repeat customers.

Personal Sales

There is a great deal of literature on **personal sales**—face-to-face sales calls. Some authors expound on the value of good grooming and a professional appearance, others go into sales psychology, and still others talk about such subjects as how to use biorhythms to make a sale. Many of these sales theories have merit and can help you sell.

However, the basics of successful personal selling can be stated quite simply. You must have thorough knowledge of your product or service, thorough knowledge of your **client's needs,** and thorough knowledge of your sales image—that is, how you come across to clients. If you know your product or service and know how to identify your client's needs, often times you can match your product/service to the needs of the client and make the sale:

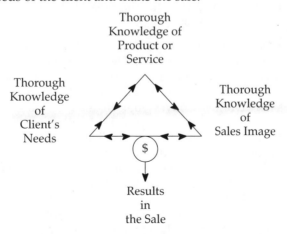

Can it really be that simple? The theory is simple, but it takes careful study and a lot of hard work to put it into practice. Let's look a little closer at the three keys of personal sales.

Key 1: Thorough Knowledge of your Product or Service. You don't possess thorough service or **product knowledge** until you know your product/service so well that you seldom, if ever, have to look up a fact or get back to a client. For example, let's say you are selling group business for a major hotel and calling on Ms. Haskell, the national sales manager for EBM Corporation. Can you readily state your hotel's room prices; amenities; meeting room sizes, set-ups, capacities, and ceiling heights; audiovisual equipment capabilities; and so on? If so, you thoroughly know your product/service.

Key 2: Thorough Knowledge of Your Client's Needs. If you have thorough knowledge of your client's needs, then you've done your homework—you know what EBM Corporation does, who Ms. Haskell is, what types of meetings she usually holds, and how much she usually spends. Even if you do not know all of this, you will find it out within the first few minutes of conversation with Ms. Haskell's secretary or Ms. Haskell herself. You should identify the client's requirements before you try to sell him or her your products/services. Even more important than this is to understand that Ms. Haskell has more at stake than you might think. A successful meeting within the stated budget makes Ms. Haskell look good to Mr. Big—remember that when you sell. The old expression, "We know you want a successful meeting; our success and yours are one and the same" should be remembered and perhaps even stated at some point whenever you are trying to sell meeting space.

Key 3: Thorough Knowledge of Your Sales Image. This is a tough thing to learn, especially if you are not looking closely at yourself. What image do you convey to clients through your dress, speech, mannerisms, and so forth? If your **sales image** and Ms. Haskell's image are not the same, you need to adjust yourself to fit Ms. Haskell's image. Yes, it may even mean getting a haircut and shoe shine. You can know your product and your client very well and still lose the sale because you aren't aware of the image you project to others, or don't adjust your image to more closely fit your client's expectations.

A Personal Sales Example. Recently, a text was published with many sales articles written by hospitality industry executives. The articles contained lots of advice on how to make a successful sales call. There were such statements as, "If you're well-groomed and wear an immaculate suit or dress, you're more than likely going to land the sale"; or, my favorite, "Convey yourself as a real swinger; most men like to be with people who are with it!" Well, you and I both know that many different attitudes and beliefs exist among prospective clients, and the sale does not totally hinge on you being a "swinger" or "the best-dressed kid."

This kind of advice reminded me of something I once saw on a flight between Boston and New York. A few rows up on the other side of the curtain was Mr. Hospitality, a hotel sales executive going first class all the way. It really hurt to watch him in action. He not only was wining and dining some decision-makers for a big medical group meeting, but he even had a better property than Ms. Tryharder, a salesperson from another hotel who was flying coach. There sat swinging Mr. Hospitality, sipping his second scotch, the entertainment of the first-class cabin. And the prospects were just eating it up—or so he thought. His grand finale

Checklist to Increase Sales

_____ 1. Shop your competition. Compare rates and make adjustments to yours when necessary.

_____ 2. Focus on maximizing revenue, rather than just rate or occupancy.

_____ 3. Communicate with reservations personnel. These employees are the hotel's front line to the customer.

_____ 4. Give every group something. To close a sale, have some items to "give"—coffee breaks, suites, etc.

_____ 5. Sell up—to a higher-rated room or better menu item.

_____ 6. Sell down. If rate resistance is encountered, try to move the function to a "valley" period and sell it.

_____ 7. Regularly review your sales files. Look to convert tentatives to definites, or check why a piece of business was lost.

_____ 8. Review all key accounts. Are they being called on regularly and by the correct person?

_____ 9. Track multi-room-night transient guests. For all transient guests producing 50-plus room nights a year, establish an account and track it; treat these guests as you would your best group customers.

_____ 10. Review the function book on a regular basis. Sell into valley periods and push weak or questionable tentatives out of prime periods.

_____ 11. Review all lost-business reports. Ask how you can get this business back next time—and do it.

_____ 12. Keep in touch with and entertain key contacts. These contacts include local car rental, airline, and motorcoach managers.

_____ 13. Develop a support letter. Ask your general manager or owner to give you a support letter. It may make the difference to a group you're going after.

_____ 14. Free yourself and all others in sales from all non-selling activities. The more time spent selling, the more sales that are realized.

_____ 15. Regularly meet with key meeting planners. Show your personal interest.

_____ 16. Send a post-meeting follow-up thank-you letter and "How-may-we-help-you-again?" questionnaire to clients.

_____ 17. Check your competitors' reader boards every day. (A "reader board" is the board on which meetings are listed in a hotel.) Make notes and prepare a game plan to land these organizations for next year or next quarter.

_____ 18. Get to know those who are in the know—your local community's newspaper, city magazine, radio, and television personalities. They are often the first to know who is coming to town or what big event is about to occur.

_____ 19. Know your transient guests. They can lead you to your next group booking. Get to know them and their local contacts.

_____ 20. Monitor and befriend the top-producing travel agents for your hotel.

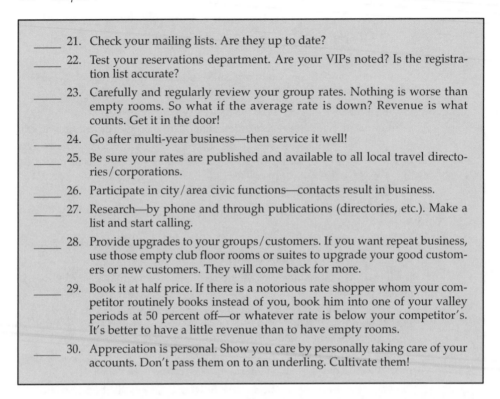

21. Check your mailing lists. Are they up to date?

22. Test your reservations department. Are your VIPs noted? Is the registration list accurate?

23. Carefully and regularly review your group rates. Nothing is worse than empty rooms. So what if the average rate is down? Revenue is what counts. Get it in the door!

24. Go after multi-year business—then service it well!

25. Be sure your rates are published and available to all local travel directories/corporations.

26. Participate in city/area civic functions—contacts result in business.

27. Research—by phone and through publications (directories, etc.). Make a list and start calling.

28. Provide upgrades to your groups/customers. If you want repeat business, use those empty club floor rooms or suites to upgrade your good customers or new customers. They will come back for more.

29. Book it at half price. If there is a notorious rate shopper whom your competitor routinely books instead of you, book him into one of your valley periods at 50 percent off—or whatever rate is below your competitor's. It's better to have a little revenue than to have empty rooms.

30. Appreciation is personal. Show you care by personally taking care of your accounts. Don't pass them on to an underling. Cultivate them!

in impressing his new "buddies" (he certainly wasn't treating them as prospects) was the old third-drink trick. As the flight attendant went past him, he extended his arm and bumped his just-about-empty glass against her back, dropped the glass, and said, "Good grief, woman, you've spilled my drink!" The embarrassed flight attendant apologized and quickly gave Mr. Hospitality a complimentary third drink. Mr. Hospitality figured this really impressed his buddies—by this point booking the business was a mere formality, he thought. When the plane landed, Mr. Hospitality sprayed his mouth with a breath spray, popped in a piece of gum, and headed for his hotel with the prospects in tow, to further impress them. Poor Ms. Tryharder had to wait until later that day to meet with these same prospects and try to convince them that her slightly inferior property with a slightly higher rate was where they should book their meeting.

In the afternoon the prospects arrived at Ms. Tryharder's property across town. Ms. Tryharder answered every question, displaying thorough knowledge of her product and thorough knowledge of the prospects' needs. Ms. Tryharder really did her homework, and it was about to pay off.

As Ms. Tryharder seated the prospects in her office and poured them a cup of coffee (which they really needed after their liquid lunch with good ol' Mr. Hospitality), she said casually, "Your attendees will be bringing their spouses, won't they?" The prospects said, "Definitely." Ms. Tryharder reached into her desk and laid out a map of the city with entertainment and shopping areas clearly marked.

The clients thanked Ms. Tryharder and asked, "What are all the red zones on this map?"

"Those are high-crime areas," Ms. Tryharder replied.

"That spot where all the red zones come together—isn't that where we were this morning, at Mr. Hospitality's hotel?" the prospects asked.

"Well, yes," Ms. Tryharder said, "but don't worry, Mr. Hospitality's hotel has excellent guards and even patrol dogs—they've thought of everything."

The next morning Ms. Tryharder's phone rang at 9:00 a.m. sharp. It was the prospects, wanting to book the meeting at her hotel. The prospects thought Ms. Tryharder's hotel might suit their needs a little better, in view of the fact that spouses were accompanying the meeting attendees.

Think about this story as you go out to sell, and remember the three keys to personal selling:

1. Thorough knowledge of your product/service

2. Through knowledge of your client's needs

3. Thorough knowledge of your sales image

Telephone Sales

Many times a hospitality industry product or service is sold without the opportunity for a direct face-to-face sales call. Booking business by telephone is an art in itself. There are a few golden rules to **telephone sales** that will help you achieve success. The first three are identical to the three keys we discussed in the previous section—thorough knowledge of your product or service, thorough knowledge of your client's needs, and thorough knowledge of your sales image. Let's look at these keys as they apply to telephone sales.

First, just as in personal sales, you should know your product or service thoroughly. You don't want to hesitate or be forced to say, "I'll have to get back to you with those dimensions." *Second*, know about your prospect by doing research before you call, not while you're talking to him or her. *Third*, make sure your sales image is professional and positive—your sales image can be transmitted and detected over the telephone by your vocal expressions and telephone mannerisms.

The *fourth* key to telephone sales is perhaps the most important of all: Listen! Think of our earlier personal sales example and imagine what it might be like if Mr. Hospitality and Ms. Tryharder had to close the sale over the telephone. There's Mr. Hospitality on the speaker phone, telling his prospects a few jokes, reminding them of his famous third-drink trick, and talking so much that he misses it when the prospects mention that their spouses will be traveling with them to the meeting. Then there is Ms. Tryharder, listening intently to the prospects, ready with information about entertainment options for their spouses, and giving the prospects a clear, accurate, and prompt response to every question. Ms. Tryharder's phone call is going to end like this: "Let me recap your needs, item by item," and then, "Now that we have all the details, should we book you on a tentative basis for the third through the fifth of next month?" Ms. Tryharder has just completed the *fifth* key to telephone sales—asking for the sale. The *sixth* key is to say "Thank you." Ms. Tryharder will then proceed to make sure the booking becomes definite, the prospects' needs are met, and the meeting is a success.

The Importance of Interdepartmental Communication ——

It is critical that all departments within a hotel communicate with each other. Communication is especially important to the sales department. After all, sales affects every department and area in the hotel. For example, if catering is not part of the sales department (i.e., it's the responsibility of the food and beverage department or is a stand-alone function), sales department communication with catering is especially critical, as both sales and catering could sell the ballroom on the same date to two different groups. While this may be an obvious example, there are many other crucial hotel interrelationships that the sales department should be constantly aware of during its daily activities.

For example, the reservations department is an often-ignored part of the overall sales process. Never forget that reservations are not just a mechanical or computerized system—it is a key point of customer contact. If you are in direct sales, be sure you spend a portion of each week talking with the reservations department. Tell the reservations department which groups are coming, what to do when the reservations start pouring in, and—if necessary—how to do it. Room availability, payment procedures, rate/revenue management, and group check-in/check-out times are some of the key areas to cover. Make sure you know the reservations personnel well enough to ask for a favor every so often. Just like other employees, reservationists like to feel appreciated, so giving them a little extra attention once in a while can really pay dividends. Horror stories about reservations are more abundant than those told about hotels or rooms. You, the sales professional, have an obligation to see that your customers' reservations are handled flawlessly.

Here are just a few more examples illustrating the importance of interdepartmental communication:

- Sales and the rooms department must be in sync on VIP needs, meeting times, etc.

- Sales and the food and beverage department must be clear about group meal functions, break times, menus, etc.

- Sales and the engineering department should review any special technical needs (lighting, HVAC, etc.) of incoming groups.

- Sales and the security department must communicate with respect to VIPs, valuable equipment, etc.

☞ Key Terms ———

client's needs—Those products and services required by the client/guest. To determine what a client's needs are, the hotel should know or find out the client's spending habits, food preferences, meeting needs, etc.

personal sales—Direct person-to-person selling.

product knowledge—A level of knowledge of your product or service wherein you seldom, if ever, have to look up a fact or get back to a client.

sales image—The image you portray to your clients—your mannerisms, habits, dress, speech, etc., as perceived by your customers.

telephone sales—A sales contact by telephone, the primary purpose of which is to obtain a reservation for a room, a group commitment, or some other sale.

Chapter 8 Outline

The Ten-Step Customer Service Process
    Step 1: Recognition
    Step 2: Identification of Problems
    Step 3: Plan of Action
    Step 4: Reallocation of Resources
    Step 5: Prioritization of Execution
    Step 6: Training of Personnel
    Step 7: Recruiting the Right Personnel
    Step 8: Communications
    Step 9: Follow-Up to Execution
    Step 10: Begin Again
Points of Encounter
    Customer Interface
Customer Service Checklist
Case Examples

Competencies

1. Identify the role of customer service within marketing. (p. 89)

2. Present a ten-step process to identify problems and solutions for better customer service. (pp. 89–96)

3. Describe sales from a consumer's perspective. (pp. 96–98)

4. Suggest methods for customer retention through problem resolution. (pp. 98–99)

5. Discuss the hierarchy of customers and identify items on an effective customer service checklist. (pp. 99–100)

8

Applying Key Marketing Methodologies: Customer Service

Customer service can be called your most valuable marketing tool for a number of reasons. It is customer service that plays a role in acquiring new customers and retaining the loyalty of existing ones. It also supports taking market share from competitors. Good customer service is most valuable if you consider that, at a minimum, it costs businesses five times as much to attract a new customer as it does to satisfy and retain an existing customer. It is most valuable if you consider that a dissatisfied customer will sometimes tell more than ten other consumers/prospects about their unsatisfactory experience. So, having a customer service strategy and a plan to execute it are very important in deploying this valuable marketing weapon. Some businesses fail to recognize customer service as a marketing weapon and under-fund the function or staff it with the lowest paid (and sometimes least trained) employees.

The Ten-Step Customer Service Process

Customer service strategies need to be in place at every point at which the customer comes into contact with your business or any representation thereof, be it personal, vocal, electronic, etc. These points" are referred to as **points of encounter**. If you examine every potential point of encounter, you are looking at all the places/processes that your image and positioning are exposed or being tested. In this discussion we present a ten-step process for customer service success, examine strategies and tactics, and look at the interrelationship of customer service with all other marketing tools. Let's begin with the ten-step process:

Step 1: Recognition

The points at which your employees encounter the consumer are opportunities to win (or lose) the consumer.

In the age of increasing customer dissatisfaction, we must take the first step toward achieving service success—**recognition**. This is not the obvious recognition after the fact in which we find that service problems have caused sales to slip or that another company has taken more market share. Such problem recognition is *reactive* rather than *proactive*. For recognition to be proactive, observation and analysis of the points of encounter must occur. Quite simply, this means that we must focus on the interaction of our product or service with the consumer.

How often have you heard, "They really have a problem here. Too bad they haven't recognized it and fixed it." *They* usually refers to top management, which has skipped the all-important thought process known as recognition. A decline in sales, employee turnover, consumer complaints—these are all *reactive* indicators.

True recognition in the proactive sense means knowing the points of encounter and assuming the customer's (also prospect's) perspective from pre-sell to post- or after-sale.

Step 2: Identification of Problems

Recognition of points of encounter and customer problems is but one proactive step to customer service success.

What is this process by which one can assure preemptive recognition and prevent loss of market share or customers? Although there are a number of approaches, placing yourself in the role of customer is one of the best. Ideally it should be done incognito and often. It will make you aware of a service problem or at least give you a fresh look at the customer's perspective. The following are some acid tests that you can run periodically. When you try them, be observant and analytical. Always record the problems and think about possible solutions.

- Call the toll-free number of one of your establishments and analyze the response.

- Visit your outlets, service centers, units, counters, or check-in desks incognito and make notes of your observations (you may need a big notepad). Ask other customers about their experiences at the points of encounter.

- Visit one of your sales offices and read your literature (after all, your name or signature is likely to be on it).

- Observe your staff. Are they empathetic with your customers?

- After making these observations, go through the entire purchasing process and/or service experience and make a list of the direct points of encounter.

  Review the list with the following objectives:

- Identification of the critical points at which the sale, loyalty, or purchase can be lost instantly if not handled properly

- Identification of the points that have to be corrected

- Identification of the points that present opportunities for making your service stand out above the competition.

Here are some additional strategies and tactics that can help you to recognize problems and opportunities and identify solutions:

- Use a shoppers' service to check on your business.

- Conduct your own service audit.

- Talk to and, more importantly, listen to your customers.

- Observe and experience the offerings of your most successful competitors.

- Experience your own service as a customer.

- Personally review a random sample of complaint letters once per quarter.

- Solicit the opinions of your service offering from a focus research group every few years.

- List all points of encounter and have your management focus on one of these points each quarter.

- Check current relevance of all points of encounter training material and procedures. Update where appropriate.

- Spend at least as much time on the point of encounter as you do on the project/development aspects of your business.

Even if you are not in the "service" sector per se, adapt these steps to check on your sales force, retailers, wholesalers, distributors, agents, etc.

Step 3: Plan of Action

Having made your incognito observations, prepared lists, identified points of encounter, and come up with several ideas, you now need a plan of action. Before implementing it on a wide scale, test it to make sure it is executed properly. To not do so can be disastrous. Test it, modify it, and implement it.

Step 4: Reallocation of Resources

Recognition, identification, and a plan of action are sometimes not enough to make the necessary change at a point of encounter. To remain competitive and successful, a **reallocation** of resources sometimes may be required. These resources may be financial-, personnel-, or equipment-related. Simple reallocations, such as putting on more phone operators to eliminate the interminable rings followed by a recorded voice telling you all lines or service representatives are busy, can set your company ahead of the competition. It is estimated that half the callers hang up when the "next available service representative" recording comes on the line—that is, if they haven't been disconnected or forgotten who they'd called in the first place!

If a firm never puts you on "hold" or if you are always connected with a professional service representative, the chances of your winning the customer is pretty good.

Step 5: Prioritization of Execution

The step least often taken and most often needed is **prioritization**. In a recent edition of the Sunday *New York Times*, two very interesting help-wanted ads appeared that serve as examples of the importance of prioritization. One fairly large block ad from Beth Israel Medical center in New York sought a "Director of Guest Relations" (new position). The other, from a nationally recognized medical clinic, read, "Wanted—Complaints Clerk." It is obvious that Beth Israel had (1) recognized that it was in a service business, (2) identified a point of encounter opportunity, (3) established a plan of action, (4) reallocated resources, and (5) prioritized the importance of its relationship with its patients. Note the difference in perspectives. Beth Israel views its patients as "guests," and the person who relates to them is at director level. These are the obvious signs of a healthy proactive service perspective. On the other hand, the medical clinic has the classical reactive mentality of looking for a "complaints" person and prioritizes this function with the label of "clerk." Which medical facility do you think will be perceived as better able to provide service? Some additional strategies and tactics to help prioritize points of encounter and reallocate resources follow:

- In order of priority, list the points of encounter that need new or additional resources.

- In order of priority, list all "projects" dollars (capital) scheduled for allocation.

- Now prepare a new list, which, in order of priority, blends the points-of-encounter items and "projects" items.

- In identifying your "projects" capital needs, first prioritize those that relate to your points of encounter.

- Review your non-point-of-encounter personnel count and payroll costs.

- Review your point-of-encounter personnel count and payroll costs.

- Allocate your resources to address the point-of-encounter personnel and related costs to do their job right on a top priority basis. Can you imagine a firm that would spend a half-million dollars on a project and deny point-of-encounter employees an increase of 50 cents per hour incentive pay or a $5,000 training program? Review all of your firm's expenses; this could be called "current shock."

Step 6: Training of Personnel

Ask yourself if your business is suffering from human incompetence (also technological incompetence). Today we are experiencing an end-product of our formal education process that frequently needs to be retrained. It is essential that every one of your point-of-encounter employees be trained or retrained. Also, make sure that your technology is functioning properly, and evaluate its ease of comprehension and use by the customer, prospect, and your employees. When your automated systems take over, do they work, and do they help or hinder the customer? Or do they simply help you lose the customer/prospect and help the competition? Reflect on your own customer experiences and you will quickly perceive the importance of assessing your automation.

Step 7: Recruiting the Right Personnel

To recruit and hire the appropriate personnel, you have to ask the right questions:

- What are the criteria for those who will be point-of-encounter employees?

- Do any of these employees sell, quote prices, or directly interface with the potential customer at the critical point of encounter—the actual purchase of your products/services? If so, what type of employee do you want to be responsible for bringing in revenue?

- Are these employees trainable?

- Are the employees sufficiently intelligent to hold such positions or are they overqualified?

If you can't answer most of these questions readily, your firm is either already in trouble or will be in trouble before very long.

Well-thought-out recruiting criteria can provide great returns and should be reviewed frequently. When did you last re-evaluate job descriptions and hiring criteria for your point-of-encounter positions? If you believe there is no need for such reviews because the products/services you offer have not changed, you are very wrong; your consumer is changing constantly. Some experts advocate turning the organization chart upside down, while others suggest that the pay scales be reversed. Obviously, there is no simple answer for all service-industry firms. All the steps must be taken into account: recognition, identification, plans of action, reallocation, prioritization, training, and recruiting.

Recruiting should be attempted only after a complete review of each point-of-encounter position. Complexity of job function as well as the types of consumers encountered on a daily basis should be thoroughly analyzed. Do you have (or want) minimum-wage clerks directly interfacing with $100,000-plus executives or large-volume purchasers?

Some additional strategies and tactics to facilitate and sharpen your recruiting are:

- Involving members of top management in at least one point-of-encounter position training session.

- Having members of top management work at least one eight-hour day (preferably an entire week) in one of the point-of-encounter positions.

- Reviewing your training resources (people, procedures, and related budgets) annually to determine if they are adequate for preparing your personnel for service leadership.

- Asking customers to evaluate (via questionnaire or direct contact) how well they believe point-of-encounter employees are trained.

- Inquiring of newly-trained employees what else they believe should be taught.

- Asking the same question of your seasoned employees.

- Instructing all recruiters of point-of-encounter employees to ask themselves whether they would want to deal face-to-face with the person they are considering for the job.

- Personally participating in at least one interview session for a point-of-encounter employee.

- Considering the upgrade of your pay scale to attract seasoned pros away from the competition.

- Ensuring that your recruiters know exactly what you expect of them and periodically verifying that they are doing exactly what you want.

Step 8: Communications

In communicating with the customer, no one is more important than the point-of-encounter employee. This employee is often the first to know when (and if) your service offering, price, policy, or procedural change is working. He or she is also a great source of information when you attempt to improve service. However, when it comes to communicating with these employees, the corporate hierarchy in general does a less than stellar job. This, in tandem with the dissatisfied consumer, works to create the environment for disastrous customer service experience.

There are many examples of good and bad **communication** in the service industry. A case in point is CEO Bill Marriott, Jr., who is renowned for his visits to virtually every hotel, restaurant, or in-flight kitchen in Marriott's multi-billion dollar empire. His visits were not mere "presidential" appearances, but detailed inspections and walk-throughs to instill motivation. Mistakes were pointed out. Employee suggestions were recorded and implemented on a broad scale if they were worthwhile.

Adherence to **standard operating procedures** (SOPs) is mandatory at Marriott. It is therefore no coincidence that Marriott's operations and services are efficient and consistent. There are other examples, but the important point is the same in all situations—good communication is good business. A conscientious CEO goes beyond motivation and inspection. The point-of-encounter employees are made aware of top management's interest in seeing not only how the job is being done, but also who is doing the job.

By definition, communication connotes a two-way flow—up and down. Small ideas turn into big winners if communication channels are open. For some reason, it is easier to inform one million customers of your offer than one thousand point-of-encounter employees. There appears to be one logical explanation. Your ad or service offer goes directly from you to the consumer, but the memo describing that offer is often handed down from the vice president of marketing through the managers, to the unit managers, to the department managers, to the shift managers and, finally to the point-of-encounter employees—plenty of opportunity for a breakdown in communication. It happens much too frequently.

One bit of advice remains valid: Never assume that your detailed memo of instructions, the training video, and manual have been read, viewed, or understood by those who must use the information. The best way to find out is to put on the consumer's hat and try to get the service you have offered. Don't be surprised at what you find. Any form of change may be difficult to communicate, and the difficulty can be compounded when the change involves behavior.

Step 9: Follow-Up to Execution

Let's go back to Bill Marriott with regard to communications. All those walk-throughs would not have amounted to much unless there had been a positive form of follow-up. In the process, either a note was sent to the unit in question reaffirming the action to be taken, or the subject was discussed during the next visit. Granted, the man had a phenomenal memory, but the key point is that because there is a follow-up, employees fix what needs to be fixed.

Follow-up steps can assume a variety of forms. Some service establishments use *shopper services,* which essentially are professional shoppers/customers. They are hired to work as typical consumers, logging their experiences for management. Intelligent use of their findings, of course, is crucial. The results can be negative (employee dismissals), or positive (improved training programs, plans to improve performance, and elimination of problem areas).

There are many effective follow-up techniques, and what is appropriate for your particular product or service offering may require special planning. But once a plan is devised, it must be implemented. You must clearly communicate the procedure to those who will implement it, and then follow-up to make sure it is done. Unless all these steps are taken, all the promises of your promotional ad will only lead to creating a more disappointed consumer.

Here are some strategies and tactics to improve communications and the follow-up process:

- Make a list of all point-of-encounter positions.

- Establish a personal communications calendar, scheduling specific, frequent dates to deliver your messages to the key point-of-encounter people.

- Decide whether to deliver your messages in person, by videotape, or in writing (in that order).

- Make sure that all of your point-of-encounter employees clearly understand that their personal contact with customers represents the most critical element to conveying a good service impression.

- Make sure you listen, listen, listen.

- Communicate the "right" way—*show* your employees. Don't simply tell them.

- Record and remember names and incidents from your own employee encounters.

- "Re-touch" those you can with a call or a note.

- Be sincere.

- Repeat all steps regularly. (Employee turnover is the most critical factor in diluting your message and communications in general.)

Step 10: Begin Again

For a number of reasons, this step is perhaps the most difficult. First, to some extent, having to repeat may imply that you have not been successful with the previous nine steps. Second, you need to go back to determine if, indeed, you did not succeed with any of the actions taken. If so, you will need to fix them or replace them. The following recap lists the necessary steps to be taken to further support your customer service success:

1. *Recognition.* Knowing that there is a service opportunity and/or problem at the points of encounter.

2. *Identification.* Determining what the opportunities and problems are.

3. *Plan of Action.* Developing the plan required to capitalize on an opportunity or deal with a problem.

4. *Reallocation.* Finding the financial and/or human resources to execute the plan.

5. *Prioritization.* Placing execution of the plan at the top of the list.

6. *Training.* Ensuring thorough preparation of those who are charged with taking action at points of encounter.

7. *Recruiting.* Finding the very best persons for execution of the plan as well as for point-of-encounter positions.

8. *Communications.* Conveying every aspect of your plan(s) accurately, thoroughly, and convincingly to all employees, with special focus on front-line personnel.

9. *Follow-up.* Periodically reviewing all the processes, beginning with the steps of recognition and identification.

Points of Encounter

Today's consumer is preconditioned and ready to challenge the product/service provider. Most surveys indicate consumers in many product/service categories have reached a level of preconditioning that leaves them cynical toward the consumption experience.

Just as there are steps your company (and management) must take, there are steps your employees must take to ensure customer satisfaction. No matter what type of service you provide, there are several keys to effective execution that will create recognition among consumers that your firm goes beyond the point of encounter.

- Expectations. Recognize that you must never deliver a service that falls short of what the customer or potential customer expects for the price they are paying. Meeting or exceeding customer **expectations** is what ultimately determines the level of customer satisfaction. Expectation levels in the mind of the consumer are influenced by the price you charge, the consumer's prior experience with your service offering, their prior experience with your competition, and what you promise in your advertising or sales message. Meeting customer expectations is absolutely critical to repeat business.

- Never blame the customer. While some may argue with this categorical statement, you cannot lose by practicing it. The customer is always right, even if he or she is not! Simply stated: *Let the customer win!* That doesn't mean you should allow the customer to take advantage of you. This means that your employees must understand that they have the flexibility and authority to bend policy when needed to satisfy a customer.

Most surveys show that less than five percent of customers will actually take the time to complain about the service received. However, these same surveys show that almost 25 percent are less than satisfied with that service. And this percentage grows dramatically when customers become increasingly cynical as a result of poor experiences with other companies offering the same type of service. When this occurs, two things can happen: (1) If you insist that your employees adhere so strictly to policy that customers are not allowed to "feel" they have won, you will lose 100 percent of those cynical customers; (2) If you have instilled in your employees the "let the customers feel they have won" philosophy, you will retain (and actually build) the loyalty of these customers.

- Clear communication with customers is essential to problem resolution at the point of encounter or purchase. Your employees must be able to tell customers precisely what they need and want to know or do. This is especially critical when you're involved in a promotional offer. After all, that is why the new customer has come to you in the first place. Make sure that supervisors and everyone who has customer-contact responsibility are thoroughly knowledgeable about all aspects of the promotion. If necessary, provide written communiqués and training videos. Augment these with in-person training sessions, and do so in a timely manner. Never start a promotion before all employees have received complete information and thorough instructions. And always provide a central resource for clarification, should questions arise.

- Organize your procedures to reduce the time it takes to purchase your service offering. The number-one peeve of today's consumer of services is *standing in line.* You must review and then revise your procedures to eliminate or at least shorten the time spent waiting in line. If the nature of your service precludes total elimination of waiting time, develop alternative plans to fill the time. This can be in the form of a customer service representative who pre-processes the customers or socializes with them. A video entertainment or informational display will attract the customer and fill the waiting time.

- Undo what the customer has done to himself. When customers discover that they are in the wrong, always avoid embarrassing them. The employee must be polite, empathetic, and tactful so that your customers save face

- Never use business jargon that is unfamiliar to your customer. You cannot assume that even those who are in the other businesses use the same terminology as you.

- **Trade-off time management** is essential in personal-contact situations. Each point of encounter must be analyzed and a determination made as to whether the strategy should be to go for optimum speed or special personal attention.

- Employee **job performance criteria** for all those in point-of-encounter positions, be they face-to-face or over the phone, should clearly focus on execution of service with efficiency and politeness. This is what it's all about, and point-of-encounter employees must know that performing their job properly is what they are being paid for.

- Reduce time where service is expected to be fast. Fast and efficient service leads to satisfaction, especially today. In essence, cynical consumers' negative conditioning has led them to expect long lines and slow, inefficient service. Beat that expectation! Provide faster service and you will convert the cynical consumer into one who is more than satisfied.

- Sincere appreciation should be expressed at virtually all points of encounter, not just at the time of purchase. This must be instilled in every contact-point employee. This will ensure reinforcement of the perception that the customer is truly valued.

These keys to successful customer service at the point of encounter translate into an acronym of customer satisfaction:

1. **E**xpectations must be met
2. **N**ever blame the customer
3. **C**lear communications
4. **O**rganize to reduce time
5. **U**ndo what the customer has done to himself/herself
6. **N**ever embarrass the customer
7. **T**rade-off time management is essential
8. **E**mployee job performance criteria fully understood by all staff
9. **R**educe service time
10. **S**incere appreciation expressed

Customer Interface

There are numerous other ways to let your customers win and let you retain their loyalty. Successful enterprises have point-of-encounter plans and policies in place that are widely communicated. These are also the firms that demonstrate lower cost of sales (expenses), higher repeat customer levels, and brand loyalty.

Finally, do not hesitate to use what is referred to as *suggestive sales*. An important form of customer service, suggestive selling is the process of suggesting merchandise or services that are related to the main item sold to the customer. The suggestion is made when, in the salesperson's judgment, the added item will provide the customer with additional satisfaction.

The salesperson who is genuinely interested in helping customers solve their problems can enhance the relationship with suggestive selling. Some of the best ways to engage in suggestive selling are incorporated in the following list. From

Exhibit 1   Customer Hierarchy

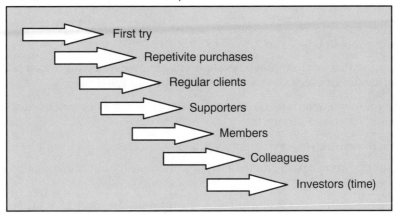

First try

Repetivite purchases

Regular clients

Supporters

Members

Colleagues

Investors (time)

studies of numerous successful companies and award winners at customer service, a number of common characteristics emerge:

- Leadership
- Formalized process or plan
- Focus on understanding customer needs
- Customer and employee feedback systems
- Responding with action on feedback
- Sales and service synergy
- Customer-retention motivational and promotional programs
- Reading the marketplace and competition and responding appropriately
- Practicing innovation through research and development and suggestion implementation
- Prominent recognition of the importance of point-of-encounter employees and giving them full support

Customer service strategies and tactics may vary for different types of customers or be tailored based on the developmental stage (see Exhibit 1).

Customer Service Checklist

There are hundreds of customer service tactics and ideas for every size and type of product and service business. The keys to successful customer service as a marketing tool can be summarized as follows:

1. Recognizing the points of encounter
2. Creating a plan for customer service success

3. Empowering your point-of-encounter employees with an armada of "let the customer win" tactics

4. Implementing a check system to verify that customer service policies are being adhered to

5. Ensuring that your employee evaluations and, where possible, compensation are tied directly to your **customer satisfaction index** (CSI).

The following checklist queries the product and service provider about the key items of customer service.

- Is there a customer service plan/strategy in place?

- Is your customer plan adequately supported with both human and financial resources?

- Are you doing everything possible to thoroughly train and support your point-of-encounter employees?

- Do you have an empowerment policy, and do all customer-contact personnel understand it?

- Is there a customer and employee (point-of-encounter) feedback system?

- Do all your personnel, vocal, and electronic points of encounter appropriately represent the image and positioning of your company?

- Are you performing customer perception audits (CPAs) either internally or with shopper services?

- Is customer satisfaction measurement an integral part of your employee evaluation and reward systems?

- Are your recruiting guidelines appropriate for each of your point-of-encounter positions? Is your level of compensation appropriate?

- Is customer service viewed as a marketing tool of the highest value?

- Do you have recognition programs in place for point-of-encounter employees who provide extraordinary service?

- Does your sales organization understand the concept of "suggestive" selling, and that it is indeed a valid customer service strategy?

- Is the leadership of your organization actively involved as a champion of customer service excellence?

- Is your customer service message clearly communicated throughout the organization?

Case Examples

Companies that recognize quality customer service as key to success in increasingly competitive business environments regularly enjoy corporate growth and positive market presence. Two such organizations—the American Express

Company and Continental Airlines—exemplify the positive effects that attention to customer service can have on the business posture of a company.

Case Example 1—American Express Cardmember Services. American Express has long believed that quality should be the goal of its businesses worldwide. The chairman of the company also carries the title of Chief Quality Officer to help convey this goal to the entire organization. American Express goes beyond the signals by supporting its quality performance with substance, all focused on one goal—better customer service.

Basic substance at American Express begins with superior training (at their Quality University) and full support of senior management. The company also publishes an annual quality management report, emphasizing that the corporation is in the customer service business. Employees are routinely expected to go beyond the normal procedures to provide outstanding customer service, and those who do are recognized by way of a corporate awards program.

Like many service organizations, American Express has numerous customer bases to address. The two largest are their cardholders and those who use their worldwide travel services. Necessarily, a lot of time is devoted to ensuring that the relationship between the two provides synergy instead of becoming a source of conflict.

American Express recognizes and successfully satisfies an immense and diverse group of customers around the globe. It focuses on customers' needs for timeliness, accuracy, responsiveness, and immediate resolution at the first *point of encounter*.

Customer satisfaction is constantly monitored and, when new customer needs emerge, new services are implemented to meet these needs. These new services come from one principal source, according to company executives, who state: "Virtually every new service introduced by American Express during the past ten years came directly from the suggestions and expressed needs of the customers themselves." In addition to listening to their customers, American Express employees are asked to spend 10 percent of their time striving to improve their job of delivering quality service. The result is many internal and procedural changes culminating ultimately in better service to the customers.

American Express sincerely believes that the key to success begins not only with pride and motivation of the employee, but with ongoing research into both job enhancement and customer needs identification. The company employs sophisticated research techniques and the latest technology to quantitatively and qualitatively assess the needs of the customer. From these assessments, delivery of service improvements and new services are developed for its card membership. Ultimately, American Express wants its customers to feel that it is the only company they want to do business with.

The common elements of the American Express success formula include getting employees involved to redefine their jobs so they can better serve the customer, a passion for listening to customers' needs, responding with action, prompt implementation of new services, addressing the needs accurately and with targeted marketing messages, reinforcing a quality image in how it promotes and markets its brand, and having the basic quality systems fully operating at all customer contact points.

American Express often "begins again," as exemplified by the innovative services introduced year after year. Many of these things customers now take for granted, because "American Express is there doing it for us." Those "things" include cash when and where customers need it, replacement of lost travelers checks, global assist programs that help cardmembers with virtually any need anywhere on earth, Gold cardholder account statements and categorizations at year-end that help customers prepare tax returns, a product/service guarantee program that makes returns simple and workable, very high credit lines, translation services, lost luggage assistance, and a host of other services that could go on for pages.

In truth, American Express quality service levels and innovative new service offerings have improved an entire industry, as competitors strive to keep up with the leader. Leadership, quality service, customer satisfaction, and marketing are what make American Express a winner and in the category of the very best at service and sales excellence, as suggested in their motto, "Membership has its privileges!"

Case Example 2—Continental Airlines—Service Plus "One Pass." Step 10 in the quality customer service process is "begin again." Continental Airlines is perhaps the ultimate proof that following this step (and all the other steps) pays off. It wasn't long ago that Continental Airlines was at the very bottom—in a category by itself—for poor service, customer dissatisfaction, and lack of management planning. In fact, at the time, Continental had just acquired People's Express and had begun to use Newark as a hub. It was a disaster. But Continental rebounded in a big way—right to the top.

What happened to pull Continental from the customer service cellar to the number one ranking in customer satisfaction? First of all, new management set out to recognize the problems and began to clearly identify each. Poor service, aging equipment, poorly trained personnel, and priorities on financial transactions instead of customer retention were among the many problems the airline encountered at that time. Things were so bad that the carrier again went into bankruptcy. Upon emerging from this dilemma, the new management developed "plans of action" (Step 3) and began to reallocate resources (Step 4) to correct the problems. They prioritized their most serious needs (Step 5) and began to address these with a new energy and attitude. Continental upgraded its equipment, improved its operational systems, recruited new personnel (Step 7), and invested in new training programs (Step 6). Moreover, the airline began a massive communications plan (Step 8), focusing on both internal and external communications.

Continental, recognizing that internal communications is vital to effective operation, found theirs lacking, and this is where their turnaround began. Management not only shared its plans with the employees but, more importantly, listened to and sought the input of employees. At first, the communications focused on the airline's problems and then moved to ways to fix those problems. Management instituted communications mechanisms to listen and seek feedback. As things began to improve, employee incentives based on everything from on-time performance, to attendance, to service measurements were implemented.

Externally, the communications were sincere and straightforward. The company admitted, "we have had problems in our performance, service levels, etc...we are fixing them...and here is what you can expect..." Continental's management was smart enough to promise they would be much better (85 percent to 90 percent), and then deliver (100 percent plus). The nationally-renowned J. D. Power and Associates ranked Continental number one in passenger satisfaction (customer service excellence) *five times*. Now, the airline was profitable and management wasn't out gulping up other airlines with that cash. In fact, Continental's board and senior management shared those earnings through a very comprehensive bonus program.

Continental followed many of the principles and concepts conveyed in this book. Its management understood that to truly turn the airline around would require employee involvement. As in any service business, the *points of encounter* would become critical to winning. This included all people-contact personnel, the interface systems (reservations, airport check-in, etc.), the product itself (aircraft, meal services, etc.), and the delivery systems (on-time performance, baggage handling, etc.).

Finally, Continental recognized the way to win back market share and build a loyal customer base. To address these strategic marketing issues, Continental enhanced its "One Pass" frequent traveler program. It offered more up-grades, discount fare opportunities, bonus points, etc. It began to treat its frequent customers, as it should have all along, as its best customers.

Key Terms

communication—The two-way (upward and downward) flow of information within an organization, from point-of-encounter employees to top management responsible for ensuring high levels of customer service quality.

customer satisfaction index (CSI)—An index (benchmark) indicating the level of customer satisfaction that point-of-encounter employees should strive to achieve.

expectations—The collective package of features and amenities customers or potential customers expect of products or services for the price they are paying.

follow-up—Any of a variety of actions—such as corrective or improvement initiatives—taken to ensure that identified problems or opportunities are being addressed appropriately.

job performance criteria—Established standards or guidelines that point-of-encounter employees must know and follow to properly perform their customer service tasks.

point of encounter—Any of numerous points at which the customer comes into contact with your business or any representation thereof, be it personal, vocal, electronic, etc.

prioritization—Establishment of levels of importance and urgency relative to reallocation of resources and schedule of completion of tasks identified as vital to improving customer service.

reallocation—Reassignment or addition of financial, personnel, equipment, and facilities resources to increase the quality of customer service.

recognition—Observation and analysis of the points of encounter: knowing the points of encounter and assuming the customer's perspective from pre-sell to post-sale.

standard operating procedures (SOPs)—Documented sets of steps to be followed by employees of an organization to accomplish job tasks.

trade-off time management—An analytical determination as to whether optimum speed or personal attention is the best approach for a given situation.

Chapter 9 Outline

Advertising
    Advertising Guidelines
    The Six-Step Advertising Process
    Do It Yourself or Select an Agency?
    Trade-Outs, Barter, and Co-Oping
    Advertising Types and Themes
    Market Coverage
    Media Selection
Summary
Case Examples

Competencies

1. Summarize advertising guidelines, and describe a six-step advertising process that can help you develop a successful advertising campaign. (pp. 107–110)

2. Describe criteria for selecting an ad agency. (pp. 110–112)

3. Review the "trade-out" and "barter" concepts. (p. 112)

4. Summarize advertising types and themes, and describe examples of hospitality industry advertising campaigns. (pp. 112–121)

5. Discuss the concept of market coverage and media selection. (pp. 121–131)

9

Applying Key Marketing Methodologies: Advertising

THE STRENGTH OF **ADVERTISING** is its usefulness in creating and/or maintaining brand awareness. It helps to position a brand, demonstrate product attributes, and provide cost efficiencies for mass-marketed products. In general, it is very useful in controlling message content and timing. Its weaknesses include low credibility, a potential for a high percentage of reach to be wasted, message clutter, and a perception of being intrusive. Advertising is ideally used for:

- Establishing awareness.
- Creating image(s).
- Creating lifestyle associations.

Advertising builds **awareness** and can positively affect attitude and initiate behavior. Selection of the appropriate media and knowing where and when to place your ad are what effective advertising is about.

Advertising

Advertising includes both the *creative* strategy and the *media* strategy. **Creative strategy** focuses on the key target market, the "promise" (why, what, etc.), the "proposition" (support for the promise), and tone (feeling, personality). **Media strategy** focuses on the planning and execution of the delivery vehicles. Media's goal is to deliver the target audience at the lowest cost within the most appropriate environment for the message.

There are many lists of "dos and don'ts" for advertising, yet few of them acknowledge the product or service itself and the role that advertising plays in the overall marketing of that product or service. However, there are some advertising guidelines that can help you acknowledge both your product or service and your total marketing plan.

Advertising Guidelines

The following list of advertising guidelines can help you put together successful advertising campaigns:

- Know your product or service.
- Advertise as part of the total marketing strategy.

- Develop a proposition.
- Create a platform.
- Be realistic about the level of expectation.
- Review for customer needs.

We briefly discuss each of these guidelines in the following sections.

Know Your Product or Service. What do you know about the product or service you want to advertise? What consumer needs does it fulfill? Do you understand how consumers currently perceive your product or service in terms of price, quality, relationship to competition, consistency, and inconsistency? Knowing the role your product plays in the market and how consumers perceive the product is essential to creating effective advertising. Without these basic facts, you cannot get a clear, realistic picture of where your product stands in the market and where you want it to be.

Advertise as Part of the Total Marketing Strategy. What role do you anticipate advertising will play in your total marketing strategy? Do you even need to use advertising as a marketing tool? If so, should you use advertising with a narrow range but direct aim, or do you want to target a large region with more general advertising tools?

Develop a Proposition. Have you developed a general **proposition** to be conveyed in your advertising message? A proposition is the strongest truthful statement you can make to the consumer on behalf of your product or service. Your proposition should agree with and support your overall marketing strategy and meet the purpose of your advertising. For example, if you are trying to persuade people to use your product or service, does your advertising include a toll-free telephone number that consumers can call to order your product or service or get further information?

Create a Platform. Once you understand your product or service, the consumer's perspective of it, the role your advertising will play as part of your total marketing strategy, and you have developed your proposition, you can then focus on the advertising **platform**. The platform is an item-by-item list of facts that support your proposition. Platform statements illustrate the strength of your proposition.

Be Realistic About the Level of Expectation. Regardless of your advertising purpose and its strategic role in your overall marketing plan, there is one key principle that you should remember when advertising products and services. *Never promise more than your product or service can deliver.* The **level of expectation** principle is presented graphically in Exhibit 1.

Keep this idea in mind when you plan advertising. Too often, companies have made the mistake of promising more than they could deliver, resulting in customer dissatisfaction.

Review for Customer Needs. Does your advertising strategy relate to your customers' needs? Your customers' needs should be the focal points of your advertising strategy. Are you reinforcing your product/service/brand attributes?

Exhibit 1 Level of Expectation Principle

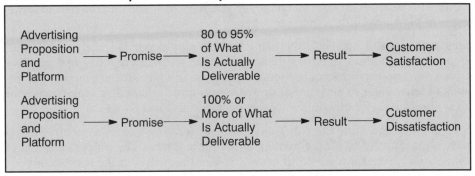

Once you understand the six guidelines just described, you can begin developing an actual advertising campaign.

The Six-Step Advertising Process

The following is a six-step advertising process that can help you develop a successful advertising campaign.

Step 1: Identify Your Purpose. Clearly identify *one* purpose you expect your advertising to serve. What do you want your advertising to do for you? Advertising is usually used to:

- Inform customers that your product or service is available and tell them how to get it.

- Persuade consumers that your product or service is better than your competitors'.

- Remind consumers to use your product or service.

Identify the purpose for advertising your product or service and then make sure that the ads you create fulfill that purpose. For example, if you want to *inform* consumers that you are offering a new service, your ads should not focus on reminding consumers you're still in business.

Step 2: Target Your Audience. Assuming you know what you want to say and why you want to say it (your purpose), the next step is to precisely *identify to whom you want to say it.* You want to advertise to people who will buy your product or use your service. "Who are these people?" and "How do I reach them?" become the next critical questions to answer. Market research can tell you who and where your target consumers are, and proper selection of advertising **media** can help you reach them.

Step 3: Select a Medium. You want to reach as many potential customers as possible with the most effective, efficient, and affordable medium you can select for advertising. Depending on your product or service, and your target consumers, it may be television, radio, or magazine advertising; in other situations, it may be direct mail, directories, outdoor advertising, or the yellow pages. Your choice of media also depends on how much money you have to spend and the role advertising is to play in your total marketing plan.

Step 4: Create the Ad. The advertising you develop depends largely on all other steps and guidelines previously cited. Despite wide interest in great creative advertising, your product or service, purpose, and budget are the practical parameters of what you can and cannot do with your creative strategy. Make sure your ad is appropriate for your audience, product, service, and budget.

Step 5: Place and Time the Ad. Thanks to your (or your agency's) creativity, you have a great ad ready for the market. Don't blow it now! The proper selection of *where* your advertising goes and *when* it is aired is critical to the success of your advertising campaign. When you select *where* to place your ad, consider:

- Markets.
- Media selection.
- Placement (where and when your ad runs).

To determine *when* to run the ad, think about:

- Time of year.
- Month.
- Week.
- Day of the week.
- Hour of the day.

Step 6: Fulfill Expectations. You ran a great ad at the right time and place, and now the phone is ringing off the hook. Is there *anyone* there to answer it? Make sure you can fulfill your ad promises after you have motivated the consumer to purchase. Meeting the expectations generated by your advertising should always be considered within the total context of your advertising strategy.

Do It Yourself or Select an Agency?

Depending on your skills and the size of your budget, you may want to do an advertising campaign yourself or contract with an advertising agency to handle the campaign for you. The scope and breadth of hospitality industry advertising is immense, ranging from local newspaper ads to national television campaigns. If you cannot afford the luxury of hiring an agency, here are a few suggestions to help you handle your own campaign.

First, start your own *master notebook*. This notebook should contain examples of clean ads that you have developed and used. The notebook will help you review the effectiveness of your ads and should include such information as how and where your ad came together. Include a section in the notebook labeled "Monitor" to record the history of your advertising and a statement of results. For example, it could read as follows:

Tues., February 20. Print Ad "A-1"—*Telegraph,* Entertainment Page
Wed., February 21. Print Ad "A-l"—*News,* Sports Page
Thurs., February 22. Print Ad "A-l"—*Telegraph,* Lifestyle Page

Results: Business up by 25% over same period last year and/or week.

or

Revenue up 16% February 22 and 28% February 23 compared with
same period last year and/or last week.

This simple procedure will give you a history of which ads were run, where
they were run, and the results.

Also, consider including in your master notebook examples of your competition's best advertising. Analyze the file to determine what advertising strategies
your chief competitors are using, trends they're following, and what you can do to
combat your competitors' moves. For example, let's say your competitor has
advertised "2-for-1" sales. Analyze their ads to determine if you can offer a similar
or better sale. Look for patterns as to when these sales are run. For example, you
might discover that your competitor runs a "2-for-1" ad the fourth week of every
month. You might counteract this strategy by advertising your "2-for-1" sale during the third week of the month.

Selecting an Agency. If you can afford to hire an ad agency, you should probably
do so, even if you believe you have the capability of running your own advertising
campaigns. Why? Because advertising professionals are best equipped to navigate
through today's complex and sophisticated marketing arena.

Selecting an agency is more like selecting a business partner than selecting just
another supplier of services, so ask a lot of questions before forming this vital part-
nership. Agencies will provide you with their credentials in terms of work they
have performed, awards they have won, current and past clients, and so on. Look
closely at these credentials and talk to the agency's former and current clients to
get a balanced perspective of the agency's strengths and weaknesses. Evaluate an
agency's strengths and weaknesses in relation to your own. Where do you or your
company need more help—for example, in creativity? in media planning? etc. The
following is a list of the major functional areas within ad agencies; keep in mind
that not every agency can be outstanding in every area:

- *Account management/account executive area.* The staff members in this area
  have the overall management responsibility for a brand, product, or client
  company; they are the primary contact persons with clients ("accounts") and
  manage the "account teams" (the persons who do the work for the clients).

- *Research.* Advertising researchers provide quantitative and qualitative data
  on the market, needs, benefits, competition, customers, etc., using an array of
  services and techniques.

- *Creative (the imagination function).* Artists and copywriters making up the creative staff generate ideas to link the brand or product to consumers' needs

- *Casting.* Members of this specialized group identify people, voices, actors: the
  ingredients that make an ad or commercial work.

- *Media.* Media specialists look for the best reach and frequency to reach your target audience, given your budget.

- *Production.* The production staff pulls together creative, media, and other agency areas and delivers the final product.

Perhaps the most important question to ask is: Who will actually work on your account—an experienced creative team or new hires?

Make sure that the agency you select knows something about your market and your customers. Good research, either conducted within the agency itself or contracted out to another research supplier, can increase your knowledge of target markets. If an agency immediately wants to talk creative strategy, media, or contract, take another look. A good agency will listen and learn as much as possible about your product or service, markets or consumers, and about you and your overall marketing philosophies before moving on to actual strategies.

One way to choose an agency is to place your business "out to bid" or "out for proposal." An amazing amount of good work done absolutely free of charge can come from "bid presentations." Consider more than one agency in the proposal stage so that you will have a basis for comparison.

Only you can judge how long to stay with an agency or how often to switch. Make changes only when your objective measurements indicate that it is time for a change. Objective measurements include declining sales, lower levels of brand awareness among customers and potential customers, negative customer feedback about your advertising, excessive errors in the advertising copy, missed deadlines, and so on.

Trade-Outs, Barter, and Co-Oping

One way to reduce your advertising costs is to exchange your product or service for advertising space or broadcast exposure. There is an infinite variety of **trade-outs** or **barter** agreements you can negotiate with advertising suppliers, ranging from a *one-for-one* trade to a *five-for-one* or even greater trade. A one-for-one trade means that you will provide a set dollar amount of products or services for an equal dollar value of space or air time, for example, $1,000 worth of your product or service for $1,000 worth of air time or space, and so on. If negotiated properly, trade-outs can be an effective way to stretch your advertising dollars and increase your business.

Another way to stretch advertising dollars is to **co-op**, or join with other companies to advertise, thereby sharing the costs (see Exhibit 2). Resort areas frequently run cooperative advertising campaigns that promote the region or area and also list or mention specific products or services. A more popular use of co-oping is seen when two or more firms advertise each other's services or products, either individually or collectively, in the same advertising campaign.

Advertising Types and Themes

An ad is not just the product of an idea. Effective advertising begins long before the "great idea" stage. As previously discussed, you need to answer some key questions regarding the purpose of the advertising, the platform, and the proposition.

Exhibit 2　Sample of a Cooperative Advertisement

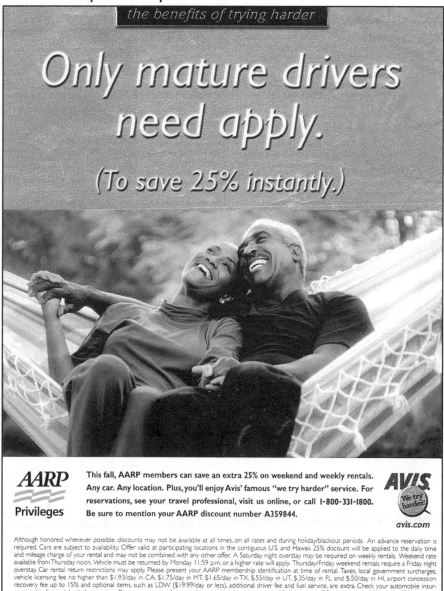

Courtesy of AARP/Avis

Even a great idea must have a purpose, or the ad campaign will be ineffective. Later in the chapter we look at some examples of great advertising ideas. "Great ideas" can backfire if the consumer's reaction to an ad differs from the reaction the

Exhibit 3   Sample of a Reputation Builder Advertisement

Courtesy of Country Inns & Suites

advertisers were trying to evoke. In selecting a type of advertisement, remember to keep in mind your target market, the needs of the individual in that market, the benefits they seek in your product or service, and your own product or service attributes. Select an ad type that is compatible with the psychographics of your market, and place it in an appropriate media vehicle. In the following sections we discuss some examples of ad campaign types or themes.

Reputation Builders. These ads feature *testimonials*, self-claims, or other-party claims, or cite leadership or professionalism as a way to enhance the reputation of the product or service advertised (see Exhibit 3). One common reputation-building technique is to have a recognized celebrity speak on behalf of the product or service, or lend his or her photo or signature as an implied endorsement of the product or service. A slightly different version of the celebrity testimonial is the self-testimonial ad, in which the CEO, president, or chairperson of the company speaks on behalf of the company's product or service. (This is also sometimes referred to as the "ego trip.")

   Another form of the reputation builder is the *professional trust ad* in which the platform itself is self-implied professionalism. The ad features the entire property or company staff in uniform, standing at attention, just waiting to professionally serve guests.

   Finally, we have the *image* form of a reputation builder, in which one or more images are used to represent your product or service, such as that shown in Exhibit 4.

Exhibit 4   Sample of an Image Advertisement

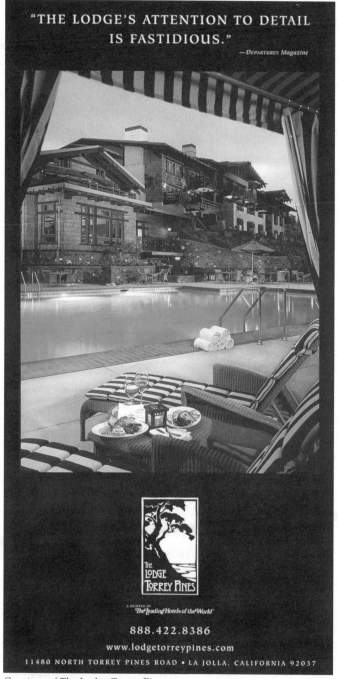

Courtesy of The Lodge Torrey Pines

Product/Service Touters. A product or service touter ad can take on a number of looks (see Exhibit 5). The *direct* look features the product or service and boldly states the reasons for its greatness. Touting the actual elements of the platform produces results similar to those of the reputation-builder ads—they both enhance the product or service. Another form of touter ad takes the *comparative approach.* Here, the ad compares your product or service with a competitor's to demonstrate that your product or service has more to offer.

A touter ad may feature an unusual product element or characteristic. For example, an amenity of unusually high quality may be the ad's focal point. Sometimes a touter ad will feature a scene, such as an elegant-looking couple or a luxury setting, as the positioning statement for the product or service. Product/service touter ads can have multiple elements, such as "we were rated highest by an independent survey, our service is extraordinary, and our facilities are world-class."

Brand Identifiers. In today's crowded marketplace, getting your brand known—also known as achieving *brand awareness*—is not an easy job. What may be even more difficult is to effectively convey what your brand stands for, or your *brand identity.* To achieve brand awareness and brand identity:

- Include statements that boldly feature the brand.

- Develop a *brand identifier*—a character, voice, image, phrase, etc., that becomes synonymous with the brand (see Exhibit 6).

- Make an introduction or announcement about the brand (see Exhibit 7).

- Develop a niche by providing a unique service.

Offers. In an offer ad, the platform becomes part of the proposition. One common type of offer is the straight *price offer*: "Newark $99 Round Trip." In a price offer, the actual price, not necessarily the product or service itself, is featured and highlighted as the key motivation for consumers to buy. Another variation of the straight price offer is the *price offer plus*—something additional is included with the product at no additional cost.

Today, one of the strongest-hitting offer ads focuses on *repeats* or *"build"* promotions, such as frequent traveler or frequent guest promotions. These ads feature offers or benefits for customers who repeatedly use one product or service.

Human Scenarios. A long-standing type of advertising is the *human scenario.* A person or group is the focal point of the ad, either directly or by identifiable event or circumstance. For example, an employee or group of employees is featured, accompanied by a gratuitous statement or slogan, or an exceptional employee is portrayed as representing the norm.

On a more sophisticated level (and more risky if it doesn't work well) is a *situation identification* (see Exhibit 8). Here, a "wrong-way" scene is shown and a statement is made that this situation won't occur with your product or service. These often humorous ads should be carefully considered, because they can backfire.

And last, but certainly not least, is the age-old *suggestive* approach, featuring or implying the promise of romance or sex to the consumer. This type of ad

Exhibit 5   Sample of a Product/Service Touter Advertisement

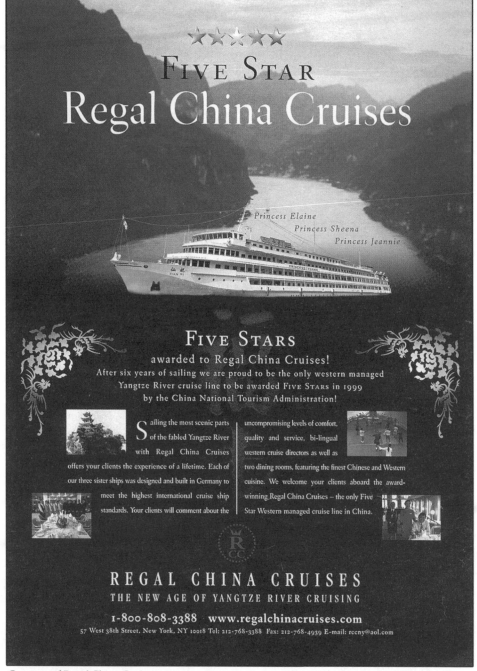

Courtesy of Regal China Cruises

Exhibit 6   Sample of a Brand Identifier Advertisement

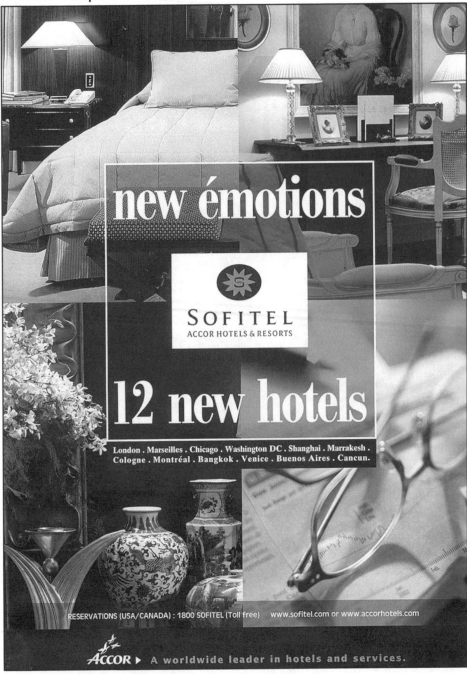

Courtesy of Accor Hotels & Resorts

Exhibit 7   Sample of an Introductory Advertisement

Introducing *Island Princess®*

THE BEST AND NEWEST SHIP TO ALASKA
AND THE PANAMA CANAL

- **More affordable private balconies** – Island Princess® features 90% outside staterooms, most with private balconies.
- **Personal Choice Dining®** – Offering seven different dining options, including the extraordinary **Bayou Café**, the only New Orleans-style restaurant afloat. Your clients can also enjoy Traditional Fixed Seating or Anytime Dining.℠

- **Universe Lounge** – Only Princess® offers the most sophisticated lounge at sea designed to educate and entertain, with high-definition televisions, three revolving stages, and daytime classes on everything from computers to cooking.

- **Island Princess** sails Alaska May '03 and the Panama Canal September '03. Sister ship **Coral Princess**℠ sails the Panama Canal December '02 and Alaska May '03.

Cruise Reservations: 1.800.421.1700 Brochure & Sales Materials: 1.888.478.6732
www.princess.com

Courtesy of Princess Cruises

Exhibit 8   Sample of a Situation Identifier Advertisement

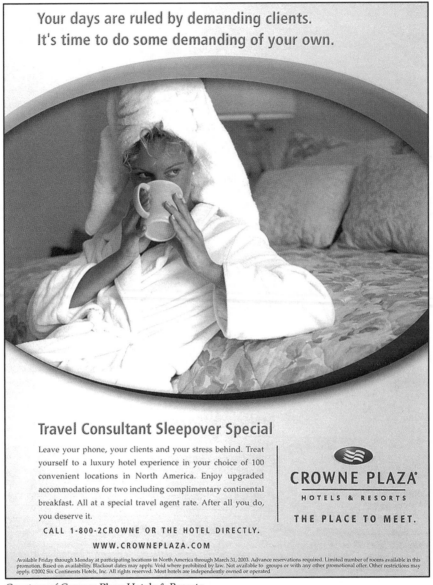

Courtesy of Crowne Plaza Hotels & Resorts

features an attractive person or implies how people who use the product or service become more attractive, successful, etc. The "hook" is a consumer's imagination.

Benefit. The *benefit* ad reflects the advertising platform in that it states, item-for-item, why consumers should purchase your product or service. Sometimes the ad will focus only on a primary benefit; at other times the benefit becomes engulfed in an overall umbrella of a more complex benefit or multiple benefits, such as those shown in Exhibit 9.

Series. *Series* ads rely on creative repetition and a similar graphic and copy theme to carry the message in a carefully planned and timed campaign. By virtue of their subtle repetition, series ads permit the reader to easily identify the product or service offered. The ad shown in Exhibit 10 is one of a series that carries the theme that many locations in Mexico are favored vacation destinations and are "Closer than ever."

Line Art and Silhouettes. More of a technique or production treatment than ad type or theme, line art and silhouettes have become more and more popular in advertising. Their popularity stems largely from their effectiveness in a newspaper or other black-and-white setting. Exhibit 11 shows an appealing application of line art in advertising.

Trade. A *trade* ad is aimed at intermediaries whose business is positioned between the end user of your products or services and the ultimate consumer. These may be agents, distributors, wholesalers, retailers, etc. Trade ads should focus on the needs of the intermediary (for example, new product information, commissions, etc.). The Hertz car rental trade advertisement in Exhibit 12 is directed at travel agents, in the hope that travel agents will preferentially reserve Hertz cars for their traveling customers.

Meetings. Selling *meeting* venues can be a challenging task, and telling potential customers about them through advertising can be equally difficult. Ads for meetings typically do not produce immediate "buys" because business meetings of the type requiring professional facilities and presentation equipment are generally scheduled far in advance. Meeting business is a major thrust in the overall selling campaign for the lodging business because most meeting venues are located in hotels. The convenience factor of having meeting attendees staying at the same hotel in which the meeting is taking place has special appeal (see Exhibit 13).

Destinations. The appeal in *destination* ads is location. Used principally to sell vacationers on the idea of visiting a particular spot, these ads are increasingly being used to inform the business market of the advantages of conducting conferences, meetings, and expositions at these locations. When the image of a destination is already established in the reader's mind, such as the promotion for Kauai shown in Exhibit 14, the ad's purpose is to strengthen the appeal of the destination.

Market Coverage

Think about where to expose your product or service to the consumer. Look at each case individually. There are no golden rules for determining how and where to cover your market. You don't always have to stick to the same media or technique. In the following sections, we discuss some different techniques for reaching your markets through advertising.

Nationwide Campaigns. Simply stated, nationwide campaigns give you coast-to-coast coverage or exposure of your product or service. If your market is nationwide or if you are trying to develop a national market presence, it might make

Exhibit 9   Sample of a Benefits Advertisement

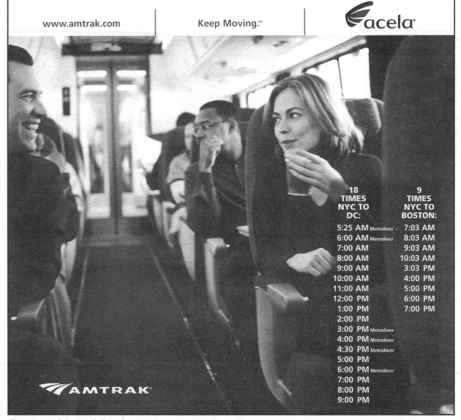

Courtesy of Amtrak/Acela

Exhibit 10   Sample of a Series Advertisement

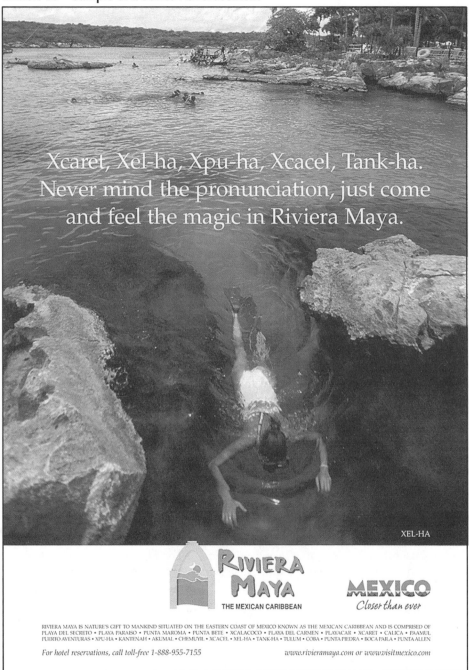

Courtesy of Riviera Maya

Exhibit 11   Sample of a Line Art or Silhouette Advertisement

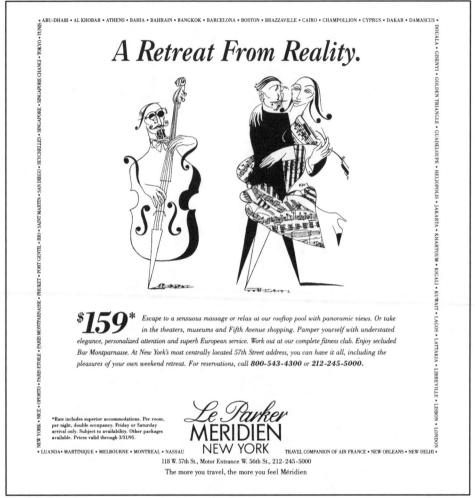

Courtesy of Le Parker Meridien New York

sense to look at this type of total market exposure. Nationwide campaigns are particularly useful for large chains seeking to increase their brand awareness levels or provide an "image" for their brand. Also, nationwide campaigns can be used to introduce a national product simultaneously in all markets.

Major Markets. Based on research or because of budget constraints, you might want to advertise only in those major markets you want to penetrate with your campaign.

Regional Markets. Advertising can be purchased or selected on a regional basis also. There are many ways to identify marketing regions for your product or service. For example, one large chain of cafeterias selects only the southwest region of

Exhibit 12   Sample of a Trade Advertisement

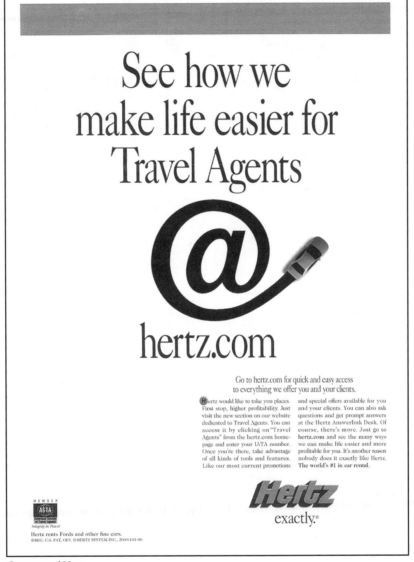

Courtesy of Hertz

the United States for advertising exposure, since this is the primary market for its locations and customers.

Population Markets. Population markets are major concentrations of population that can be categorized according to size, such as standard metropolitan areas with populations of over 1,000,000, over 750,000, over 500,000, and so on. Populations

Exhibit 13   Sample of a Meetings Advertisement

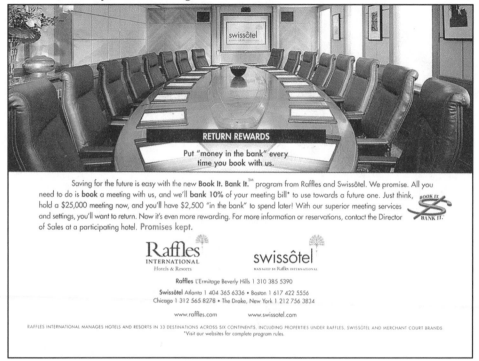

Courtesy of Raffles/Swissôtel

may be measured in terms of viewers, readers, listeners, exposures, etc., depending on the type of media you are considering.

Viewer/Reader/Listener/Subscriber Market Areas. Television stations, radio stations, magazines, and newspapers can provide detailed descriptions of the number of people within their range or on their circulation lists. In addition, they can provide you with various *buyer characteristics* that will help you choose the media that best match the needs of your product or service consumer. Using this advertising method allows you to better define a market area for your advertising message.

Feeder Markets. Feeder markets are geographical areas (markets) from which customers originate and that represent likely targets for your advertising.

Cities. Advertising can be placed in individual cities or even in areas within an individual city. Local market research can be a valuable aid to selecting the proper media for each city.

Media Selection

Carefully evaluate media before creating your advertising. *Broadcast media*, which include television and radio, provide one type of exposure for your product or

Exhibit 14   Sample of a Destination Advertisement

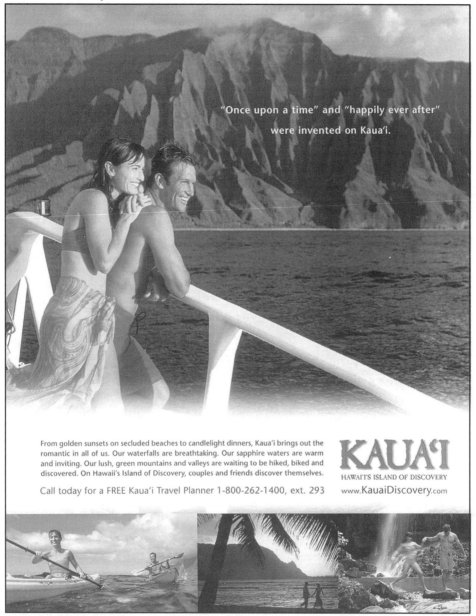

Courtesy of Kaua'i Discovery

service. *Print media*, which include magazines, newspapers, supplements, catalogs, directories, yellow pages, brochures, flyers, and so on, provide other types of exposure for your product or service.

Before you select media for delivering your advertising message, carefully analyze the various media to determine the number of potential customers they can reach, your expected return on investment, and the best, most cost-effective method to convey your advertising strategy. Again, consider your needs, purpose, and budget as part of your media analysis.

Media Strategies. Media strategies can be viewed or subdivided into planning, executing/buying, and measuring delivery. The overall goal is to deliver the target audience at the lowest cost in the most suitable environment for the message. Media *planning* simply involves selecting and sorting the various media in combinations and support levels that produce the most efficient and effective *plan* to achieve the marketing objectives. Media *execution* is the actual process of negotiating/buying and placing the media after the plan and budget have been determined. *Measuring delivery* is the process that determines if types and weights of media have performed to deliver the target audiences initially calculated. The *target audience* is the target market simplified by listing key strategic and demographic descriptors.

An advertising media plan, like any plan, should contain a media objective, media strategies, a media plan calendar, and budget. Your plan should answer such questions as:

- To whom is the advertising aimed (target audience description)?

- Where will the advertising go (market coverage desired, expressed geographically)?

- When will the advertising appear?

- How much advertising is needed for optimum communication (weight/impact)?

Selecting media involves both qualitative and quantitative decisions. Key questions to consider include:

- What is your target market's media behaviors and patterns (what do they watch, read, listen to, etc., and where)?

- What are their buying behaviors and patterns (when do they purchase your product/service)?

- When and where are the best times and places to reach the target market (direct mail to the home, drive time radio, late news on television, etc.)?

- What alternative media do the target consumers use (special-interest cable channels, trade magazines, etc.).

Strategic decisions must be made with respect to *media mix*—the different types of media to be used (television, magazines, radio, etc.) that produce the most efficient and effective plan/results. Further, *medium use* must be addressed, which includes the ad sizes, part of the day (day part), length of the commercial, type faces, etc. Also, calculations will need to be made to determine the cost per thousand (CPM) (MIL = 1000) to reach your audience. Finally, determinations will have to be made with respect to geographic weighing (distribution of your advertising

Exhibit 15   Major Data Sources

Medium	Audience Data	Cost Data
Direct Mail	Direct Mail Standard Rate and Data Services (SRDS) Dun's Marketing Services	Direct Mail SRDS Dun's Marketing Services
Magazines	Audit Bureau of Circulation (ABC) Simmons Market Research Bureau (SMRB) Mediamark Research Inc. (MRI) Individual Magazine Representative	Magazines SRDS Magazine representatives (Ad position is usually negotiable, but cost usually is not)
Newspapers	Simmons/Scarborough Report Newspaper Association of America Local newspaper representative	Newspaper SRDS (space costs national products) Local rate cards via newspaper representatives (lower cost for local business advertising than national products)
Outdoor	Traffic Audit Bureau (TAB) Local representative	Outdoor SRDS Outdoor representatives (costs are sometimes negotiable and board position is usually negotiable depending on availability)
Radio	RADAR—Network Arbitron Research—Spot	Network/station representatives Media Market Guide Radio SRDS (costs are negotiable)
Television	Nielsen Research Services (NTI, NSI)	Network/station representatives Media Market Guide Spot Quotations and Data, Inc. (costs are negotiable)

geographically), seasonality (purchasing patterns), relationship of media selected to product/market distribution, and the overall right time and right place to run your advertising.

In order to facilitate decision-making, agencies subscribe to services and organizations that provide data on audiences, readership, etc., and on costs. Some agencies develop *models* based on the data of your product's or service's market characteristics. These models then provide various choice options. Exhibit 15 provides a listing of some of the major data sources.

Media Scheduling. In viewing media **scheduling**, it is good to first determine how much *frequency* you need for your specific product/service/brand. The table below provides an overview for frequency determination.

More Frequency	Less Freqency
• New campaign	• Established leader/brand/ product/service
• New product/service	
• New brand introduction	• Strong market/strong competitive position
• Trial offer	• Simple message
• Promotion or sales event	• Established campaign
• Complex message	• Reminder messages
• Short product purchase cycles	• Low or less crowded
• Crowded/highly competitive advertising market	• Competitive advertising levels
	• Longer purchase cycles

Once your overall frequency is identified, there are a number of options for advertising media scheduling, including:

• *Continuity Schedules.* Continuous run at a relatively fixed level—non-seasonal, non-promotional levels.

• *Flighting in Scheduling.* Generally three to six weeks of continuous advertising, followed by periods of no advertising.

• *Front Loading.* Running heavier weight levels with the commencement of a media schedule (kick-off).

• *Heavy-up Schedules.* Incorporate incremental media weight to support periods of higher market activity.

• *Pulsing Schedules.* Run in continuous on/off patterns.

Media Measurement and Terminology. Not every media selection is evaluated or measured in the same way. *Rating points* for broadcast media are usually determined by a formula involving percent "reach" and frequency. Rating points may be expressed as **gross rating points (GRP)** or **target rating points (TRP)**. A rating point is defined as one percent of the universe being measured. GRP provides a common term of measurement to help assess how much weight is going into a specific marketplace and allows for comparisons among media selections. To determine total GRP, *reach* (defined as how many homes/persons your message has reached, expressed as an absolute percentage) is multiplied by *frequency,* (how often the homes/persons have been reached on an average basis). The total GRP formula follows:

$$\text{Percent Reach} \times \text{Frequency} = \text{Total GRP}$$
$$(\text{e.g., Reach of 75} \times \text{Frequency of 10} = 750 \text{ GRP})$$

As previously referenced, there are different methods to measure specific types of advertising media. These are summarized below:

- *Broadcast* (TV, radio, etc.) uses GRP to assess viewership/listeners in a defined marketplace. Percentage reach multiplied by frequency equates to GRP.

- *Direct mail* uses percent coverage for reach (number mailed/total market, target households, or target persons) and number of mailings for frequency.

- *Magazine* uses percent coverage for reach (circulation/total market households or total readers/target persons) and number of insertions for frequency.

- *Newspaper* uses percent coverage for reach (circulation/total market households or total readers/target persons) and number of insertions for frequency.

- *Outdoor* uses a standard four-week showing time frame, reach, and showing (e.g., 50 showing = 85 reach and 15 frequency). Many view traffic counts as another key indicator of outdoor value.

There are other evaluation and measurement techniques to help quantify overall media goals. These include what is referred to as the *macro method*, in which advertising is used as a percentage of sales based on an industry (specific to your product or service category) average. Here, **share of media voice (SOV)** is compared to **share of market (SOM)**. The *micro target method* determines the amount of GRP media weight necessary to effectively reach (communicate) with large portions of your target market to assure that consumers understand the message to a degree to support a sale. Two other popular overall indicators are the **brand development index (BDI)** and **category development index (CDI)**. BDI is determined by dividing product sales by the percent of households in a given market. CDI is the percent of category (product category) sales divided by the percent of households in a given market.

Summary

Developing your advertising message requires detailed planning, establishment of objectives, plotting of strategy, and a plan of execution. Objectives should be established for increasing awareness levels and changing attitudes and behaviors. Advertising strategy must address the overall *promise, proposition* (support for the promise), and *tone* of the message. Advertising execution is based on key research information (data) and takes into consideration specific creative requirements, legal considerations (claims and disclaimers), etc.

Exhibit 16 is an advertising checklist that can be adapted to your own advertising efforts and can be a useful tool for your organization. Such a checklist can do more than save you money: it can help you determine if your advertising is organized and effective and provide a cross-check to ensure that advertising, sales, and public relations personnel are all working together to execute your marketing plan.

Exhibit 16   Advertising Audit/Checklist

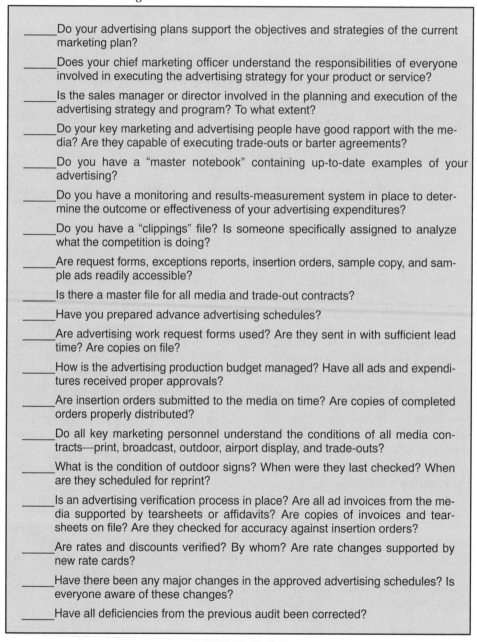

_____Do your advertising plans support the objectives and strategies of the current marketing plan?

_____Does your chief marketing officer understand the responsibilities of everyone involved in executing the advertising strategy for your product or service?

_____Is the sales manager or director involved in the planning and execution of the advertising strategy and program? To what extent?

_____Do your key marketing and advertising people have good rapport with the media? Are they capable of executing trade-outs or barter agreements?

_____Do you have a "master notebook" containing up-to-date examples of your advertising?

_____Do you have a monitoring and results-measurement system in place to determine the outcome or effectiveness of your advertising expenditures?

_____Do you have a "clippings" file? Is someone specifically assigned to analyze what the competition is doing?

_____Are request forms, exceptions reports, insertion orders, sample copy, and sample ads readily accessible?

_____Is there a master file for all media and trade-out contracts?

_____Have you prepared advance advertising schedules?

_____Are advertising work request forms used? Are they sent in with sufficient lead time? Are copies on file?

_____How is the advertising production budget managed? Have all ads and expenditures received proper approvals?

_____Are insertion orders submitted to the media on time? Are copies of completed orders properly distributed?

_____Do all key marketing personnel understand the conditions of all media contracts—print, broadcast, outdoor, airport display, and trade-outs?

_____What is the condition of outdoor signs? When were they last checked? When are they scheduled for reprint?

_____Is an advertising verification process in place? Are all ad invoices from the media supported by tearsheets or affidavits? Are copies of invoices and tearsheets on file? Are they checked for accuracy against insertion orders?

_____Are rates and discounts verified? By whom? Are rate changes supported by new rate cards?

_____Have there been any major changes in the approved advertising schedules? Is everyone aware of these changes?

_____Have all deficiencies from the previous audit been corrected?

Developing your media plan requires establishing media objectives related to your target audience, geography, seasonality, weighing and impact goals, and overall qualitative judgment. Media strategies must address media mix, specific

Exhibit 17   Media Plan Checklist

_____Will your plan provide a competitive advantage?

_____Is the media plan based on a factual assessment of your market and competition?

_____Is the media plan synergistic with the overall marketing strategy?

_____Is the advertising media plan interlinked with all other marketing tool plans and strategies?

_____Is the media plan appropriate for the "creative" message that was developed?

_____Will the media plan support the promotional objectives, and is it interlinked with the promotions calendar?

_____Is the media plan in sync with the geographic and seasonality patterns?

_____Is the type of "scheduling" appropriate to the objectives and overall expenditure levels?

_____Is the media plan delivering more (e.g., GRP) than in previous years based on the level of expenditures?

_____Are evaluation and measurement processes in place to assess performance?

_____Are alternatives developed and ready for implementation?

_____Have all organizations' functions been briefed about the media plan?

medium usage, and scheduling. A media plan checklist such as that shown in Exhibit 17 will ensure that you are addressing key media plan concerns and questions.

Let's look at two case examples of advertising strategies.

Case Examples

Case Example 1: Extreme Target Market Execution. A small upscale hotel and resort company trying to compete with much larger chains such as Hyatt, Hilton, and Westin needed to employ an advertising media/strategy we will call "extreme target market execution." The scenario was that the small chain's budget was one-fifth to one-tenth that of the competitors'. Its brand awareness on an unaided basis was less than one percent, compared to its competitors' whose unaided awareness levels were at 70-, 80-, and 90-percent levels.

With a very limited research budget, the small chain discovered that by _looking within_ its core customer base, it found that over 85 percent of all customers arrived by air. Further, through some cooperative research with American Express, it discovered over 75 percent of these core customers used the American Express card. These cardholders were then profiled, resulting in demographic, psychographic, and benefits/needs findings. In essence, these core customers displayed a consistent habit of reading and viewing very specific media. Most of their reading was done while traveling, either on a plane or in their hotel room at night.

Most of their television viewing during the week was limited to CNN Headline News or the Weather Channel. In fact, they were very consistent about the weather. They indicated that they checked the weather for their home location and the cities they were traveling to on a daily basis and sometimes up to three times a day. They also indicated that they carried with them a pocket edition of the airline timetables (*Official Airline Guide* or American Express *Skyguide*). Almost all belonged to the airline VIP clubs. Further, when questioned about their specific reading habits, nearly all indicated they read *USA TODAY* and the *Wall Street Journal* daily and when on planes would read or scan the major business publications such as *Forbes, Business Week,* etc.

Given this base of information, the small chain decided to drastically modify its media plan. It reduced and eventually eliminated all television advertising, except for a heavy schedule on CNN Headline News (time slots at the weather forecast) and an even heavier schedule on the Weather Channel. The small chain also dramatically changed its print media plan by eliminating most sports/golf/tennis publications, most ads in travel magazines, and all ads in consumer magazines, except *Forbes* and *Fortune*. With this reduction in media advertising, the small chain had the funds necessary to focus on dominating media related to air travelers and weather watchers.

In the course of the next twelve months it had signed agreements providing it exclusive advertising rights with *USA TODAY*, where it created a new advertising space called the "weather band" (a 4 ½-inch horizontal bar at the bottom of the weather page) and *The Wall Street Journal*, where it provided a special weather forecast (through an agreement with the Weather Channel) in the upper right corner of page three of the paper. The company also:

- Signed contracts for the back cover ad space of the pocket edition of the *Official Airline Guide* and the American Express *Skyguide*.

- Purchased the inside front cover ad space and additional space in *Frequent Flyer Magazine,* providing monthly weather data.

- Contracted with the company that supplied all the consumer seat-back magazines to all the airlines (44 titles in all, including the business magazines), with rights to the cover ad inside the back cover of the cardboard "wraps" or binders placed on the magazines.

- Supplied these same magazines to all the airlines' VIP clubs.

- Secured the on-board video advertising rights in the "hotel" category with ABC Video, which supplied video programming to most of the major airlines at the time.

- Purchased ad space (including inside front, back covers, and center spreads) in the East-West network and other major airlines' on-board airline magazines.

- On occasion, purchased the rights to insert a mini-version of its directory in the plastic bags holding the headphones on board the major airlines.

This concentrated target market media plan cost the same as its previous plan and still was one-fifth to one-tenth of what the small chain's major competitors were spending. For these dollars, the small chain was everywhere its target market customers and potential customers were in terms of their daily viewing and reading habits. In fact, their advertising was on all the television stations serving their target market and in the complimentary newspapers placed at the door of the competition's hotels. The results included:

- A dramatic increase in brand awareness to parity levels with competition on an aided basis and to within 10 to 20 percentage points on an unaided basis.

- Strong gains in market share, average rate, and occupancy increases.

- A perception that this small chain was actually five times its size (as perceived by the target market).

Case Example 2: Icon Power. Icons can take on many different shapes, forms, and personalities. Consider Mr. Clean, Colonel Sanders, the Eveready (Energizer) Bunny, and Ronald McDonald. Perhaps one of the more recent examples of successful advertising deployment of an icon is Jack of the Jack In The Box fast-food chain. Here is an icon that changed not only its personality and character, but also rescued a fatally wounded fast-food chain. The original Jack was a wise-guy radical character who did his swan song with an attempt to blow up the boardroom. Shortly thereafter, disaster in the form of four deaths resulted from e. coli bacteria that was linked to hamburger meat consumed at a Jack In The Box restaurant. Sales plummeted, and Jack No. 1 was shelved.

To resurrect the brand was going to be a very difficult task. After all, you don't want to talk about your hamburgers and remind everyone of the previous problem. The old Jack #1 was an unlikely candidate to bring back, as his character related to a younger, youth-orientated market. Research indicated the hamburger business had changed and so too would the character the new Jack (Jack #2), if he were to come back and be on target and successful. According to the research, the market was now more complex and older. There were some distinct categories of burger eaters. These included what were referred to as the "cravers," or individuals that had to have their burger everyday. There were the "dealers," those who wanted the most food for the dollar. And, there were the "quality seekers." How would the "new" Jack come back, and how would he relate to these distinct types or segments?

The world-renowned Chiat/Day agency recreated Jack (the new Jack) as a new breed of executive, clearly in charge and with a wonderful new personality as a smart-talking no-nonsense executive/CEO. The character, with its ping-pong ball head and yellow hat, is readily recognized and easily distributed as a giveaway fixture for auto aerials across America. Jack #2 has become an icon with the personality "power" to bring back the brand. His character allowed for more than a hundred different spots, each aimed at the three market segments or newly emerging segments. The results have been a remarkable turnaround for a brand many wrote off as deceased. The power of Jack the icon is a tough ad concept to beat if it is executed as well as Jack In The Box has executed it.

🗝 Key Terms

advertising—Printed or spoken matter that calls attention to or praises a product or service publicly, as through newspapers, handbills, radio, television, etc., so as to make people want to buy it.

awareness—In advertising, making your brand known to your markets, achieved through information campaigns that boldly feature the brand and creating a brand identifier or image, etc.

barter—An exchange of products or services for advertising space or broadcast exposure.

brand development index (BDI)—An evaluation and measurement technique to help quantify overall media goals. BDI is determined by dividing product sales by the percent of households in a given market.

category development index (CDI)—The percent of category (product category) sales divided by the percent of households in a given market.

co-op—A technique for reducing advertising costs in which two or more companies join to advertise complementary products or services.

creative strategy—A core element of advertising that focuses on the key target market, the "promise" (why, what, etc.), the "proposition" (support for the promise), and "tone" (feeling, personality).

feeder market—Those geographical areas (markets) from which customers originate. They are likely targets for advertising.

gross rating points (GRP)—A common term of media measurement that helps assess how much weight is going into a specific marketplace and that allows for comparisons among media selections.

icon—An image, figure, personage, or representation created to identify and promote a product or service

level of expectation—The quantity or quality of your product or service, as expected by your customers; a basic premise of advertising is that you never promise more than your product or service can actually fulfill.

media—The vehicles—newspapers, magazines, radio, television, and so on—by which you can advertise.

media strategy—A core element of advertising that focuses on the planning and execution of the delivery vehicles.

platform—The item-by-item list of things that directly support your ad proposition.

proposition—The strongest factual statement you can make on behalf of your product or service.

scheduling—The overall strategy of ad placement. Scheduling defines the frequency of the appearance of ads, based on a number of options (continuity, flighting, front loading, heavy-up, pulsing) available to the media planner.

share of market (SOM)—That portion of a specific market captured by an advertiser, expressed in a percentage.

share of media voice (SOV)—A macro-method media evaluation and measurement technique, in which advertising is used as a percentage of sales based on an industry (specific to your product or service category) average. Share of media voice is compared to share of market to arrive at the media measurement statistic.

trade-out—An exchange of your product or service for advertising coverage.

target rating points (TRP)—In broadcast media evaluation and measurement, the increment or index used as the common term to express the portion of the target market covered by a given television or radio station, based on a formula involving percents of *reach* and *frequency.*

Chapter 10 Outline

Public Relations
    What Public Relations Is
    How Public Relations Can Be Applied
    Internal Public relations
    How Can Public Relations Be
        Measured?
Publications
    Trade Media
Case Examples

Competencies

1. Describe public relations.
   (pp. 139–141)

2. Explain how public relations can be
   applied, summarize tips for
   direct–contact PR, and describe
   strategies for successfully dealing with
   the press. (pp. 141–147)

3. Describe internal public relations,
   explain how public relations can be
   measured, and list examples of
   hospitality industry publications.
   (pp. 147–152)

10

Applying Key Marketing Methodologies: Public Relations

THE PURPOSE OF THIS CHAPTER is to help you understand how public relations can help improve sales and boost employee morale. We will focus on internal or "within-the-house" public relations applications as well as the full range of external public relations techniques and methods. We will also take a look at types of public relations opportunities that have proven their worth in the hospitality industry. Finally, we will discuss how to tie your public relations effort to your marketing strategy and how to measure the results.

Public Relations

Public relations is a marketing tool. It is a communications vehicle connecting your marketing message to a variety of audiences. The public relations perspective must include the *total audience*, which includes the investment community, shareholders, and franchisees, among others, as well as intermediaries and individual consumers of your products and services. Public relations can effectively reach and affect everyone in this broad external audience. Furthermore, public relations can prove to be a very effective internal marketing device to communicate and motivate employees.

You may frequently hear that "so and so really got publicity from that event." But **publicity** is only one facet of public relations. Publicity can be free, but it can also be negative as well as positive—think of all the publicity surrounding hotel or casino fires. We will discuss publicity in more detail later in the chapter.

There are many fallacies about public relations: "PR is B.S.;" "Public relations is undefinable—it doesn't do anything and can't be measured;" "It's a waste of time and money;" "Anyone can do PR work." People who make these comments either do not understand public relations or have only been exposed to disorganized public relations efforts. It's true, public relations does not directly make sales; however, it can be very influential in seeing that sales are made. Let's look at some ground rules for various aspects of public relations and explore what public relations is, how it can be applied, and how it can be measured.

What Public Relations Is

Public relations is a powerful marketing tool that is capable of reaching all marketing audiences. In positive applications, public relations can provide a strong defensive strategy.

Public relations involves dealing with all publics, including individual consumers and potential consumers, the financial community, the local community, the media, and even your own employees. Effective public relations can provide a competitive advantage within your own business area—be it hotels, airlines, restaurants, or travel services. This competitive advantage is frequently overlooked, even by public relations personnel. In essence, a well-executed public relations program can provide a good image within your industry segment. That image pays dividends in consumer preference for your product or service, and it may also result in attracting and retaining good employees.

Public relations can create a favorable environment for your company, product, or service. It creates this favorable environment most effectively if it is part of the firm's overall marketing plan. Objectives, strategies, target markets, expected results, timetables, and measurement can and should be established for all public relations programs. Of equal importance in a formal plan for public relations is the selection of the trained professionals to create and execute the plan. It is an absolute fallacy to believe "anyone can do public relations."

The resources that can be used in public relations are unlimited. Here is a brief list of some of the vehicles public relations personnel use to reach various audiences:

- Announcements
- Broadcast media (TV and radio)
- Print media (newspapers, magazines, etc.)
- News conferences
- News releases

- Civic, social, and community involvement
- Employee relations
- Speeches
- Interviews
- Photographs

In addition, there are many different public relations techniques that can be employed to obtain media **exposures.** Numerous articles and texts provide list after list of ideas and suggestions for generating positive publicity, but many authors forget one basic thing—the planned purpose or strategy for achieving such exposure. Even if your relationship with the media is superb, the use and placement of publicity must support your overall marketing strategies. The caution is simply stated: "Make your PR count." Some ideas for making your PR count are included in Exhibit 1. Each of the ideas listed in Exhibit 1 should be placed within the context of an overall marketing strategy. Your public relations effort is your best marketing tool for establishing creditability and building trust. Exhibit 2 depicts a simple way to help you remember the six tools or focal points of public relations.

Exhibit 1   Suggestions for Public Relations Opportunities

- Accomplishments of employees or firm
- Activities involving your company employees
- Anniversary dates
- Appointments of key people
- Awards received by firm or employees
- Celebrities who visit you (obtain their approval)
- Community awards
- Contributions to charities and the local community by the firm or employees
- Displays of all types
- Entertainment appearing at your facility
- Events occurring on your property
- Events of special interest—humorous or creative
- Grand openings of all types
- Groups of interest meeting or eating with you
- Guests of interest (obtain their approval)
- Industry-related events
- Interviews with visitors, guests, etc.
- New management, ownership, employees, etc.
- Openings of all kinds
- Operating changes of major significance to the public
- Organizational changes
- Public service events/activities
- Receipt of certificates, awards, etc.
- Recognition of people, places, things, etc.
- Special displays, features introduced, etc.
- Special events of all types
- Speeches of employees, groups meeting at your facility, etc.

How Public Relations Can Be Applied

Once the ideas and objectives for your public relations plan have been established and tied into the overall marketing plan, it is time to consider how to apply or execute those ideas. You must first answer some questions:

1. What medium can best execute this strategy?

2. Who are the key contacts for this task?

3. Is it necessary to establish or re-solidify any personal relationships with the media before executing the strategy?

4. Is our approach carefully thought out? What are the potential downside risks?

5. Do we have a delivery package ready for the media?

Exhibit 2   Public Relations Tools

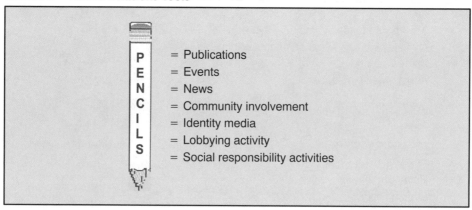

P = Publications
E = Events
N = News
C = Community involvement
I = Identity media
L = Lobbying activity
S = Social responsibility activities

The **delivery package**—a package for the **press** containing news items, names of contact persons and their phone numbers, property information, photographs, brochures, and so on—is essential. Although there is no guarantee your copy or materials will be used, it is much more likely that your public relations message will correspond to your intentions if you make a delivery package available. The list in Exhibit 3 will aid you in compiling a package that will be useful to the media.

Some public relations opportunities—speeches, press conferences, meetings, interviews, and so on—involve personal contact with media personnel and others. If you are going to employ one of these direct-contact PR methods, you need to prepare the individual(s) who will be making the direct contact with the media. *Thorough preparation is essential for successful direct-contact public relations.* Ground rules and suggestions abound as to how to prepare a speech or other public presentation. Assuming your spokesperson follows the rules and makes a good presentation, there is still one critical mistake that can be made—using the wrong person. Simply stated, be sure you put the right speaker in front of the media. If the talk is on technical matters, be certain that the speaker has total command of the technical terms. If the talk is on corporate strategy, be sure the individual has enough authority within the corporation to be credible. If the talk is on your own product or service, make sure the speaker can relate it to the audience's perspective. The following is a brief list of public speaking do's and don'ts:

Do's

- Carefully organize and allow yourself enough time to prepare.
- Be prepared—write out the talk, memorize it, and keep notes.
- Rewrite, review, and rewrite again.
- Create an outline or plan for your speech and follow it.
- Use pauses for emphasis.
- Check and double-check the visuals, equipment, room, visibility, etc.
- Speak clearly and deliver smoothly.

Exhibit 3   Delivery Package Requirements

- Addresses and phone numbers of key media contacts
- Addresses and phone numbers of key corporation personnel
- Approval procedures and required forms
- Biographies of key personnel
- Briefing sheets on individuals, company, product, etc.
- Brochures, if applicable
- Cancellation procedures and policy
- "Canned" formats, releases, letterheads, logos, symbols, etc.
- Confidentiality statements/procedures
- Contacts list and phone numbers/procedures
- Copy samples and actual copy
- Displays, podiums with logos, etc.
- News conference procedures list
- One person to call and his or her phone number (usually public relations contact)
- Photo inventory of product, people, etc.
- Photo library and selection ready for press
- Previous problems files and checklist
- Previous questions files and checklist
- Price/rate information
- Procedures for distribution
- Product/service procedures and policy
- Promotional package on firm or product
- Request forms—data, photo, product information, etc.
- Scrapbook or clipping files
- Speech copies for distribution

Don'ts

- Don't speak on subjects about which you are not qualified.
- Don't ad lib.
- Don't guess or estimate numbers.
- Don't read in a monotone.
- Don't use excessive pauses, either in number or length of time.
- Don't prepare unreadable visuals.
- Don't mumble, slur, laugh to yourself, etc.
- Don't wait to read what you are going to say until the plane ride or cab ride there.

Dealing With the Press. Dealing with the press is one of the most difficult tasks marketing and public relations personnel undertake. It is difficult for many reasons, but most of all because the press is *powerful.* It reaches many consumers with a message in writing, so you must be absolutely certain that the press has your facts correct.

Again, many good articles have been written on public relations and the press, many golden rules laid down, and many do's and don'ts have been listed. The recognition factors that follow represent a composite of a number of such lists. These are not all-inclusive, nor are they intended to be golden rules. They are factors that may keep your public relations efforts on a positive note—on the offensive rather than in a defensive position:

Recognition Factors

1. *Identify your purpose.* What is your purpose or reason for seeking the public relations exposure? If your purpose is to make others aware of your new product/service, be sure that is exactly what you convey—don't let it be lost in a story about your production process. Be precise and be sure your intent is communicated.

2. *Identify your target and objectives.* Who is your target? Is it prospective consumers of your product? Is it the local financial community? Is it your employees? What are your objectives? Do you want to boost employee morale? Do you want to increase food sales, beverage sales, room sales, or brand awareness? Think it out and identify how and where in the media you will best achieve your objectives.

3. *Understand the press's perspective.* You know your purpose and your target; that is your perspective. What is the press's perspective? Identify and understand the press's interests. Determine how you can place your purpose and target within a package that directly meets the interest of the press or other media. Think about what will help increase their circulation.

4. *Tailor your preparation.* Having identified your purpose, your target, and the media's perspective, tailor your preparation to include all three. Be sure to include everything that the press will need to convey the story—photos, names, and releases. Be sure your story is typed, double-spaced, and in the style the medium is currently using. Follow the editorial style of your selected medium at all times.

5. *Know the **transmission channels**.* Knowing where to send your material means knowing the difference between news and a feature story. News should be directed to the city desk, and feature stories should go to the appropriate editor. Better yet, get to know the editors who can be of most help to you, and cultivate those relationships (but don't wear them out).

6. *Deal with the human element.* People do not like extra work or being pressured, and most cannot afford the time to tell you the ground rules. People basically want the easy way out. This sounds cruel, but it should help you understand how to deal with the human element. Find out the media's deadlines in advance. Do not waste your time or the valuable time of media contacts. Do as much of their work as you can. Remember, if your material is well prepared and you do most of the work for them, your material may be used. If

you do not do the work, you can expect nothing to appear. Also, remember to be available to respond to any media questions or requests for clarification. If you are unavailable, your material may be scrapped or come out wrong.

You will also need some guidelines for answering questions from media representatives. The keys that follow are not all-inclusive, nor are they original, but they are very practical:

1. *Tell the truth.* The message you want to convey should be pure fact. The media want credible, straightforward, and truthful material and relationships. This simply means your materials should be thorough and honest. It does not mean you need to reveal confidential data or private sources, nor does it mean you should violate confidentialities.

2. *Be responsive.* You may not have all the answers at your fingertips for every question or inquiry. Do not lie or guess; say, "I do not have that information with me; however, I will call you and provide it today." Then get the information fast and provide it accurately.

3. *Provide the facts and follow up.* Supply the key facts in print to lessen the chance of being misquoted on key data. If at all possible, follow up with media personnel by going over the facts or key numbers with them to ensure accuracy. If you do not have a requested statistic, get it and call or send a note to the person who requested it. Be sure accurate numbers reach the media.

4. *Be concise.* People usually get into trouble with the media for what they say, not for what they do not say. Provide the facts in a concise, uneditorialized, and unexaggerated manner. Be precise and accurate. Ranges may be okay, but pulling numbers out of the sky is a disaster.

5. *Build the relationship.* If you follow steps 1 through 4 by being truthful, responsive, factual, and concise, you are on your way to achieving the fifth practical key—building good relationships with media personnel. Hostile attitudes, a reactionary statement to sensitive questions, aloofness, or a combative position damages relationships with the press. Work hard at being in control of yourself and your responses, no matter what you think of the media or a particular media representative. After all, someone who dislikes you is not going to be eager to give you space or air time.

Tools of Public Relations. A **press kit** is usually two-sided folder of high quality, often customized with the firm's logo or other identification markings. Background materials are normally placed in the left side/pocket, timely news items in the right. Examples of background information might include biographies of key property personnel, property fact sheets, and photographs. Timely news items include the actual **press release(s)** (see Exhibit 4). The cover of the kit should not only convey your firm's image, but also be of a practical weight, size, and nature to protect photos. Photos should be clearly labeled on the reverse side. Few things are more embarrassing to marketers than to have the wrong photo get picked up with a press release.

Exhibit 4   Sample Press Release

NEWS RELEASE

Hospitality Industry Hall of Honor

For Immediate Release

HOSPITALITY INDUSTRY HALL OF HONOR ANNOUNCES 2002 INDUCTEES: JENNIE GROSSINGER, ELAINE GROSSINGER ETESS & WILLIAM NORMAN

Houston --The Hospitality Industry Hall of Honor is pleased to announce its 2002 inductees: Jennie Grossinger & Elaine Grossinger Etess of Grossingers Resort and Country Club and William S. Norman, President & CEO of the Travel Industry Association of America. Tom Curley, President & Publisher of USA TODAY and Joseph McInerney, President & CEO of American Hotel & Lodging Association will serve as Masters of Ceremony.

The original Hospitality Industry Hall of Honor is located in the University of Houston's Conrad N. Hilton College of Hotel & Restaurant Management. Within the complex are displays and memorabilia related to the life, career and accomplishments of each inductee. Dr. Ronald A. Nykiel, Chairman of the Hospitality Industry Hall of Honor stated, "…from the moving portraits in the 'Leaders Gallery' to the visual displays and historic documents, a true 'learning from leadership' educational environment is provided."

The 2002 Hospitality Industry Hall of Honor Induction Ceremony will take place on Wednesday, October 2 at the Conrad N. Hilton College of Hotel & Restaurant Management.

Contact: Ronald Nykiel
            (555) 123-4367

            Laura Sutherland
            (555) 124-5678

Press releases may sometimes be picked up verbatim. Therefore, all releases should be "in form" and grammatically flawless. "In form" means the release should be exactly in the form you would want a publication to present your story. More often, the press release will be used as background or a resource from which the magazine or newspaper editor or reporter will work to mold an actual "story." Here are seven keys to creating a press release with the proper form:

Key 1: The top right or left corner is almost always used for the name of the "contact" person(s); sometimes the contact person(s) appear at the end of the release. These contacts are the people who are readily available to provide more information. This means they should be knowledgeable enough to speak to the press. Under the names should appear their phone numbers, fax numbers, and addresses.

Key 2: A specific release date should be noted at the top of the page, slightly below the contact information. If the information is for a feature story that can appear at any time or is otherwise not date sensitive, the words "FOR IMMEDIATE RELEASE" should appear there, usually capital letters and sometimes underlined.

Key 3: The headline should be presented in capital letters and underlined (if desired) about one-quarter to one-third down the first page. Considerable effort should go into developing the headline, because it is the "hook" that might catch the editor's eye or make your release stand out from any others seeking the same precious space.

Key 4: The "dateline"—city and state in capital letters followed by the month and day—should be the lead into the actual text of the release. Datelines are important because they tell the reader where and when an event is occurring.

Key 5: The "body" or main part of the release should always be double-spaced. Paragraphs should be short, journalistic, and to the point. Like the headline, the first few sentences or lead is a "hook" that must grab the attention of the reader and address the key questions (who, what, where, when, and why—the five w's).

Key 6: Including a few quotes is almost standard procedure with a press release. Whether the quote is from an internal source (someone employed by the organization issuing the release) or an external source, it is imperative that the individual quoted is aware of and approves of the quote. It is best to also let the individuals being quoted know of the date and time of the release so there are no surprises. When multiple quotes are used, it is usually best to alternate direct quotes (those in quotation marks) and factual non-quoted information.

Key 7: Photographs almost always enhance a story. You cannot always read the minds of those picking up your releases/stories; therefore, if you do not know the specifications, it is usually better to provide black and white photos as well as color photos. Color slides or negatives (assuming the publication uses color) are generally better, but send the actual photo to help the editor see what is on the slide or negative.

Internal Public Relations

The jobs of many people in the hospitality industry are challenging and require long hours. Keeping employees motivated and proud of their jobs is a difficult task. One of the most effective devices for combating these problems is a well-organized internal public relations effort. This does not mean promoting the goods or benefits of the company to the employees. It can take many shapes and forms. An especially effective technique is to promote or provide special recognition of employees, their efforts, or even their interests. "Employee of the Month" awards, posters, photos, and so forth, all work well. Special incentive awards and related public relations also are valuable motivational tools. Giving cash, prizes, or even novelty awards or plaques to deserving employees will help boost morale. Activities and events employees and managers do together—a bowling club or a joggers' group, for example—will help build a team spirit. Common goals, such as company-wide support of a selected charity, is another type of internal PR device for building unity. Perhaps most important of all is the continual recognition of employees' human dignity, pride, and desire for respect. Make internal public relations one of your key strategies for helping your employees be productive and happy.

How Can Public Relations Be Measured?

You frequently hear this comment: "PR is useless because you can't measure it." This is absolutely false! If a public relations program is well organized, it can be measured in many ways. One way is to measure the number and type of media exposures received. Keep a scrapbook of clippings and a current log of exposures—newspaper stories, magazine articles, mentions on the local television news, and so on. Set goals for the number and type of exposures, and then measure actual performance versus targets.

A second measurement method is geared to evaluating the effectiveness of internal PR efforts. Look at questionnaires that assess employee morale, as well as employee turnover rates, breakage, pilferage, etc. If your internal PR is working, certain quantifiable trends should emerge. Do not, however, ignore a more subjective yardstick of your efforts: have you improved the esprit de corps in your organization? Are employees busy and enthusiastic?

Specific public relations activities may be measured by increases in sales. For example, if a major event or product is promoted through PR, and sales volume directly increases as a result of additional customers coming in for the event or for the product, you know public relations is likely working for you.

The checklist on the following page can assist in managing the public relations function.

Publications ⎯⎯⎯⎯⎯⎯⎯⎯⎯⎯⎯⎯⎯⎯⎯⎯⎯⎯⎯⎯⎯⎯⎯⎯⎯

Most industry sectors have publications dedicated to the types of firms, products, and services within the industry sector. These are referred to as "trade" publications. They are often widely read by those who have an interest in your industry, such as wholesalers, distributors, agents, and other intermediaries. These are excellent vehicles in which to publicize a new product, explain a change in policy or management personnel, etc. And in most cases, it is usually less expensive to advertise in the trades and easier to obtain coverage for your releases, stories, etc.

Public Relations Checklist

_____ Does a PR plan exist and does it support the current priority areas of marketing?

_____ Do the director of marketing and all staff members understand their responsibilities with respect to the press, PR firm, and other outsiders?

_____ Do key managers have good relations with the local media?

_____ Are press release mailing lists up to date, accurate, and readily available?

_____ Are *fact sheets* readily accessible to all and near the phones?

_____ Are *photo files* up to date and fully stocked? Is there an up-to-date black-and-white photo file?

_____ Are brochures and other collateral material accessible?

_____ Are there definite plans, budgets, reviews, and measurement procedures in place for PR?

_____ Is there a property or product press kit? Is it up to date?

_____ What is the quality of photos and stories, and how are they to be used?

_____ Are all key employees briefed and knowledgeable about the value of public relations? Do they know the procedures to follow for press inquiries?

_____ Are PR network memos kept on file? Where? How often are they looked at or discussed?

_____ When was the last PR audit? What were the results, and were all follow-up steps completed?

If your product or service lends itself to advertising in consumer-related publications, make sure your ad agency and public relations function/agency work together. Frequently, in order to secure your advertising, consumer publications will provide "advertorial" type space or agree to include your product or service in a story or article. The synergy of advertising and public relations working together is a win-win scenario.

The types of items you can "pitch" that publications may pick up and run are many and varied. They include news releases, announcements for an event, feature stories, concept articles, opinion pieces, and public service announcements (PSAs). Remember that publicity is a non-paid media communication that helps build target market awareness and positively affects attitudes for your products and services, brand(s), and firm. Like all other marketing tools, public relations should be planned to work in concert with your total marketing strategy.

Trade Media

The hospitality industry is fortunate to have excellent **trade media** in the form of industry-related publications. These publications are widely read not only by those within the industry, but frequently by travel consumers. Some of the major hospitality industry publications that public relations personnel should be aware of are listed in this section.

Major Hospitality Industry and Trade Publications

Association & Society Manager
825 South Barrington Avenue
Los Angeles, CA 90039

Association Management
1011 16th Street, N.W.
Washington, DC 20036

Association Trends
7204 Clarendon Road
Washington, DC 20014

ASTA Travel News
Travel Communications, Inc.
488 Madison Avenue
New York, NY 10022

Aviation Daily
1156 15th Street, N.W.
Washington, DC 20005

Business Travel News
CMP Publications, Inc.
600 Community Drive
Manhasset, NY 11030

Canadian Hotel and Restaurant
Maclean-Hunter Publishing
   Company, Ltd.
481 University Avenue
Toronto, Ontario
Canada M5W 1A7

Club Management
8730 Big Bend Blvd.
St. Louis, MO 63119

The Cornell Hotel and Restaurant
   Administration Quarterly
School of Hotel Administration
185 Statler Hall
Cornell University
Ithaca, NY 14853

Corporate Meetings & Incentives
747 Third Avenue, 7th Floor
New York, NY 10017

Corporate Travel
A Gralla Publication
1515 Broadway
New York, NY 10036

FIU Hospitality Review
Florida International University
Miami, FL 33181

Food & Service
Texas Restaurant Association
1400 Lavaca
Austin, TX 78701

Food Executive
International Food Services
   Executives Association
508 IBM Building
Fort Wayne, IN 46815

Food Service Director
Restaurant Business, Inc.
355 Park Ave. S.
New York, NY 10010

Hospitality Lodging
Penton/IPC, Inc.
614 Superior Avenue, West
Cleveland, OH 44113

Hospitality Restaurant
Penton/IPC, Inc.
614 Superior Avenue, West
Cleveland, OH 44113

Hotel and Motel Management
Advanstar Communications
7500 Old Oak Blvd.
Cleveland, OH 44130

Hotels
1350 E. Touhy Ave.
Des Plaines, IL 60018

Incentive Marketing
633 Third Avenue
New York, NY 10017

Incentive Travel Manager
825 South Barrington Avenue
Los Angeles, CA 90049

Insurance Conference Planner
695 Summer Street
Stamford, CT 06901

Lodging
American Hotel & Lodging
   Association
1201 New York Ave. NW #600
Washington, DC 20005-3931

Lodging and Food-Service News
Hotel Service, Inc.
131 Clarendon Street
Boston, MA 02116

Lodging Hospitality
1100 Superior Ave.
Cleveland, OH 44114-2543

The Meeting Manager
Meeting Professionals International
1950 Stemmons Fwy.
Dallas, TX 75207-3109

Meetings & Conventions
8773 S. Ridgeline Blvd.
Highlands Ranch, CO 80126-2329

Meetings & Expositions Magazine
22 Pine Street
Morristown, NJ 07960

Meetings News
600 Harrison St.
San Francisco, CA 94107

Motel/Motor Inn Journal
Tourist Court Journal, Inc.
306 East Adams
Temple, TX 76501

Nation's Restaurant News
Lebhar-Friedman, Inc.
425 Park Avenue
New York, NY 10022

Promo
47 Old Ridgefield Rd.
Wilton, CT 06897

Resort Management
Box 4169
1509 Madison Avenue
Memphis, TN 38104

Restaurant Business
355 Park Ave. S.
New York, NY 10010

Restaurant Hospitality
1100 Superior Ave.
Cleveland, OH 44114-2543

Restaurants & Institutions
Cahners Publishing Company
275 Washington St.
Newton, MA 02158-1630

Restaurants, USA
National Restaurant Association
1200 17th St. NW
Washington, DC 20036-3097

Sales and Marketing Management
Sales Management, Inc.
633 Third Avenue
New York, NY 10017

Successful Meetings
355 Park Ave. S.
New York, NY 10010

Tableservice Restaurant Operations Report
National Restaurant Association
One IBM Plaza
Suite 2600
Chicago, IL 60611

Texas and Southwest Hotel Motel Review
Texas Hotel & Motel Association
8602 Crownhill Boulevard
San Antonio, TX 78209

TravelAge East
TravelAge Mid-America
TravelAge Southeast
TravelAge West
Travel Magazines Division
Official Airlines Guides, Inc.
100 Grant Avenue
San Francisco, CA 94108

Travel Agent
American Traveler, Inc.
2 West 46th Street
New York, NY 10036

Travel Management Daily
An Official Airlines Guide
Publication, Inc.
888 Seventh Avenue
New York, NY 10106

Travel Master
645 Stewart Avenue
Garden City, NY 11530

Travel Trade
Travel Trade Publishing Company
605 Fifth Avenue
New York, NY 10017

Travel Weekly
Reed Travel Group
500 Plaza Dr.
Secaucus, NJ 07094-3626

Trends in the Hotel Industry
PKF
425 California St., Ste. 1650
San Francisco, CA 94104

World Convention Dates
Hendrickson Publishing Company
79 Washington Street
Hempstead, NY 11550

Worldwide Lodging Industry
Horwath & Horwath International
  & Laventhol & Horwath
919 Third Avenue
New York, NY 10022

In addition to the printed version of the publications, many maintain on-line versions, as shown in the following list. Also, there are numerous on-line sites where press releases may be picked up.

Food & Service News (TRA Magazine)	http://www.restaurantville.com
Food Service Today	http://www.foodservicetoday.com
Hospitality Technology Magazine	http://www.htmagazine.com
Hospitality Upgrade	http://www.hospitalityupgrade.com
Hotel & Motel Management	http://www.hotelmotel.com
Hotel Business	http://www.hotelbusiness.com
Hotels	http://www.hotelsmag.com
Hotels-On-Line	http://www.hotelonline.com
Lodging Magazine	http://www.lodgingnews.com
Meetings Network	http://www.meetingsnet.com
Michael Pollock's Gaming Observer	http://www.gamingobserver.com
Nation's Restaurant News	http://www.nrn.com
Newspaper Links	http://www.newspaperlinks.com
Prepared Foods	http://www.preparedfoods.com
QSR (Quick Service Restaurants) Magazine	http://www.qsrmagazine.com
Restaurant Marketing	http://www.restaurant-marketing.net
Restaurants & Institutions Magazine	http://www.rimag.com
Travel Weekly	http://www.twcrossroads.com
World Gaming Live	http://www.casinojournal.com

Case Examples

Case Example 1—Sources and Experts. One of the many goals of public relations is to extend brand awareness and support overall marketing strategies. Achieving press/media coverage is not an easy task: against a backdrop of limited print space and air time, there is virtually unlimited demand for that space and air time. One major lodging chain, however, mastered the art of garnering space in local, national, and international media. It developed a multifaceted plan for its public relations program with a goal of enhancing its reputation and achieving the highest top-of-the-mind awareness. The "plans" were interlinked with other marketing tools, such as research and advertising. The chain capitalized on its research capabilities by conducting a series of surveys and questionnaires on a variety of topics. Each time a newsworthy finding was discovered, a series of steps was taken to assure broad distribution and related name awareness for the lodging chain. This strategy relied on both primary and secondary research to create items (findings) that would generate media attention (for example, the number of people who prefer king-size beds, the number who prefer room service, etc.).

Case Example 2—The Power of the Survey and Award. There are two ways to use the power of the survey or award. One is to be fortunate enough to be ranked number one in an external objective consumer survey of products or services in your category. The other is to conduct and report on your "own" survey. Politicians and political parties frequently use the latter practice to create perceptions that their policies are on target or to create momentum for a candidate. The former is an extraordinarily valuable marketing tool when used to its fullest extent and maintained consistently (remember the level of expectation concept).

Continental Airlines won the J. D. Powers and Associates number one ranking in customer service in 1997 and went on to win it again in both 1998 and 1999. This is a highly visible award/survey, but once it is released, it could be yesterday's news unless it is reinforced in a methodological manner. Continental Airlines did a masterful job of doing just that, reinforcing its accomplishment with all constituencies: employee-based "internal" public relations programs and incentives; external advertising campaigns; and constant reminders in its promotional literature, timetables, frequent traveler programs, etc. In fact, its CEO even wrote a book, *From Worst to Best*, that further publicizes the achievement. In a business where service *is* the business and a major competitive advantage, Continental captured the edge as a result of reinforcing its achievement through an aggressive internal and external public relations program that is interlinked to its other marketing initiatives.

Key Terms

delivery package—The essential tools, including required forms, copy, photos, fact sheets, and biographies, that ensure that you are ready to effectively execute public relations programs.

exposures—The number of consumers actually hearing or seeing your advertising.

press—The collective name given to printing and publishing establishments, embracing the art, business, or practice of printing newspapers, magazines, etc., in general, or the persons who write for them.

press kit—A communications folder usually containing two pockets, the left used for background information, the right used for a press release.

press release—A formatted document, usually one or two pages, presenting concise and pertinent information on a topic/event deemed newsworthy.

publicity—One facet of public relations, it comprises the gratuitous mentions or exposures a company receives from announcements, events, and press releases.

public relations—A marketing tool that is the communications vehicle between your firm and current customers, potential customers, and the variety of other audiences in the marketplace.

trade media—A group of publications and broadcast media that follows a specific industry.

transmission channels—The routing network that public relations specialists create to get their material to the appropriate person, publication, or broadcast medium. News should be directed to the city desk, feature stories to the appropriate editor.

Chapter 11 Outline

Competencies

1. Explain the keys to successful promotions. (pp. 158–159)

2. Identify the different types of promotions. (pp. 159–163)

3. Describe methods of executing promotions. (p. 163)

4. Describe the benefits of internal promotions, identify the elements that determine a successful internal promotion, describe how to determine desired payback from promotions, and cite case examples of good and bad promotions in the hospitality industry. (pp. 163–170)

11

Applying Key Marketing Methodologies: Promotions

Promotions have been used widely in many industries for a long time, and they are a very powerful and effective marketing tool for the hospitality industry. Perhaps the earliest promotion ever used in the hospitality industry was the offer of the first free cup of coffee. Since then, Promotions have become increasingly sophisticated.

Promotions are an integral part of and should support the organization's overall marketing effort and be linked to the strategic marketing plan and other marketing tools wherever possible.

Promotions

Promotions can be defined as activities offering added incentives to stimulate incremental purchases or trial purchases of products or services. Promotions may be aimed at target market consumers or trade intermediaries. Incentives to purchase include price, incremental product/services, merchandise or gifts, experiences, and *allowance*s (cash, credit, etc.). They may be "immediate" (on the spot), "*chance*" driven, or of the instant or delayed-payoff nature. Promotions are measured in terms of incremental volume (sales, units, revenue, profit, etc.) or desired behavioral outcomes. Promotions may be delivered via the media, through sales personnel, or in or near the package/unit/outlet, etc.

The parameters for promotions include causing incremental consumer behavior over what is normally anticipated. They are *time specific* and usually have a specific singular identifiable goal that can be measured quantitatively or qualitatively. Promotions may also be limited by geographic focus. They typically are designed to affect target market behavior by way of capturing repeat business from current users, increasing new user business, boosting purchases by current users, and obtaining repeat usage from trial customers.

Promotions fall into two general categories: *open* and *closed*. In an **open** promotion, the business offers an added incentive to purchase with no specific behavior required to take advantage of the offer (for example, a 40 percent discount sale). In a **closed** promotion, an added incentive to purchase is offered to consumers, but they are required to do something in order to take advantage of the offer (for example, clip and present a voucher or coupon).

There are seemingly an infinite number of different promotions, with their diversity limited only by the boundaries of the promoters' imaginations. However, the single element common to all promotions is that they are designed to fulfill a marketing need. This need may be to build new business, gain a greater share of existing business, keep business, or gain repeat business. Regardless of the type of promotion, the objective is to support the overall marketing effort and it should be linked to the organization's comprehensive plan and other marketing tools, where possible.

Keys to Successful Promotions

Just as there are many reasons for promotions, there are many keys to making promotions successful, such as the following:

1. *Purpose.* Why is the promotion needed? Answering this fundamental question is the start of executing a good promotion. Is the promotion necessary to create new business? To stimulate demand in a down period? To take business from a competitor?

2. *Target identification.* To whom is the promotion directed? Be specific in identifying your target. Is the promotion geared toward potential first-time users of your product or service? Is it geared toward previous users? Are they young or old, male or female, upscale income or low income?

3. *Type match-up.* What is the best type of promotion for the purpose and target identified? There are many types of promotions, and not every one will be compatible with your creative idea or, more important, with your marketing objective. Some key questions to ask are: What is it I want to promote, and to whom? What is the demographic and psychographic profile of my target?

4. *Execution determination.* Once you know the purpose of the promotion, its target, and the type of promotion required, it is time to determine how to carry out the promotion. To do so, you must answer these questions: What is the best method to reach the target? When is the best time to promote? Where is the best place to promote?

5. *Fulfillment.* Anticipate the needs the promotion will create and make certain that you can fulfill them. Ask yourself this critical question: If this promotion works as planned, will I have enough available products or services to meet the demand? Does my promotion plan include adequate provisions for **fulfillment**? If you are promoting a food item, drink, weekend, seat, or space, be sure it is there when your customer arrives to accept your promotional promise. Otherwise, you may well lose that sale or customer for good.

6. *Fallback.* No one is ever completely correct in predicting the response to every promotion. If your promotion is a greater success than expected, you may not be able to fulfill the expectations created by the promotion. To avoid customer dissatisfaction in this situation, plan a **fallback**. It can be a menu-item substitution, an upgraded room, a first-class seat, or something else, but provide it. An important key when planning a fallback is to ensure it is of like or better

value than the promoted item. Even if you use the "rain check" fallback, consider adding some extra value to that rain check to offset the customer's inconvenience.

7. *Real expectation.* Promote only what you intend to deliver. Never lie, exaggerate, or make false promises. Always remember that the level of expectation your promotion creates must be fulfilled for the customer to be satisfied.

8. *Communication.* Don't forget to tell everyone at your company exactly what you promoted and how it is to be fulfilled. Be sure you clearly communicate in writing such key items as price, quantity, acceptance procedures for the promotion, dates, times, and other key details. Nothing is more irritating to a consumer than responding to a promotion only to find that no one at your company knows about it.

9. *Measurement.* Why did you go through the entire promotion effort? Establish a goal or goals and measure the results of your effort. Did the promotion do what you wanted it to do? Did it accomplish more or less than expected? If more, will it work as well again? If less, what went wrong?

10. *Recordkeeping.* Write down what you did for the promotion and how it worked. Don't be forced to reinvent the wheel next time. How often have you heard, "What was that promotion we ran so successfully a few years ago?"

Types of Promotions

Many different promotions have been used in the hospitality industry. Most of these can be grouped according to the following types or classifications:

1. *Price.* This is a promotion in which the incentive to purchase is based on price. The price is the main attraction and is featured prominently in the promotional message (see Exhibit 1).

2. *Trial.* This is a promotion designed to get your target to try your product or service. Price is one method that is frequently used to motivate customers to give a product offering a **trial**. Sampling is yet another technique.

3. *Share.* This is a promotion geared toward taking market **share** away from the competition through some form of incentive. Lower price, an upgraded product, or an advantage is clearly established over the competition and is the focus of the promotion.

4. *Introductory.* This is a promotion designed to introduce a new product or service to the market. An **introductory promotion** may also be designed to build repeat purchases (see Exhibit 2).

5. *Build.* This is a promotion designed to **build** repeat business through an increase in the reward or payoff for multiple purchases. Today's frequent flyer and frequent guest promotions are forms of build promotions (see Exhibit 3).

6. *Give-away/sweepstakes.* This is a promotion geared toward getting people to buy your product or service by offering the chance of a monetary award or a

Exhibit 1   Sample of a Price Promotion

Courtesy of Carnival Cruises

give-away item. **Give-away/sweepstakes** item promotions are referred to as premium promotions (see Exhibit 4).

7. *Ego/recognition.* This is a promotion designed to appeal to an individual's desire to be valued. These promotions may offer customers special recognition in the forms of first-class upgrades, special product customizations, and complimentary suites.

Exhibit 2   Sample of an Introductory Promotion

Hawaii.   25% Off.

Introducing "Mix 7 Rates" from Aston.

Guests spend 7 or more consecutive nights with Aston and save
25% off rack. Any room. Any price category. Any combination adding
up to 7 or more consecutive nights. Choose from 31 Aston Hotels
and Condominium Resorts in Waikiki, Maui, Kauai, Molokai,
and the Big Island of Hawaii. Offer valid 4/17-6/30/95.
For more information and reservations, call 1-800-922-7866.

ASTON.
Hotels & Resorts
Relax and enjoy the value.™

Courtesy of Aston Hotels & Resorts

Exhibit 3   Sample of a Build Promotion

Since it's football season,
consider this the 350-pound lineman of offers.

The Marriott Rewards® "Take Two" promotion is about as big as they come. Because when you make
three stays by January 31, 2003, you'll get two weekend nights free at any of 2,100 hotels in the Marriott
family plus Silver Elite status. For details or to register, call **1-888-MARRIOTT** or visit Marriott.com

Marriott® Hotels, Resorts and Suites • Renaissance® Hotels • Courtyard®
Fairfield Inn® • Residence Inn® • SpringHill Suites® • TownePlace Suites®

Marriott
REWARDS.
Your Marriott Awaits™

©2002 Marriott International, Inc. Marriott "Take Two" promotion good 10/14/02 - 1/31/03. Registration for this promotion is required. A "stay" is defined as consecutive nights spent at the same hotel, regardless of check-out/check-out activity. Weekend night awards expire June 30, 2003, and are valid Friday through Sunday at category 1-4 hotels. Nights spent while redeeming an award are not eligible for points/miles, free weekend nights or toward Elite level status. A maximum of two free nights may be earned per member for this promotion. Free night certificates will be mailed at the end of the promotion. All Marriott Rewards program terms and conditions apply.

Courtesy of Marriott International

8. *Tie-ins.* This is a promotion of a product or service that ties into another company's product or service. Usually a tie-in is undertaken when there is a clear benefit to both parties.

9. *Refunds/rebates.* This is a promotion designed to provide a cash incentive (equivalent to a discount) to purchase. **Refunds/rebates** are often used to stimulate sales or clear out items (for example, automobile rebates).

Exhibit 4   Sample Sweepstakes/Giveaway Promotion

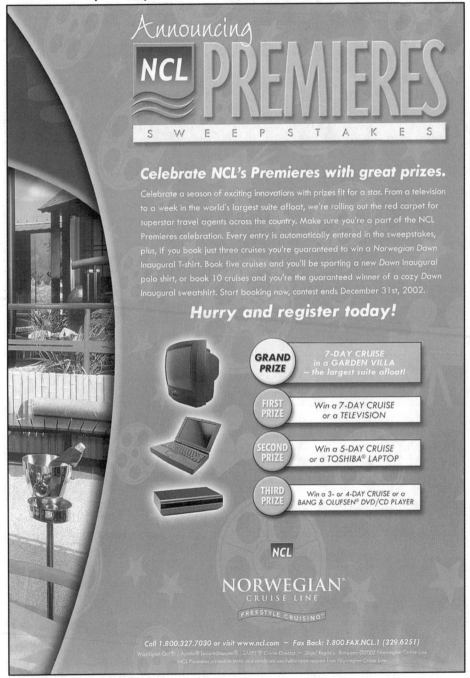

Courtesy of Norwegian Cruise Lines

10. *Trade allowances (commissions/discounts).* These are promotions providing a monetary incentive to the trade or intermediaries.

11. *Events.* This is a promotion built around a specific event (for example, the appearance of an entertainer, concert, designer, etc).

12. *Cooperative.* This is a promotion similar to a tie-in in which two firms cooperatively promote a product or service for a mutual benefit (see Exhibit 5). The **cooperative** promotion may be undertaken because of the limited budget of each firm or because the products or services are of more value when promoted together. A cooperative promotion in the hospitality industry could be one involving an airline and a rent-a-car company.

There are many other types of promotions or variations of the promotions listed here. Some may be intended to build goodwill, others are designed as paybacks for the use of your product or service, and still others are designed to expand the awareness of your product or service into new market areas or expose new market segments to your product. Always keep in mind your *purpose* for entering into a promotion and the *benefit* you will receive from the promotion.

A word of caution, however: do not enter into a tie-in, cooperative, or other joint promotion without determining the impact that the promotion will have on your base business, your image, or your overall market. While it is enticing to be offered a low-cost tie-in into someone else's package or promotion, it may not always be beneficial. In fact, it could be detrimental. Look closely at your own image and reputation and make it your rule of thumb not to enter into a joint promotion unless the other parties have an equal or better overall reputation.

Methods for Executing Promotions

One of the key reasons promotions fail is that the wrong method of execution is used. Take the time to determine the best promotion method for reaching your target and achieving your purpose. These methods include advertising (outdoor, displays, TV, radio, and print), direct mail, tent cards, publicity, personal selling, handouts, telephone sales, a special benefit to loyal customers or club members in monthly billings, on-line offers, and so forth.

You may promote your purpose and reach your target yourself by directly appealing to the end-users of your product or service, or you may reach your target through appropriate intermediaries such as agents, retailers, wholesalers, suppliers, organizations, associations, bureaus, franchise affiliates, and distributorships. You may use credit-card mailing stuffers, mailing lists, someone else's outlets, and posters and flyers of all types. Just make sure you select the methods that most efficiently and effectively reach your target and accomplish your purpose.

Internal Promotions

To this point, the chapter has covered some general aspects of promotions. Frequently, a major way to increase the revenue and profit yield from your existing customers is to promote to them after they are inside your door. This can be achieved in many ways, but should be done selectively and with a specific purpose

Exhibit 5   Sample of a Cooperative Promotion

Courtesy of Radisson Hotels & Resorts/American Express

or goal in mind. Internal promotions should be created and executed with the same care given external promotions. In fact, there are additional considerations to take into account when promoting internally. Assuming all the keys to successful promotions have been followed, consider these additional items:

- *Compatibility.* Is your internal promotion compatible with how your customers perceive your product or service? Never cheapen the image your loyal customers have of you by using a slapped-together, poorly thought-out, poorly executed promotion.

- *Benefit.* Will your internal promotion meet your purpose and offer a perceivable benefit to the customer? Will it keep the customer as a friend, or will the customer be offended?

- *Value.* Does the internal promotion provide your customers with a perceived value for their money? Value means quality at a fair price, not cheapness.

- *Clutter avoidance.* Will your internal promotion piece clutter or detract from the table, desk top, wall, or other area where it is presented? Be sure your overall product quality is not cheapened as a result of the physical promotion piece or content of the promotion.

These considerations should be thought out prior to doing any internal promotions of your own or allowing anyone else's promotions to be viewed by your customers.

Cost/Payback

In developing a promotion, it is essential to plan your **costs** and determine the desired **payback**. To do so requires identifying all your "redemption costs," such as the *value* of the discount (coupon), the *number of coupons* distributed, the estimated *redemption rate*, the *number redeemed*, and the *dollar value* or offer (the number redeemed times the value of the coupon). In addition, advertising and media costs need to be factored into the equation. These include the printing, mailing costs, envelopes, and any design or legal costs. After arriving at the total cost of the promotion, a payback calculation can be made. Included in this calculation are estimated sales with and without the promotion (to arrive at the promotional impact on sales in dollars or units), estimated gross margin dollars for the period with and without the promotion, and estimated net margin dollar increase with the promotion. The same rationale—calculating with and without advertising and media costs—should be applied. Also, any incremental advertising and media costs attributable to the promotion should be factored into the calculation. The payout factors also need to include incremental margin sales, incremental advertising and media expenditures, and contribution to fixed overhead.

The promotions checklist shown in Exhibit 6 provides some key questions that should be addressed before undertaking a promotion.

A short list of the many types of promotions you can draw ideas from is included in Exhibit 7.

Exhibit 6   Promotions Checklist

- Are your promotions part of your total marketing effort/plan?
- Are your promotions scheduled at the optimum times to produce the desired results?
- Are your promotions interlinked in a synergistic manner with your other marketing tools?
- Do your promotions support your image and positioning?
- Is the promotion appropriate or matched to the objective/strategy or purpose?
- Can your competitors readily match or "one up" your promotional offer?
- What are the quantifiable expectations (results)?
- How much will the promotion cost, and how much return do you expect/desire?
- Is the promotional "incentive" strong enough to evoke the behavior change/incremental purchase desired?
- How will the promotion be delivered in the most effective and efficient way?
- Do you have a "fallback" planned and ready to go?
- Have you communicated the promotion with and trained those who need to know about the promotion?
- When will the promotion begin and how long will it remain in effect?
- Have you checked with your legal department with respect to the promotional offer?
- Have you maximized the distribution of the promotional offer?
- Is there a specific geographic area in which you desire the promotion to be run?
- Can you fulfill the promotional offer if it succeeds beyond your response estimate?
- How will the promotion be communicated to the sales force, distributors, agents, etc.?
- How will you actually measure the promotional results?
- If the promotion does not work, do you have a "cut-off" plan?
- Is the promotion consistent with your overall positioning for the product, service, or brand?
- Have you reviewed the history of the specific offer or like offers?
- Is there a logical partner to co-op with that will give you a stronger promotion or extend your reach?

Case Examples

Case Example 1: The Great Idea. In a medium-sized New England city, an independent motel owner/operator was trying to compete with a nearby national-chain motel. Overall, this was a good occupancy sector of the market, averaging 80 percent. The chain motel had a slightly better location, but the independent motel

Exhibit 7   Promotion Types and Tools

• Contests	• Refunds/rebates	• Introductory
• Couponing	• On pack/in pack	• Share
• Bonus offers	• Premiums	• Tie-ins
• Build promotions	• Sampling	• Cooperative
• Events	• Trial offers	• Ego/recognition
• Sweepstakes	• Price	• Give-aways

had a better physical property. The chain motel was running 83-percent occupancy, the independent motel a 73-percent occupancy. Mr. Owner/Operator watched that occupancy percentage weekly and was getting frustrated. He came up with what he thought was a logical "great idea," but he didn't research it.

He called a friend who painted signs, and he ordered a large sign with red letters reading "Low Discount Rates—Stay Here," with a large red arrow pointing to his motel's entrance. This "great idea" resulted in Mr. Owner/Operator's occupancy gradually declining to 63 percent and his bottom line sinking even further. In desperation he called in a marketing consultant.

The consultant examined the market and determined that rate was of less significance to consumers than quality of the facility. Mr. Owner/Operator had a high-quality facility; however, his great idea had given his property the image of a cut-rate, low-quality independent motel. The consultant recommended that Mr. Owner/Operator change the name of the motel to "The Lexington Inn," incorporating the name of the city, and that he replace the homemade price-war sign with a permanent high-quality sign made of brick and brass with the motel's new name on it. The consultant also recommended that Mr. Owner/Operator improve the landscaping and lighting, paint the entry façade, install a new awning canopy, and implement a new rate structure $2 above the chain motel's rate structure. The final touch was a promotional slogan on the marquis: "The new Lexington Inn—the finest in town."

The results were dramatic. Occupancy jumped to 83 percent, with a rate averaging $2 higher than the franchise motel and $7.50 higher than a year earlier for the same independent motel. The chain motel's occupancy dropped to 74 percent.

Case Example 2: The Simple Idea. Often, the simpler the promotion and the less complicated its execution, the more successful it is. Two national chains have succeeded in getting a large share of the summer family market with very simple promotional concepts. Holiday Inn's "Kids Stay Free" program and Ramada's "Four for One" program have both succeeded. "Kids Stay Free" simply means that children under age 18 accompanying their parents at a Holiday Inn stay free in the same room as their parents. Ramada's "Four for One" program permits four people to stay in the same room for the price of one person.

These promotions are successful for two basic reasons. First, each meets the needs of the summer family market segment by offering a tangible, perceived value. Second, each is straightforward and easy for both the consumer and the operations to understand. Other hotels and motels have tried similar promotions, but have confused consumers with such restrictions as "only children under 12 years," "no extra beds allowed," and "only at the following Inns…" But both Holiday Inn and Ramada have kept it simple for their consumers and their front desk agents. They have offered a plain value and have succeeded.

Case Example 3: The Addicting Idea. The fast-food industry is tremendously competitive. Market share and repeat business factors are constantly measured and monitored. Advertising and promotions demand the best creative ideas. A major challenge for fast-food restaurant operators is to increase market share without having **price promotions** put major dents in their restaurants' financial statements. McDonald's creates extremely effective promotions based on a simple concept—give people a reason to come in and come back. McDonald's "Build a Big Mac" promotion, for example, gave customers puzzle pieces of a Big Mac when they made certain purchases. When they put a complete Big Mac together, they won a cash prize. The idea that only one more piece of the puzzle was needed to win up to $100,000 instantly kept people coming back and helped McDonald's build volume during a recessionary period.

Case Example 4: The Pay-Off. Pay-off promotions blossomed in the 1980s and continued to be extremely popular in the 1990s (see Exhibit 8). There are many examples of this type of promotion: airline frequent traveler programs such as United Airlines' Mileage Plus, American's AAdvantage, and Continental's One Pass, and hotel frequent guest programs such as Marriott's Honored Guest, Hyatt's Gold Passport, and Stouffer's Club Express. The pay-off works along these lines. A "cost" is figured, such as five percent. This is a marketing expense that is applied to cover the cost of awards. The awards are then equated to points, credits, miles, or other measurements applied on a scale. Achievement of points, etc., on the scale corresponds to award levels or the "pay-off" back to the loyal customer. The pay-off increases with the volume of consumption. For example, customers flying 30,000 miles receive a free first-class round-trip ticket, while those flying 50,000 miles receive two free first-class tickets.

Case Example 5: Left Brain/Right Brain. One frequently-used generalization is that people who are financially and analytically oriented are dominated by the left side of their brain and those who are more marketing and creatively oriented are driven by the right side of the brain. One hotel chain discovered that its customer base was equally divided between "left brainers" and "right brainers." This posed a dilemma in terms of what the awards should be in its promotional offer. The solution was to view this information as a research and marketing opportunity. Focus groups drawn from the two factions revealed very contrasting perspectives and little commonality. Left brainers categorically preferred the lowest rates, and right brainers consistently wanted a payoff-type reward: either upgrades to suites, executive levels, or other "ego"-driven recognition. Left brainers wanted to "beat the system," and right brainers wanted to "break the rules." As the focus groups evolved, however, a few common perspectives did emerge. Both wanted to be appreciated for their patronage. Both wanted to pay "corporate" or "preferred"

Exhibit 8   Sample of a Payoff Promotion

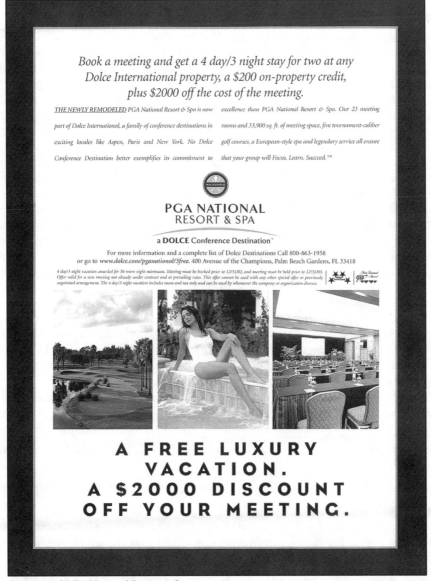

Courtesy of PGA National Resort & Spa

rates for their volume. Both wanted to be treated differently than other guests. Both wanted to be recognized by some sort of "club" or membership program.

Based on this research and focus group input, a new frequent guest program was developed to appeal to both the left brainer and right brainer points of difference and points of commonality. The "club" membership was provided to both at no cost by waiving the initial fee, "compliments of a co-op partner" (airline, credit card company, rental car company, etc.). This established a perceived *value* to the membership. To the left brainer it was "paid for by someone else." To the right brainer it was "they recognize my importance." The reward structure presented a real challenge. Awards would have to appeal to both and have to be perceived on a corporate and preferred rate. The solution was found in the research, which indicated that the left brainers responded to the "beat the system" concept and the right brainers to the "break the rules" notion. Each was offered an automatic upgrade to the executive/club level or a suite (if available) at the corporate or preferred rate for a regular room. In fact, although never indicated or promised, each could receive the Presidential Suite under certain circumstances. For example, if the guest (or guests) is a CEO or is eligible under a key corporate or group meetings account, the hotels had the option of placing them in the (usually unoccupied) Presidential Suite. You can imagine what that did for brand loyalty. The left brainer paying a corporate rate of $89.00 looks on the door and sees that he or she is staying in the $1,200.00 per night Presidential Suite: that is "beating the system." The right brainer is *ego satisfied* and considers his or her weight/clout helped "break the rules." Both are highly satisfied.

As for awards, the ultimate for a left brainer is free cash or as close to it as he or she can get. For right brainers it is a prestige gift they can use for themselves (as determined by the research), so the "club members" had their choice: either U.S. Savings Bonds or American Express Gift Certificates. It was no surprise to the company that the left brainers went for the U.S. Savings Bonds (more than 85 percent of the time) and the right brainers for the American Express Gift Certificate (more than 95 percent of the time). The promotional concept was successful primarily because it was based on sound research that looked into the psyche and motivations of the guest/customer. The hotel chain responded by directly meeting guest needs and providing the benefits they sought.

Key Terms

allowances—Promotional incentives to purchase a product or service in the form of cash rebates, credit, etc.

build—A promotion designed to build repeat business through an increase in the reward or payoff for multiple purchases. Airlines that recognize passengers for patronizing their airline frequently is a form of a build promotion.

chance—A promotion geared toward getting people to buy your product or service by offering the chance of a monetary award or give-away item.

closed—A promotion type in which an added incentive is offered, but consumers are required to do something in order to take advantage of the offer (redeeming a coupon or voucher, for example).

cooperative—A promotion in which two firms cooperatively promote a product or service for mutual benefit (an airline and a car rental company, for example).

cost/payback—The promotional equation that calculates the relationship between what a planned promotion costs and what is expected to be achieved in monetary returns. Promotion planners must identify all "redemption costs" (for example, value of discount coupons, number of coupons distributed, estimated redemption rate, number redeemed, and total dollar value) and media and advertising costs. Planners can then calculate payback by estimating sales (with and without the promotion), gross margin dollars for the period (with and without the promotion), and net margin dollar increase with the promotion.

fallback—A backup measure used when response to a promotion overwhelms the ability of the organization to accommodate the promises. The fallback can be in the form of a menu substitution, another type of room, a different size of rental car, or an airline upgrade. In such situations, the fallback must be of like or better value than the promoted item.

fulfillment—Anticipating and planning for the expected number of items needed for a promotion and ensuring that enough are available to fulfill the promises.

give-away/sweepstakes—A "chance" type of promotion in which the opportunity to win a monetary award or a give-away item is directly tied to the purchase of a product or service.

introductory promotion—A promotion designed to introduce a new product or service to the market.

open—A promotion in which an added incentive is offered to consumers to purchase a product or service, with no specific behavior required to take advantage of the offer.

price promotion—A promotion whose incentive to purchase is based solely on the price of the product or service.

promotions—Activities offering added incentives to stimulate incremental purchases or trial purchases of products or services.

refunds/rebates—A type of promotion designed to provide a cash incentive (equivalent to a discount) to purchase.

share—A promotion geared toward taking market share away from the competition through some form of incentive, such as lower price, an upgraded product, or a clear product advantage over the competition.

trial—A promotion whose purpose is to get consumers to try a product or service. Price adjusting is one of the effective tools in this type of promotion.

Chapter 12 Outline

Competencies

1. Describe the origins of data base marketing, explain three key elements of the data base systems, and summarize keys to successful data base marketing. (pp. 173–177)

2. Summarize keys to successful direct mail. (pp. 177–179)

3. Cite marketing applications for which marketing/direct mail is an effective tool. (p. 179)

12

Applying Key Marketing Methodologies: Data Base Marketing

COMMUNICATING YOUR SALES OR PROMOTIONAL MESSAGE is more challenging in today's crowded media marketplace. Getting your message directly into your target audiences' hands is what data base marketing is all about. This chapter will discuss why data base marketing has become increasingly popular, the components of a data base system, and keys to selling through direct mail.

Data Base Marketing

In 1884, Montgomery Ward mailed its first catalog. Soon other retailers began using catalogs to reach customers. By 1902 Sears produced over $50 million in catalog sales. America was experiencing an incredible explosion in **direct mail** sales.

No one in the early 1900s could have imagined what would occur in direct mail sales in the second half of the century. In the 1950s, a concept arrived that would further increase direct-mail sales and lead to the birth of **data base marketing:** the credit card. As consumer acceptance and use of credit cards grew, so did the "data" to form a "base" list of prospective customers. Then in the 1970s came a technological development that really allowed data base marketing to take off: the computer. By the 1990s, computer technology, optical and electrical scanning devices, and a multitude of software programs and other technological advances propelled data base marketing to the forefront of many businesses' marketing plans. Today, data base marketing is a multibillion-dollar business influenced by many factors (see Exhibit 1).

More than technology has contributed to data base marketing's success. Geographic segmentations of the U.S. population (such as by zip code) and more sophisticated demographic information from the U.S. Census Bureau have helped shape the growth of data base marketing. Demographics and psychographics have also played key roles in influencing the acceptance of this marketing tool. With the increasing demands placed on people's personal time, the weakening of the traditional television networks, and the overabundance of product and service offerings, new ways to reach potential customers directly with marketing messages became essential. Shifting and declining brand loyalties also supported the need for direct mail's personal and targeted marketing approach. Getting direct mail

Exhibit 1   Influences on the Development and Popularity of Data Base Marketing

messages into the hands of consumers in a cost-effective manner and breaking through the advertising clutter with response-generating, creative direct mail pieces are the challenges facing data base marketing today.

Data Base Systems

To make a data base system work, you need three key elements: technology, accurate information, and prioritization.

Technology. Simply defined, data base marketing "technology" is computer hardware and software capable of supporting data base marketing. The degree of technological sophistication you need depends on the complexity of your marketing needs. The more **mailing lists** you use, the more customer data you store, and the greater your frequency and measurement of responses, the greater your technological needs will be.

Accurate Information. A data base is only as good as the integrity of the data it contains. Valid records, including correct addresses, correctly spelled names, most recent purchase activity, and so on, are all essential components of accurate data base information. **Clean lists** (lists free of invalid or out-of-date information) increase response rates, reduce costs, and improve return on investment. When purchasing lists, always seek to verify the last date the list was cleaned. Also **purge** (remove) duplicate records—few things turn off a prospect more than two personalized letters arriving on the same day that offer a "once-only" opportunity.

Prioritization. Having a conceptual understanding of which prospects and customers are the most likely to respond to your direct mail will help you improve return rates and increase revenues. In general, people who have recently purchased your product or service are most likely to remember you; they make great first-priority targets for a direct-mail piece urging them to make another purchase (see Exhibit 2). The second likeliest response group would be those who have made multiple or frequent purchases. The third would be those who have spent the greatest amount of total revenue with you historically. The fourth likeliest group to respond is made up of those prospects that reside in areas or purchase from locations similar to those of your best customers. These priority categorizations will help you select likely responders to your direct mail and help you develop realistic response expectations.

Exhibit 2 Group Priorities for Direct Mail

Group A—Recent Purchasers
Group B—Frequent Purchasers
Group C—Large Purchasers
Group D—Similar Purchasers

Keys to Successful Data Base Marketing

Like all other marketing methodologies, data base marketing requires planning to be on target and successful. Exhibit 3 lists ten keys to data base marketing success.

1. *Preplan.* To successfully use any marketing tool, especially a very targeted one like a data base mailing, you need to preplan. Preplanning not only includes developing objectives, return estimates, and a budget, but also should include determining where data base marketing fits and what role it plays within your total marketing effort.

2. *Specify targets.* Unless you are very specific in lining up your target market(s), your direct mail will be wasted. You'll need to specify your audience in terms of size, locale, and make-up (psychographic profile, demographic profile, benefits sought, needs, and so on). Once you have identified this target market, you're ready to take the next critical step.

3. *Select an appropriate message.* Selecting the correct message and presenting it in a manner that will entice your target market to respond will increase your chances of connecting with prospects. For example, if you are mailing to price-sensitive individuals, a strong financial incentive within your product/ service offering will probably produce better results than one that offers no discount. On the other hand, if you mail a discounted offer to individuals who are more sensitive to ego and status issues, your chances for success may actually hurt if your discount is viewed as cheapening the product or service. Selecting the right message to get the job done the first time is better than sending the wrong message and having to start all over again. For one thing, before you can get a corrected message out, someone else might connect with your prospect and eliminate you from the competition.

4. *Predetermine return on investment.* Ask yourself how much return you need to generate to cover your basic mailing costs. Then ask, how much more return you will need to achieve an adequate **return on investment (ROI)**? You should always try to predetermine your ROI and compare your direct-mail ROI with that of the other marketing tools you use.

5. *Maintain creative consistency.* Maintaining creative consistency with your direct mail pieces provides multiple benefits in direct mail marketing. Some of these benefits include: clearly perceived brand identity, clearly perceived positioning, increased association/recognition from mailing to mailing (when multiple mailings occur), and carry-over brand awareness to other media.

Exhibit 3   Ten Keys to Successful Data Base Marketing

1. Preplan
2. Specify targets
3. Select an appropriate message
4. Predetermine return on investment
5. Maintain creative consistency
6. Integrate your mailings with your overall marketing program
7. Use clean lists
8. Know when to mail
9. Repeat your message
10. Track the results

6. *Integrate your mailings with your overall marketing program.* Multiple marketing methodologies working in concert and orchestrated within a total marketing program are much more likely to succeed than are hit-or-miss, uncoordinated marketing efforts. Be sure to integrate your data base marketing efforts with the overall marketing program for your product or service offering.

7. *Use clean lists.* Always use "clean" mailing lists. This is the best way to improve ROI and **response rates**. A clean list has a minimal number of duplicated, erroneous, or false addresses.

8. *Know when to mail.* The best way to decide when to mail is to determine when responses are needed. If you need business in December and you know it takes six weeks to get results from a mailing, sending out your direct mail pieces in December or January isn't going to help you. It is always good to prepare to mail sooner than you need to. Build in a **time cushion** to allow for correcting errors, fine-tuning or redoing the direct mail piece, and dealing with problems such as delays at the printer. Preparing early makes it more likely that you will be ready to go when your mailing date arrives.

9. *Repeat your message.* Use the power of repetition throughout each direct mail package. The synergy of multiple messages and calls to action can only increase the chance that your prospects will see your message and respond. Use the outside of the envelope, front and back; use the response card or other reply vehicle; use every opportunity in the direct mail piece itself to convey the message. Try to get your message out in like or identical form at least five times somewhere in each direct mail package.

10. *Track the results.* How will you know how well or poorly a direct mailing did if you don't track the results? Tracking results will help you justify future mailings, compare direct mail to other marketing methods, evaluate the effectiveness of the direct mail piece(s), etc.

Exhibit 4   Keys to Direct Mail Success

- Good mailing lists
- A good direct mail piece
- Knowing when to mail
- Knowing when to stop mailing
- Timely fulfillment

Always remember to alert all of the departments within your business that will be affected by a direct mail campaign. If you're mailing out a large promotional offer, be sure staff members understand what the offer is, when they can expect customer responses, and what they are supposed to do to fulfill the offer. Exhibit 4 recaps the keys to direct mail success.

Sales Through Direct Mail

If you were to look closely at all of the direct mail pieces you receive in a week, you would be examining the results of great creative energies. Unless you look closely at your direct mail, you might not be aware of all of the things you "may" have won—from cashier's checks, to cars, to lifetime memberships, to your own vacation home. If you're like most people, when you open your charge card or gasoline credit card bill, a handful of fantastic offers "too good to refuse" fall out of the envelope.

Keys to Direct Mail

Selling your products and services via direct mail presents special challenges and requires special knowledge. In direct mail sales, you do not have the chance to personally talk to your prospects, as you do in face-to-face or telephone sales. For direct mail to be successful, it must be sent to prospects that have needs that your product or service can meet. Therefore, starting with a good mailing list is vitally important. Then you must develop a good direct mail piece—a communications vehicle that relates prospects' needs to your product or service offering. It is also necessary to know when to mail and when to stop mailing. Last but not least, when prospects respond, you must fulfill your direct mail offer promptly and accurately. In the following sections, we will briefly discuss each of these keys to direct-mail success.

Good Lists. Knowing to whom your sales letter or other direct mail piece is going is of primary importance. A simple thing like the correct spelling of a manager's name means a lot if you want your letter read. Lists should constantly be "cleansed" or "purged" of invalid or out-of-date information. Lists should be updated each time a new piece of information becomes available. Verify names, titles, and addresses from your most recent contact with each sales prospect. Constantly strive to be accurate.

The Direct Mail Piece. You can develop checklist upon checklist of do's and don'ts for direct mail promotion literature. There is no single "best" approach. Sometimes a very personal approach is appropriate; at other times, a formal approach should be used. Some general rules for promotional literature are helpful, but if rules are strictly followed, they may inhibit an engaging personal touch. For example, when using a sales letter, one good guideline is to be sure to send an "original"—or at least have it appear to be an original. No one wants to read a "personal" letter that has been photocopied. Also, be sure to include the key to any direct mail sales message—relate the prospective customer's needs directly to your product or service. If possible, place your message on one page. Time is important to everyone, and a personal one-page letter has a lot better chance of being read by Ms. Decision-maker than a multi-page direct mail package containing flashy but lengthy promotional pieces.

Knowing When to Mail. Knowing when to mail is important. Consider the example of a large publishing company that just came out with a terrific consumer-oriented book about saving money on federal income taxes. The publisher is excited because this is a super book—new ideas, right price, and so on. So why doesn't the publisher promote it in June and July when the press runs are complete? The answer is timing. People buy books about the federal income tax in October through March, not in June, July, and August. So time of year is sometimes a consideration when you are deciding when to mail. Day of the week is also a consideration. If possible, when mailing to a business address you should time your direct mail piece to arrive on a Tuesday, Wednesday, or Thursday. You know what Mondays are like in a busy office. You also know if your direct mail piece arrives on Friday afternoon, it may not even make the reading file. So, think it out—when do you need the business and when is the best time to send that letter?

An example of *not* knowing when to mail is provided by Mr. Go-Getter, an enthusiastic sales manager for a large New York hotel. Mr. Go-Getter compiled a list of prospective customers and prepared a personalized letter for each customer that concluded with, "I'll call you later this week to set up an inspection tour and complimentary luncheon." All 150 letters went out in the 4 p.m. flight to Los Angeles for a four-day sales blitz. The moral is simple. Think! Be there when your letter says you will be, and call when you say you will. Otherwise, you will have to start all over again to land that prospective customer, only now you will be battling a credibility problem.

Knowing When to Stop Mailing. Promotional materials and sales letters are expensive; it is estimated that it costs up to $8 to create and send out a letter today. Thus, knowing when to stop mailing makes a lot of "cents." Many mailings may be sequential, with up to four or five pitches to the same mailing list. Be sure you have a system that will eliminate the portion of the list that has already responded "yes" or "no" to an earlier mailing.

Timely Fulfillment. Once you get a positive response, be sure you are in a position to fulfill what you promised on a timely basis. If you offered Mr. and Mrs. Jones a weekend vacation any weekend in May with the proviso that an advance reservation be made, be sure you handle their reservation properly and have their room ready when they arrive. If you fail to fulfill your offer, you may as well eliminate Mr. and Mrs. Jones from your "good" list, along with the names of their friends and neighbors—they won't be responding either.

Strategic Marketing Applications

Data base marketing/direct mail is an effective tool for many marketing applications, including:

- Customer retention programs
- Acquiring incremental business from existing customers
- Introductory/trial offers to prospective customers
- Establishing ongoing product/service dialogue
- Building marketing promotions
- Product/service information updates
- Changes in policy
- Announcements for events, new products/services
- Customer information gathering
- Customer feedback
- Test offers

As you organize, validate, and prioritize your data base, measure it against the questions in the following data base checklist and keep in mind what management expert Peter Drucker once stated: "A data base, no matter how copious, is not information...for information it must be organized for a task, directed toward specific performance, or applied to a decision."

- Is your direct marketing program part of your total marketing strategy?
- Are your mailings interlinked and supportive of your other marketing tools?
- Are your lists up to date/accurate?
- Have you prioritized your mailings based on response patterns for optimum returns?
- Does your direct mail reflect the positioning and image of your brand(s)/product(s)/service(s)?
- Is your direct mail campaign appropriate for the offer?
- If you are using a purchased list or outside vendor, have you checked the accuracy of the lists?
- Is your direct mail being sent/delivered on a timely basis?
- Have you calculated your return on investment/expected results?
- Have you maintained creative consistency throughout your mailings?

Case Examples

Case Example 1: The Check Is In the Mail. Knowing the habits of your target market can be of immense value in data base marketing. A problem many direct mail marketers face is simply getting the message opened and not thrown away. True, many put the central message or a "teaser" message on the outside of the envelope, and to some extent this helps. One technique for overcoming this problem is that used to reach travel agents. Travel agents, like many commissioned workers, rely on payment checks from their clients. Many of these checks come by mail. Agents are inundated with all kinds of direct mail every day. Yet if you could observe what happens to that mail upon delivery, you can learn the "magic" step that gets the envelope opened. Agency managers are experts at sorting their mail into two stacks. One stack goes directly into the wastebasket or to the floor for later action. The other stack goes directly in front of them and is opened immediately. The key is visual. It is the "pay to the order of" message that can be seen on check-like paper. These envelopes rise to the top and are opened immediately. The message is simple: know your target market's habits, know how to get their attention, and design your direct mail so it gets immediate attention.

Case Example 2: By Invitation Only. Promotion pieces flood our mail every day, but invitations come only for special occasions. People open invitations and discard promotional offers before they are opened. Think of the numerous credit card mailings you receive on a monthly (or even daily) basis. Many of these you never open because you already know it is a credit-card solicitation with the teaser/trial period percentage printed in large type on the envelope. What you *do* open is the typed or handwritten envelope that looks like an invitation to a special event (wedding or social engagement). People like to receive invitations and are curious enough to open an envelope that appears like one. Designing your direct mail piece with the look or appearance of an invitation, personal letter, or check will help improve the chances that your message/offer isn't trashed before it is opened. Sounds simple, but it works.

☞ Key Terms

clean lists—Lists free of invalid or out-of-date information.

data base marketing—A sales and marketing methodology that sells and promotes by selective direct mail with the objective of increasing sales and profits.

direct mail—Promotional letters, advertising pieces, catalogs, or any other sales-oriented correspondence mailed to prospective customers.

mailing lists—Collections of names and addresses maintained on a computer to generate mailings.

purge—The act of removing duplicate, invalid, and outdated records in a mailing list.

response rates—The percentages of the total audience(s) mailed to that replies.

return on investment (ROI)—The monetary return in the form of sales revenue compared with the amount of money spent to generate the sales revenue.

time cushion—A period of time incorporated into direct mail campaigns that allows for correcting errors, fine tuning or recasting the direct mail piece, and dealing with problems such as delays at the printer.

Chapter 13 Outline

Electronic Marketing
    The Internet
    Web Sites
    Email and Fax
Hospitality and Tourism Sites
Case Examples

Competencies

1. Delineate the role of electronic marketing. (p. 183)

2. Describe Internet uses. (pp. 183–184)

3. Identify key points for web site development. (pp. 184–185)

4. Discuss email and fax marketing. (p. 185)

13

Applying Key Marketing Methodologies: Electronic Marketing

Electronic Marketing

Eʟᴇᴄᴛʀᴏɴɪᴄ ᴍᴀʀᴋᴇᴛɪɴɢ can take on a number of looks. It can be vocal, as in telemarketing, visual, as in television shopping, or written or digital, as in electronically transmitted email offers or fax mail. It also includes advertising and promotions via the Internet, web sites, etc. Web sites, in particular, provide the benefits of electronic ease and speed to numerous marketing channels—retail store sites, catalog sites, home shopping Internet sites, direct manufacturer wholesaler sites, customer service sites, and intermediary sites such as hotels.com or travelocity.com.

The Internet

In an age where value is being redefined to include speed and convenience, **electronic marketing** via the **Internet** is right on target in meeting major consumer needs. The use of the Internet as a marketing tool for your products and services could well prove to be a valuable marketing strategy. Exhibit 1 lists some of the ways in which the Internet can be used for marketing.

As with other marketing tools, electronic marketing should be deployed as part of the total strategic marketing plan and by design be in concert with the image and positioning of your brands, products, and services and be interlinked to your other marketing strategy tools. Electronic marketing tools are ideal for building and actively managing and communicating with your customer base. Developing a clear concept of how to take advantage of the Internet is a must for most businesses today. To get your message to your markets, consider developing your own site, placing your banner and **logo** on related web sites, and having a strategy for easy access and quick response to customer calls.

While much of what is included in the strategy of data base marketing has applicability to electronic marketing, each of the many electronic marketing tools has its own nuances. Just as you would preplan your data base marketing strategy, you should take care in preplanning your electronic marketing strategies. Irrespective of the electronic marketing tool you select, you will have to take into account

Exhibit 1   Internet Marketing Uses

- Conduct research
- Gather information
- Buy and sell on-line
- Auction goods on-line
- Barter, trade, exchange on-line
- Participate in discussion forums
- Receive training
- Transmit and receive data (bits)
- Establish effective customer-service function (two-way communication with customers in real time)

the return on investment, measurement of the results, and overall benefits to the customers targeted. You will need to maintain creative consistency (site design, logo usage, etc.) to build awareness levels and familiarity with consumers. You will need to be sure that you can fulfill your promotional offers, that you do not undermine your pricing strategies, and that you constantly monitor and track the results. You will have to remember that when you are on the Internet, you have removed geographic boundaries and must address your strategy in terms of **currency translation**, pricing, delivery, languages, etc.

Web Sites

View your **web site** as you would a combination of your television/print advertising, your catalog, and your customer service/sales functions all rolled into one.

To help make your web site marketing effective, make it easy to read (type font sized for quick reading and limited information per screen), use large visuals (small photos project like postage stamps), select good contrast between your background and print/type colors, and always keep the user's perspective in mind. Remember, although you may have had a technical professional design your web site, it is being used by someone (your customers or potential customers) whose knowledge base of computers is very distant from that of your designers/ programmers, etc. It is good practice to pre-test your site and response/order mechanisms/processes with average consumers. Listen, accept suggestions, and make changes. If your site has been on line for a period of time, you might want to freshen the photos and the look. You may also want to run a flag or banner indicating "new" or "update."

Internet marketing should include a special focus on **links**. Develop a comprehensive list and plan to achieve maximum cross-references, co-op linkages, and banners on other related sites. Make sure you include your fax and phone numbers (800 number, etc.) for those who just need help to complete a transaction or have the need for information they cannot find on the site.

Exhibit 2   Electronic Marketing Checklist

- What role does electronic marketing play in my overall marketing strategy/plan?
- What level of resources will be needed to execute this strategy? What will it cost? What will be the return on investment?
- Should telemarketing be part of my overall marketing effort? Do faxes and email play any role?
- How does my Internet site compare to the overall image and positioning of my business, brands, products, and services?
- How does my Internet site compare to my competitors'?
- Is my Internet site user- (consumer-) friendly?
- How will I monitor the external vendors I select to handle my electronic marketing needs?
- Where should my site be listed? Where should my links be built to and from?

Email and Fax

Email and fax offers should be presented to existing customers in a service-oriented manner, and the customer always should be offered the option of not receiving the message if they prefer. Remember to check the law where you plan to use faxes or telemarketing. Telemarketing should be scripted—not prerecorded—messages and also follow strict guidelines and stay within the law. Review these electronic marketing tools carefully before implementing them, and ask if they will do more harm than good for your business. Remember that poorly executed or even flawlessly executed faxing, email pitches, or telemarketing calls are viewed by many as annoying. The result could be a lost customer versus a potential sale. If you believe these electronic marketing tools will work for you, train your personnel well and constantly monitor the efforts of organizations you contract with to provide the service.

Finally, keep in mind the uses of the Internet when developing your electronic marketing plan. Ask yourself if you can market your products or services in a way that addresses the *uses* of the Internet (for example, does it provide information and offer a quick link to purchase, etc?). *Packaging* and (site) *presentations* are two of your major keys to Internet marketing success.

Hospitality and Tourism Sites

Your site is your image around the globe. Make sure it is a good one. Review the questions in the checklist in Exhibit 2 and remember to design your site around the user. Access the websites in Exhibit 3 to see how some organizations in the hospitality and tourism industry use electronic marketing.

Case Examples

Case Example 1: Making It Work For You. One of the keys to electronic marketing is good linkages to other sites. For example, if yours is a lodging product, can

Exhibit 3   Travel and Hotel Web Sites

Airlines		**Crowne Plaza**	www.crowneplaza.com
Air Canada	www.aircanada.ca	Days Inn	www.daysinn.com
Air France	www.airfrance.com	Doubletree	www.doubletree.com
Air Tran	www.airtran.com	Embassy Suites	www.embassysuites.com
Alaska	www.alaskaair.com	Hampton Inn	www.hamptoninn.com
All Nippon	www.fly-ana.com	Hilton	www.hilton.com
America West	www.americawest.com	Holiday Inn	www.holiday-inn.com
American	www.aa.com	Homewood Suites	www.homewoodsuites.com
ATA	www.ata.com	Howard Johnson	www.howardjohnson.com
British Airways	www.british-airways.com	Hyatt	www.hyatt.com
China Southern	www.cs-air.com	Inter-Continental	www.intercontinental.com
Continental	www.continental.com	Le Meridien Hotels	www.lemeridien.com
Delta	www.delta.com	Marriott	www.marriott.com
Frontier	www.flyfrontier.com	Omni	www.omnihotels.com
Japan Airlines	www.japanair.com	Quality	www.qualityinn.com
JetBlue	www.jetblue.com	Radisson	www.radisson.com
KLM	www.klm.com	Ramada	www.ramada.com
Lufthansa	www.lufthansa.com	Regal	www.regal-hotels.com
Midwest Express	www.midwestexpress.com	Renaissance Hotels	www.renaissancehotels.com
Northwest	www.nwa.com	Residence Inn	www.residenceinn.com
Qantas	www.qantas.com	Sheraton	www.sheraton.com
Southwest	www.southwest.com	Westin	www.westin.com
Swiss	www.swiss.com	Wyndham	www.wyndham.com
United	www.united.com		
US Airways	www.usairways.com	**Car Rental Agencies**	
Vanguard	www.flyvanguard.com	Alamo	www.alamo.com
Virgin Atlantic	www.virgin.com	Avis	www.avis.com
		Budget	www.budget.com
Hotels		Dollar	www.dollar.com
Best Western	www.bestwestern.com	Hertz	www.hertz.com
Comfort Inns	www.comfortinns.com	National	www.nationalcar.com
Courtyard	www.courtyard.com	Thrifty	www.thrifty.com

prospective clients locate you with a link on the convention and visitors bureau site, the regional and state tourism sites, the area or city directory site, etc.? Having your product or service linked to as many other related sites as possible is a great way to extend the reach of your electronic marketing and make the Internet really work for you. One resort in Southern California developed over 25 separate links to extend its reach.

Case Example 2: The Major Mistake. This example describes what can happen when key information is not electronically synchronized and not effectively communicated. While this example is not from the hospitality industry, it points out well the many mistakes that can be made by not keeping your marketing tools all running on the same information. Remember, your web site, advertising, 800 telephone number, direct mail, and sales staff need to have important information such as rates/prices, availability, etc., as up-to-date as possible in an electronic world.

Recently, a customer attempted to purchase a designer fashion watch as a gift for mother's day. The watch was featured as a new item in a major woman's magazine in the gift selection section. The photo, wristband style, and $295.00 price were clearly visible on the magazine page. The customer went to a nearby mall that had the designer's store in it to buy the watch. In fact, he even brought the page from the magazine to be sure he purchased the exact watch desired. The store personnel, including the manager, stared at the magazine page and stated, "that must be a new item, we don't have it." No attempt was made to contact their office or another store in the area.

The customer returned home and called a number of other designer brand retailers who carried the company's products, only to hear the same message: "We don't have it" or, "It must be new." Undaunted, the customer turned to their web site (something anyone in any of the stores could do, but didn't). The customer clicked on watches and immediately saw the identical watch featured on the web site. A small flag said the item was in stock but be sure to call to verify express shipping if needed soon. The customer thought this a wise thing to do in view of the fact that mother's day was just a week away. One problem immediately surfaced, however: the price on the web site was $429.00. Another problem also arose: no 800 telephone number was listed anywhere. Still desirous to purchase the watch, the customer located the store's 800 number through information and asked to speak to customer service to order the watch. The customer service representative stated that she didn't have access to the web site as it is operated by someone else for them, and also they do not have a computer terminal from which they can access outside sites. The representative was well trained and told the customer she would research both the magazine and web sites and call back. The next day she called back to state she located the watch and could Federal Express it in time for Mother's Day. The customer then asked, "Okay, how much is it?" The service representative replied $429.00. The customer stated the magazine listed it for $295.00. The service representative then put on a "supervisor" who stated: "Someone in merchandising or new products must have given the wrong price to the magazine. It's not our fault, and the price is $429.00." The customer, still wanting the watch, purchased it over the phone, and it was delivered as promised.

The customer then wrote to the president of the company and included the magazine page and a printout of the web site page. The letter delineated the customer's experience and also pointed out that the web site and the magazine showed the identical watch at two very different prices. The customer also pointed out the fact that he was a loyal customer who had purchased numerous products over the years. Neither the president nor anyone from the organization responded. The customer (after six weeks) decided to call and was told that the customer service manager in the public relations area handled complaints. The call was transferred before any other words could be spoken. The spokesperson then stated: "We have had quite a few calls on that, and unfortunately it is the magazine's fault." (Did she really expect the customer to believe that the national woman's magazine ran a photo and price on their new watch without anyone from the company being involved?)

The message here is multifold and simple. Be sure what you advertise on your web site agrees with what is in print. Be sure your sales personnel and customer service personnel can readily access the same information as the customer. And, finally, *respond* appropriately or lose a customer for life—as did this company.

Key Terms

currency translation—A service of the electronic marketer wherein monetary conversion factors are included on the web site so that foreign customers can translate dollar values into currencies of other nations.

email—Electronic mail, that enables users to communicate rapidly whether the receiver resides in the same building, across town, out of state, or elsewhere. Its content is a message or document composed, mailed, received, and read through computers. As an electronic telemarketing tool, it is used for product, service, and brand advertising. The most effective messages are scripted, as opposed to prerecorded, and always offer the customer the option of not receiving them.

electronic marketing—A general term describing the use of the Internet, web sites, email, fax transmission, and other electronically created and transmitted advertising, promotional, and customer service messages from the manufacturer, intermediary, or retailer to consumers.

Internet—A large and complex series of computer networks designed to provide universal access to information and communication services around the world. It is used effectively by marketers to reach vast audiences at a fraction of the cost of traditional media.

links—An Internet system of cross-referencing that enables users to move quickly from one document to another, regardless of whether the documents were located on the same computer or on computers on opposite sides of the world.

logo—The name, symbol, or trademark of a company or publication used to identify the company in advertising, promotion, and image-building.

web site—One page or many pages of information linked together in a single package. Web sites can be organized very simply, in a hierarchy that progresses from general to specific information, or they can be complex, having pages that seem to link randomly to other pages on the site. Documents within a site can be linked to any other document on the site and even to documents on other sites.

Chapter 14 Outline

Packaging in the Hospitality Industry
    Packaging Benefits
    Packaging Participation
    Types of Packages

Competencies

1. Define "packaging," and explain packaging benefits to consumers and hospitality firms. (pp. 191–192)

2. Summarize some questions hospitality businesses should ask themselves before participating in a package. (pp. 192–193)

3. List and briefly describe common types of travel packages. (pp. 193–198)

14

Applying Key Marketing Methodologies: Packaging

T ODAY MORE THAN EVER, people are buying a complete product or service, such as all-inclusive cruises, weekend accommodations that include a rental car, and so forth. A travel or vacation experience, be it for a single weekend or for several weeks, can also be presented to consumers in a complete "package." Packages may contain every component or just some of the components of the total travel experience. Packaging makes the purchase more attractive to the consumer: it simplifies a multiple purchase and may even offer price advantages. Packaging is an important marketing tool that is becoming increasingly popular in the hospitality industry. In this chapter, we will examine the benefits of packaging, then look at some examples of typical travel packages.

Packaging in the Hospitality Industry

In the hospitality industry, **packaging** can be defined as combining two or more travel products and/or services and offering them to consumers for one price. Packages range from simple "escape weekends" that may include rooms and meals to more elaborate packaging schemes, such as "fly-drive-cruise" packages that include air travel, car rental, the cruise ship cabin rental, meals, entertainment and other services.

Packaging has become a very useful and widely applied marketing strategy within the hospitality industry. Packaging is more than just a promotion concept; it involves every step of the marketing process, from pricing to identifying customer needs. As travel and the products and services of the hospitality industry continue to grow, the acceptance and need for simplified purchasing will increase. Packaging directly meets that need. While packaging employs the marketing tools of advertising, promotion, and sales, it is also a tool unto itself.

Packaging Benefits

A typical travel package should offer benefits to consumers and to the participating hospitality firms. Consumers should feel that they are benefiting from the package offer by (1) having many travel-related decisions simplified and (2) saving money or otherwise receiving value. While these consumer benefits seem straightforward, providing them presents a substantial challenge to hospitality firms.

What are packaging's benefits to hospitality industry product or service suppliers? There are many potential benefits. A package can:

- Increase sales.

- Fill fringe or down periods with sales.

- Make your product easier for consumers to acquire because it is part of another, better-known product.

- Make your product or service appear more attractive than if it were offered on a stand-alone basis.

- Help you achieve economies of scale because your product or service is being offered through many sales channels.

- Gain recognition for your company or build your reputation in a new market.

- Help you introduce a new product or service.

Besides consumers and the participating hospitality firms, who else profits from packages? The person or firm that puts the travel products or services together. Packagers may buy travel products and services, put them together in a package, and sell the package directly to consumers—this is known as **retailing** a package. Packagers may also perform another role—contracting for the travel products and services, packaging them together, and selling the packages to others to sell directly to the public. This is known as **wholesaling** a package (see Exhibit 1).

Regardless of whether a package is offered directly to consumers or wholesaled through other retailers to consumers, it must be attractive to consumers from a marketing perspective as well as a financial one—that is, the package must meet the needs of consumers. These needs are often complex, and defining them requires considerable thought.

Packaging Participation

Not every hospitality industry product or service lends itself to packaging. Also, there are times when participating in a package at a discounted rate can hurt you. Let's consider some questions to ask yourself before you put a package together or participate in someone else's package:

- What benefits will my business receive from participation? More room nights? When? In season? Or in the off-season when I need them most?

- Will my participation in and identification with the package be advantageous or detrimental to my business's image? In other words, am I the Cadillac among Fords or the Ford among Cadillacs?

- What is the downside risk in including my product or service with the package?

- Are my "partners" in this package going to do their part to keep our customers happy?

Exhibit 1   How Packaging Works

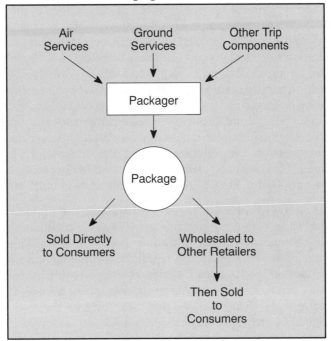

- Who is handling the details? Will I have enough control over my portion of the package to keep my customers satisfied?

- How will my business be paid for providing its share of the package?

Let's assume that your answers to those questions point to your participating in a package. Perhaps you even want to put one together and reap the benefits of being the packager. Let's also assume you have the financial resources, the key contacts, and the willingness to accept the risks of being a packager. How do you create a package? This question should lead you to think about such marketing issues as: Which market segment is my package going to go after? What are the needs of that market segment? Where do I go to reach that market segment? What kind of pricing structure will that segment respond to? A package must be thought out with all the skill and care you would put into a marketing plan, because a package is just that—a plan to bring your products or services to the market for purchase.

Types of Packages

There are virtually limitless applications of the packaging idea. In the following sections, we will look at some common types of travel packages. Be aware that these packages sometimes overlap; for example, some weekend packages can also be considered special-interest or special-event packages.

All-Inclusive Packages. All-inclusive packages are complete in that they include air services, lodging, **ground services,** car rental, admissions to attractions, taxes and gratuities, and so forth. Examples of all-inclusive packages include the following: "One week for two adults at Walt Disney World via Delta Air Lines" (hotel, car rental, and admissions included), or "Complete three-day Las Vegas Spree—$399" (air fare, deluxe rooms, meals, and shows included). All-inclusive packaging lends itself to destination trips, since it simplifies the purchase of the complete trip.

All-inclusive packages may be offered directly to consumers via local newspaper ads; through clubs, churches, or civic organizations; or through retail travel agents. Or, a package wholesaler may supply an all-inclusive package to one or more retail outlets that in turn sell them to consumers. Frequently, price discounts for all-inclusive packages can be arranged as a result of averaging off-season and in-season rates, purchasing hotel rooms or airplane seats in bulk, and so on.

Fly-Drive Packages. Fly-drive packages (see Exhibit 2) are popular and continue to grow in number. In a fly-drive package, air services and auto rental services are combined. For example, one airline's "California Fly-Drive" package included air fare to Los Angeles or San Francisco, a rental car for five days, and return airfare from San Francisco or Los Angeles. The concept was to offer consumers a way to fly to California, drive up or down the coast, and return home—all for $499 per person. For many years, air carriers and rent-a-car firms on the east coast have successfully marketed fly-drive packages to Florida. Fly-drives are particularly popular in markets where renting cars is difficult—for instance, in-season in Florida—or where many of the destination's attractions are best seen by automobile.

Fly-Cruise Packages. A variation on the fly-drive package is the fly-cruise package (see Exhibit 3). Originally conceived to eliminate cold days at sea for cruise passengers, the fly-cruise package flies consumers to a warm seaport where they begin the cruise. For example, vacationers from the northeast might fly from Boston to Miami, from where they sail to the Caribbean and back to Miami, then return to Boston by air. Recently, the struggle to maintain long-distance cruising (for instance, transatlantic cruises) has resulted in a fly-cruise variation in which consumers fly first-class one way (say, from the United States to Europe) and then cruise back across the Atlantic. The packaged transatlantic fly-cruise offers the cruise experience consumers seek, while reducing the total cruise time by offering air travel one way.

Weekend Packages. Perhaps the most common and one of the simplest forms of packaging centers on weekend promotions (see Exhibit 4). Convenience and price are important, but the main reason consumers purchase weekend packages is that they offer a much needed getaway or escape. Examples of weekend packages include "family escape packages" geared to family fun and value (for example, the kids stay free Friday and Saturday nights, or four stay in the room for the price of one); second-honeymoon escape packages (which typically include a deluxe room, champagne, breakfast in bed, and so on); and hundreds of other escape-weekend concepts, from ski packages to sporting-event packages.

Exhibit 2   Sample Fly-Drive Package

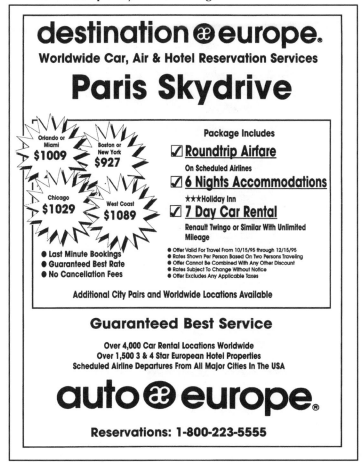

Courtesy of Auto Europe

Special-Interest Packages. A package can be successfully created to appeal to people's special interests. The concept behind a special-interest package is to combine a basic hospitality service or product (lodging, for example) with a special interest such as boating, golf, tennis, swimming, skiing, or horseback riding. Special-interest packages need not be limited to sport or recreational activity tie-ins, however. They may also relate to history, religious interests, or hobbies.

Examples of successful special-interest packages are weekend "foliage" bus tours of New England to see the changing landscape as fall unfolds. Meals and rooms at quaint New England inns are usually packaged along with the bus tour; the tour usually features photo-taking opportunities at scenic overviews along the highway. Another example of a special-interest package is "Friday Night at the Races" in which consumers are taken to the racetrack via motorcoach, with dinner, cocktails on board, and general-admission tickets all included in one price.

Exhibit 3   Sample Fly-Cruise Package

Courtesy of Cunard Line Ltd.

Special-Event Packages. Packaging around a special event is another form of package marketing. Each year tens of thousands of people purchase special-event packages to the Super Bowl, Mardi Gras, college football bowl games, major boxing events, the World Series, and many other special events. The event is the reason for the trip; the package provides the easiest method to purchase everything in one step.

Some creative individuals have developed not only special-event packages but even the special event itself. These types of packages include transcontinental balloon flights, nationwide bike races, and weekend dinners or festivals honoring people or places.

Special Destination/Attraction Packages. There are special places that lend themselves to being promoted via a package (see Exhibit 5). These include the Holy Land; the Vatican; Israel; Washington, D.C., and capitals in general; theme parks (Disney World, Six Flags, and so on); Atlantic City and Las Vegas; mountains (the Catskills, for example); beaches (Myrtle Beach, Virginia Beach, Cape Cod); Alaskan cruises; and so on. One of the best examples of a special destination that is

Exhibit 4   Sample Weekend Package

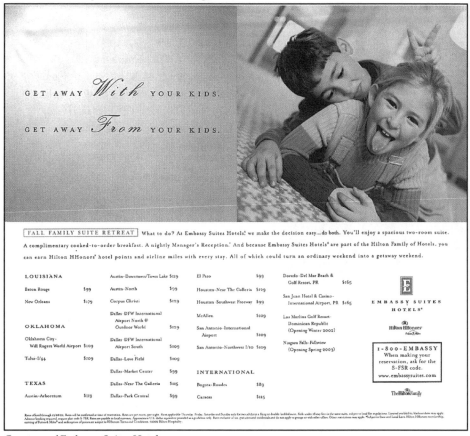

Courtesy of Embassy Suites Hotels

packaged for the young (school-aged children) as well as the old (retirees) is Virginia's Colonial Williamsburg Village.

Theme Packages. With a theme package, the packager literally creates the reason for the package. For example, a number of New York City hotels looking for weekend business have created successful packages on the theme of "a weekend in New York, including dinner in Central Park and an evening at the theater." This theme requires the package to include rooms, theater tickets, and meals; most of the packages also include a buggy ride through Central Park or a limo ride to and from the theater as part of the attraction. Other theme packages have related to art shows, cultural displays at museums, gambling, and even "celebrity weekends," which center on the appearance of a celebrity.

Holiday Packages. "Winter vacation week of 12/28 to 1/5 in sunny Florida via Delta only $469 air fare, room (double occupancy) included" is a frequent type of

Exhibit 5   Sample Destination/Attraction Package

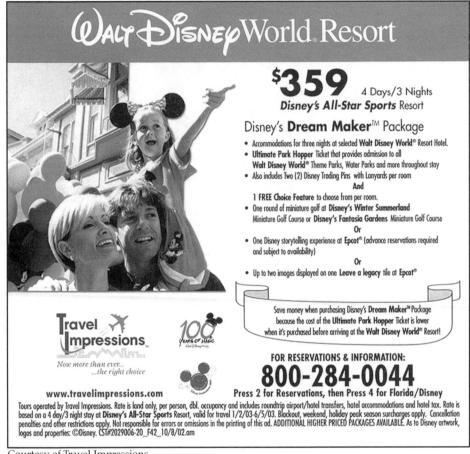

Courtesy of Travel Impressions

holiday package promoted on college campuses in the Northeast. Other holiday packages include everything from "Easter in the Holy Land" to "St. Patrick's Day in Dublin" to a week in sunny Spain to witness Pamplona's running of the bulls. While the reason to travel is the holiday event itself, the packaging of that event with other hospitality industry products and services for one price is the key to making the sale.

"Price" Packages. There are many types of "price" packages (see Exhibit 6). With price packages, the marketing message focuses on value. One successful concept in price packaging is the "give-away," frequently called the "two-for-one" concept, in which the purchaser's spouse or significant other goes along "free." Other typical price-oriented travel packages include weekends at 50 percent off, a free suite, the second week is free, "two extra days on the Costa del Sol included at no cost," and so on.

Exhibit 6   Sample Price Package

HOTELS & RESORTS

Why do so many people choose Sol Meliá?
The Best Beach Experience • Ultimate Relaxation • Luxurious Accommodations • Exquisite Cuisine • World Class Pampering • Incredible Diving • Ageless Activities • Championship Golf Course
That's why!

Mexico & Dominican Republic

MEXICO

CANCUN   4 Days/3 Nights

Meliá Turquesa • *Guaranteed Room Upgrade* $189

Meliá Cancun • *$50 Food & Beverage Credit per room* $195

Paradisus Riviera Cancun • *ALL INCLUSIVE* $369

PUERTO VALLARTA

Meliá Puerto Vallarta • *ALL INCLUSIVE • Guaranteed Room Upgrade* $245

LOS CABOS

Meliá Cabo Real • *Guaranteed Room Upgrade* $249

Meliá Los Cabos • *Guaranteed Room Upgrade* $305

Meliá San Lucas • *Guaranteed Room Upgrade* $309

MEXICO CITY

Gran Meliá Mexico Reforma • *Guaranteed Room Upgrade* $275

COZUMEL

Paradisus Cozumel • *ALL INCLUSIVE • Guaranteed Room Upgrade* $299

IXTAPA

Meliá Azul Ixtapa • *ALL INCLUSIVE* $359

DOMINICAN REPUBLIC

PUNTA CANA

Meliá Caribe Tropical • *ALL INCLUSIVE* $279

Paradisus Punta Cana • *ALL INCLUSIVE* $395

ALL PACKAGES INCLUDE: • Roundtrip Airport/Hotel Transfers • 4 Days/3 Nights Hotel Accommodations • Hotel Tax & Service

ALL-INCLUSIVE PACKAGES ALSO INCLUDE: • All Meals, Drinks & Snacks • Non-motorized Watersports • Entertainment & Much More!

AmericanAirlines
MORE ROOM *THROUGHOUT COACH*

Airfare Available from Cities Nationwide...
Call For Details!

Travel Impressions™
Now more than ever... ...the right choice

1% BONUS COMMISSION WHEN YOU BOOK THROUGH: SABRE CHANGE KEY | CHANGE KEY | TIP APOLLO LSSI V TIP & WWW.TRAVELIMPRESSIONS.COM

Tours operated by Travel Impressions. Rates are land only, per person, dbl. occupancy and include roundtrip airport/hotel transfers, hotel accommodations and hotel tax. Blackout, weekend, holiday peak season surcharges apply. Rates valid for travel 9/1/02 through 12/20/02. Cancellation penalties and other restrictions apply. Not responsible for errors or omissions in the printing of this ad. ADDITIONAL HIGHER PRICED PACKAGES AVAILABLE. CST#2029006-20_XS4_7/5/02.am.

For Reservations & Information, CALL: 800-284-0044

Courtesy of Travel Impressions

Key Terms

ground services—All the services received at a destination (excluding method of travel to the destination), such as rooms, food, beverage, and local tours

packaging—The combining of more than one hospitality product or service into a single purchase item for a single price.

retailing—With regard to hospitality packaging, the selling of a travel product, service, or package directly to the consumer.

wholesaling—With regard to hospitality packaging, the selling of a travel package to travel agencies, airlines, and other travel companies who, in turn, sell it directly to consumers.

Chapter 15 Outline

Collateral Materials
    Types of Collateral Material
Employee Motivation
    Employee-of-the-Month Programs
    Employee-Interest Promotions
    Employee Community Service
        Recognition
Clubs
    VIP Clubs
    Administrators/Secretaries
        Appreciation Programs
    Salesperson Appreciation Clubs
    Meal-of-the-Month Clubs

Competencies

1. Explain eight key points for preparing and presenting collateral materials. (pp. 203–204)

2. Describe several types of collateral materials used in the hospitality industry. (pp. 204–212)

3. Give examples of employee motivational programs that help make a property more marketable, and explain how they are used. (pp. 212–213)

4. Describe the club concept as a marketing tool and give examples of successful uses of the club concept. (pp. 213–215)

15

Applying Key Marketing Methodologies: Collateral Materials and Promotional Support

To MARKET YOUR ESTABLISHMENT EFFECTIVELY, you need to use a variety of tools. This chapter examines some very specific types of marketing tools: collateral materials, employee motivation programs, and club concepts.

Collateral materials are printed items such as brochures, maps, guides, flyers, posters, tent cards, etc. They help advertise your property or the services within it.

Employee motivation programs help make your property more marketable by motivating your primary resource—your employees. These programs help make your employees more committed to their jobs and to making sure that the property succeeds.

Club concepts have taken a variety of different forms, but all of them succeed by giving the customer extra recognition. A club concept tells a particular market segment that it is special, and that your property values its business.

Collateral Materials

Collateral materials are the print support materials that help market your product or service. In the hospitality industry, they include brochures, maps, guides, menu inserts, tent cards, photo displays, and posters. The cost of preparing, printing, and distributing collateral materials is easily measured.

It is important to approach the preparation of each collateral piece with the same care you would give your best advertisement and most important sales call. Your potential market and customers are always viewing your collateral materials. The same "do's and don'ts" that apply to general promotion pieces apply to collateral materials. There are eight key points to keep in mind when preparing and presenting collateral materials:

1. *Identification of purpose.* Your first step—before you determine whether you need color, what quality of paper **stock** to use, or what shape, size, etc., you should make an item—is to ask yourself what the primary purpose of the piece is and who the intended audience is.

2. *Fallacy about quality.* There is a fallacy about quality that states: "If it's four colors on a high-quality stock, it's got to be good." Remember that the true value of a collateral piece is its marketing purpose, not its physical appearance.

3. *Compatibility.* Your collateral materials should reinforce the image you are trying to establish or maintain regarding your product or service. Don't let it contradict that image. If you are running an upscale gourmet restaurant, be sure your materials are compatible with that image. There are times when you might try to improve on your establishment's image by improving the collateral materials. An example might be creating a new brochure that portrays a better image than that currently being portrayed. A word of caution, however: if you allow a new brochure to build a level of expectation beyond what the product can deliver, you could be doing yourself more harm than good.

4. *Consistency.* The single greatest fault with most collateral material is its lack of consistency. Is your collateral material consistent with your other marketing and image-related visual aids? Simple things such as the use of a logo, certain colors, print styles, and so on will help build consistency. You may want your piece of collateral material to stand out, and it should, but not by detracting from your image.

5. *Practical detail.* Does the collateral material accomplish the marketing purpose it was designed to meet? Too often things like picture selection take precedence over clear directions and a useful map. The result may be great photos, but customers who can't find you! Remember to review the materials and be sure every detail is accurate and useful.

6. *Visibility.* If you want customers to pick up and respond to your collateral materials, don't hide them! Check often to see that these materials are where they belong—somewhere where the customer or potential customer can clearly see them and pick them up.

7. *Clutter avoidance.* Be sure you are not a victim of "the-more-the-better" syndrome. Yes, it's great to have good information for your hospitality customers, but too much collateral material in one place results in clutter. You may even find that the customer has left you to spend time and money at an external attraction you promoted overzealously.

8. *Keep it clear.* Make sure that the purpose of each piece is clear. Do not overload it with too much copy or detail or it will lose its purpose as a marketing vehicle. A customer or potential customer picks up the material to get a message. Don't bury that message in fine print or, worse, too much print.

Types of Collateral Material

Given these key points, let's look at some specific types of collateral materials employed in the hospitality industry.

Brochures. A brochure is a highly specialized piece of collateral material. Its preparation requires careful thought. It is not simply a collection of sexy photos and some copy. A successful, well-prepared promotional brochure for a property should contain the following ten elements:

1. Identification of the property, including its logo
2. Descriptive facts about the property
3. Directions on how to get to the property
4. A map with travel times
5. The property's telephone number(s)
6. The property's address
7. The person or individual to contact for more information (sales director, the catering department, etc.)
8. Amenities within the property (recreational, food and beverage, etc.)
9. Nearby attractions and items of interest to the guests/customers (e.g., shopping, tourist attractions, etc.)
10. Transportation information (limo service, buses, airlines, rail, interstates, rental-car companies, etc.)

Including these ten elements will not necessarily guarantee that your brochure is successful. You must also consider the eight key points to preparing successful collateral material mentioned earlier and, of course, use professional photos, art, design layout, and copy to produce a quality final product.

Directories. There are both large-volume reference directories and pocketsize or briefcase directories. If you produce a directory that you want the traveling consumer to use, be sure that it fits in a briefcase or purse. No one wants to (or will) carry an oversized book. Make it easy to use. Follow a format that is logical—to the customer, not you—and include an index and a key. Put your phone number wherever possible, preferably on every page, as well as on the front and back covers.

If you list your property in someone else's directory, observe the following points:

• Proof everything twice.

• Be careful about being too specific with prices or rates; use ranges (especially if it is an annual directory).

• Check and double check your address, phone and fax numbers, and telex number (if applicable).

• Ask to review the final copy.

• Ask to review the actual placement.

• If a photo of your product or service is used, be sure it is up-to-date, representative, and a sales tool; otherwise, do not use it.

Today there are more than 5,000 different reference directories, ranging from the local yellow pages to *A Directory of Directories,* many of which are available in CD-ROM format or on-line. In order to determine which directory listings are most helpful to you, you will need to analyze *where* your business is coming from, *how* potential customers find out about you, and *what* type of business you are getting.

Answer the following questions to help determine which directories you should list in for the most exposure of your product or service:

1. Do I currently receive business as a result of a directory listing?

2. Does my competition receive business as a result of a directory listing that I do not receive?

3. Will I receive enough business from a directory listing to offset the cost for the listing? This is especially applicable with respect to fees for computerized directories and CD-ROM distribution.

4. Are there any key directories in which my competitors are listed and I am not?

5. Is my product or service compatible with the directory format (e.g., one line, block ad, a photo ad, etc.)?

While these five practical questions should provide you with some rationale for whether to list in a directory, often trial and measurement will be the best test. If you decide directory listings will be helpful in marketing your product or service, be sure that the content and the **placement** of that listing are well thought out to convey your marketing message. Directory listings often require similar information from all contributors. It is to your advantage to fill in every line in the listing questionnaire. If the directory you select allows leeway, be sure to include the following:

• A landmark reference along with your address—for example, "next to the Metro Station in Crystal City"

• Your phone number

• Any special information that will give potential customers a reason to call you (this reason can be referred to as the "why statement")

Insist that you review the placement of your listing—the actual spot in the directory where your listing will appear—and, most important, that you have an opportunity for a final review of the copy that goes into the directory. Do not scan it—read it word for word and number for number. Once in print in a directory, the listing is widely circulated—errors, wrong phone number, and all. Again, if you must list rates or prices, use a range. Most directories are published annually, and you may not want to commit to specific rates (especially during times of high inflation).

Fact Sheets. A fact sheet is an abbreviated version of a hotel's brochure. It is usually in a one-page, bulleted format. It contains brief descriptive phrases that convey the key information about the property (see Exhibit 1). It is used as a "stuffer" in mailings, as a self-mailer, or (in less expensive form) as a handout for people making inquiries at the property.

Gift Certificates. Another very useful application of collateral materials is the gift certificate. Gift certificates let consumers buy your product or service for someone

Exhibit 1   Hotel Fact Sheet Format

Name	Name of hotel.
Location	Include street address, distance from airport, and attractions.
Physical structure	Design, number of floors, and number of rooms per floor.
Number and type of rooms	Number of guest rooms and description of the bed types and decor of the rooms.
Number and type of suites	Same information for suites as given for standard rooms.
Club floor	If hotel offers a "concierge" level, description of accommodations and services.
Function space	Location and number of meeting rooms, including dimensions and capacity for each (a capacity chart may be used).
Food and beverage outlets	Names and descriptions of each food and beverage outlet, including type of cuisine, seating capacity, price range, and hours of operation.
Recreation	A list of all recreational facilities.
Amenities	A list of all other hotel amenities, such as turndown service, complimentary *Wall Street Journal,* shoe shine, barber/beauty shop, etc.
Parking	Description of facilities and cost.
Transportation	Description of transportation service to the airport and area with accompanying cost. Does hotel provide complimentary van or limousine service?
Secretaries club	If it exists at the hotel, description of the program.
Frequent guest program	If offered by the hotel, a brief description of its advantages and disadvantages in relation to your hotel.

else. Gift certificates can take on many different forms and be promoted in many ways. One example is seasonal promotion of books of gift certificates sold by McDonald's as Christmas gifts. Another example was executed well by a lodging property that sold "gift boxes" containing escape weekend tickets and empty champagne glasses that would be filled on a complimentary basis. Restaurants offer "dinner-for-two" gift certificates with all sorts of variations. These programs have become increasingly popular, fulfilling people's need to give an unusual and much appreciated gift.

Entertainment Pieces. Collateral materials supporting entertainment come in many shapes, forms, and levels of quality. Most entertainers will supply photos, posters, or flyers (a one-page formatted message). Most hospitality properties use these as supplied. This is fine if the quality and the *taste* in the collateral material are compatible with the establishment's image. There are no standard criteria by which to screen entertainment collateral materials; however, there are some steps that can be taken to ensure the materials are compatible with the establishment:

1. Consider developing a standard poster display case.

2. Ask entertainment groups to supply appropriate photos or posters to fit the display case.

3. Reject all "homemade" posters, signs, or other wall hangings that are of low or mediocre quality.

4. Consider your print advertising as part of the total campaign for the entertainment—make it stand out from the rest.

5. Be sure that the supplied photos, copy, and any related public relations or press releases are in good taste and compatible with your establishment's desired image.

6. Be sure the entertainment itself is representative of how you want your customers to perceive your establishment. Think of your image at all times.

Flyers. Flyers are announcements usually printed for quick distribution to stimulate interest in a special event or promotion. Flyers may be reminders or even an announcement of an event when time does not permit using another method. If you use flyers, take care that they have a professional appearance and are compatible with the other materials used to promote the event. It is important that you control distribution to ensure that potential customers (and not your parking lot) get the message. Flyers are an inexpensive method to reach the local market. Image concerns may make flyers an inappropriate delivery vehicle for some users or messages.

Guest Services/Guestroom Collateral Materials. There are two approaches to guest services collateral materials: the clutter method and the organized approach. The clutter method is best depicted by a hotel room dresser or desk-top full of everything from credit card applications to room service menus, all set up alongside instructions on how to work the TV, save energy, and so forth. The net result is a cluttered guestroom.

There are many ways to organize guest services information. One method is to use a folder with inserts related to the various services (e.g., room service menu, amenities, and so on). The second method is to use a display made of laminated plastic with slots for inserts. Either is acceptable, and both are preferred to the clutter approach. The guestroom materials should reflect some consistency in color and print style, and—most important of all—they should be readable. Often too much is squeezed on an instructions card with print too small to be of help to the guest, resulting in unnecessary calls to your telephone operator. One final note: Be sure a pen or pencil is included with the collateral materials in the room, preferably one imprinted with the name and phone number of your establishment. Guests will not only appreciate it and use it—they'll probably take it!

Lounge Materials. Collateral material promoting a lounge at the property should adhere to the same guidelines as the materials used to promote the property itself.

The lounge materials should convey not only the lounge's environment, theme, and so on, but also a marketing message that relates to the needs of the consumer. The message can be "a place to relax," "a place to unwind," "a place to discuss business or pleasure," or whatever.

If there is something special about the lounge, say so in the collateral material. Collateral material promoting the lounge should tell the reader where the lounge is in the property, indicate any dress requirements, and be placed in visible locations throughout the property. Visible places include, but are not limited to:

- The restaurant.
- The elevator lobby.
- The hotel lobby.
- Guestrooms.

Collateral materials for the lounge should convey, via photos, the reason to come to the lounge, whether it is relaxation or the promise of intimate conversation. A photo of four walls does not sell or motivate consumers. People visit lounges to get away from their rooms, seek companionship, or relax. Be sure your collateral materials communicate that your lounge meets these needs.

Maps. A good map will indicate a clear way to reach your establishment. It will also identify landmarks, key roads, and distance or travel time. Use the distance or travel time indicator that is most advantageous to you. If you are three miles from the airport, but it takes 25 minutes to travel the distance, indicate three miles. If you are nine miles from the airport, but only 15 minutes via the expressway, indicate 15 minutes. If you can get your establishment listed on other maps, do so—it is additional exposure for you. Rent-a-car company maps, chamber of commerce materials, Realtor maps, bank maps, on-line direction services, and sight-seeing maps are but a few of the opportunities available to get your establishment noticed.

Menu Specials. Advertisements for special food or beverage promotions are a frequently used type of collateral material. These promotions take many forms, ranging from the photocopied menu clip-on to multicolored menus and tabletop displays. Regardless of the formality of the collateral piece, its objective is to increase sales by getting guests to opt for the special. Potential customers can perceive these promotions as adding "value." The promotion can be on a regularly scheduled day of the week, week of the month, or month of the year. If you use the material as part of an ongoing program, you can more easily implement and control the promotion and measure its effectiveness. Many restaurant chains use this type of collateral sales material. These restaurants regularly promote a number of items as specials, using collateral material clipped to menus. Although the specials frequently change, the clip-on material should be well prepared with quality that is comparable to the menu's quality.

You can design menu specials to achieve many objectives. The purpose may be to increase volume by offering a relatively low-priced special, or it may be to build "trial" (new) business by offering a low-priced special to attract new clientele. You may also design specials to increase profits by promoting low-cost items that provide a higher profit margin, such as pasta dishes. Other specials may be designed to build volume for a specific item, increase beverage sales, increase the average check amounts through dessert promotions, etc. Menu specials can help you meet your objectives if you:

- Clearly identify the purpose and the result expected.
- Conscientiously and methodically measure your results.
- Carefully plan your collateral promotion piece.

Finally, remember to tell the servers, hosts, and hostesses about the special and *how* to promote it to customers. A server who answers, "I don't know" when your customer asks about a special is not going to make the sale.

Meeting Facilities Brochures. If you decide to prepare a brochure about the meeting facilities in your establishment, be sure to include the items of interest to meeting planners. This means every detail, not just photos. Details may include:

- Room sizes/dimensions.
- Ceiling heights.
- Seating capacity, referencing different setups (theater style, classroom, U-shaped, etc.).
- Audiovisual equipment.
- Display capacities (maximum width and height of entries).
- Sketches or diagrams of the rooms.
- Breakout room and additional conference room information.
- Adjoining banquet facilities.
- Meeting and meal setups.
- Special features (acoustics, tables, technical capabilities, etc.).
- Service procedures and policies, focusing on the human aspect rather than the physical facility.
- Rate and discounts.
- Location of the facilities.
- Proximity to transportation (subway, airports, etc.).
- Group transportation services.
- Other property amenities that will help sell meetings.
- Telephone number and name of the person to contact.

Make the meeting-facilities brochure easy to read and responsive to the meeting planner's needs. Include the banquet menu and any other related collateral materials as support information for the meeting planner.

The meeting-facilities brochure should answer every question a potential customer might ask about the physical facility and services available. Include a "things-to-do" section or attachment to help sell your facility. This section or attachment should mention nearby or in-house shopping, entertainment, cultural attractions, recreational attractions, etc.

Most important of all, be certain that there is a telephone number and person to call. If that person is not available, be sure that the person answering the telephone is completely prepared to answer questions or that the appropriate salesperson can quickly contact the potential customer. Finally, be certain that there is an adequate stock of all materials on hand to supply potential customers. If volume merits it, consider a CD-ROM version of the information; it is more likely to be retained by the requesting individual or organization.

Rate Cards. Perhaps the single most debatable piece of collateral material today is the rate card. Rates change frequently and are often discounted or tailored for special types of business (for instance, corporate clients, airline crews, families). If rate cards are used, plan to replace them frequently and design them to allow flexibility in selling. The best rate cards:

- Use price ranges.

- Clearly define special rate programs and qualifying rules.

- Clearly state dates for which the rates are in effect.

- Define any special policies.

Printing your rates may not always legally compel you, but it certainly builds expectations among your potential customers about what your products and services cost. Always have a disclaimer, such as "rates subject to change," but, more importantly, strive to have the correct, current rate clearly defined for your customer. Likewise, be sure every employee who has contact with potential customers knows the current rate policy and procedures and has the current rate card accessible at all times.

Recreational Facilities Guide. Attractions, be they within the hospitality facility or in nearby areas, are an asset to promote. Internal collateral materials can promote attractions that help satisfy guests and attract repeat visitors. Reference materials for nearby local attractions can especially benefit a property that lacks internal amenities or facilities. The caution here is to avoid the clutter of having many different collateral pieces that vary in quality. Also, discard out-of-date brochures. Cooperative programs between lodging facilities and nearby attractions (in which program participants refer to one another) can work very well to increase the exposure and perceived value of all program participants. Give careful thought to consistency and image before you enter into such cooperative promotions.

Shopping Cards. Shopping ranks consistently high on the list of needs expressed by leisure travelers. Collateral materials pointing out nearby or special shopping areas can thus add another perceived value to the hospitality property. Getting your establishment identified within a local shopper's guide as a reference point or map point can provide additional marketing exposure.

Tent Cards. Tent cards are another popular form of collateral material. They can promote everything from a restaurant within a hotel to a drink or dessert special within the restaurant. Tent cards come in all shapes, sizes, and forms. Some practical considerations are:

- Use all sides of the tent card.

- Design it in a practical manner to rest on a table or a desk.

- Make it look attractive.

- Avoid the temptation to use a "totally unique" tent card—it will usually be costly to produce, difficult to use, and constantly in need of replacement.

- Be sure that size and placement of the tent card are consistent with the purpose or message on the card.

- Monitor and measure the results of each tent card promotion to determine its real value to you.

- Avoid clutter or promotions that cheapen your overall product or service offering.

Employee Motivation

Customers are often impressed when an establishment recognizes good employee performance. You can keep your customers informed and motivate your employees through a number of in-house marketing methods. As a labor-intensive industry, motivated employees with good service attitudes are very often the keys to a successful operation. Ensuring employee motivation is a very difficult task in the services business. In-house materials that help employee morale are important and have a direct impact on the sale of your product or service. Do not ignore strategies for improving employee motivation; such strategies are key marketing tools. Some examples are included in the following sections.

Employee-of-the Month Programs

One of the more successful applications of motivational principles in the hospitality industry has been "employee-of-the-month" programs. The visual execution of these programs is important; often, a photo poster is prominently displayed in a high-traffic employee area.

An even more meaningful—and potentially more beneficial—method is to establish a permanent display case for such a poster, thereby allowing your guests to also see this recognition award. This placement method provides even further recognition for the employee and fosters additional feelings of goodwill among both employees and guests. A successful employee-of-the-month program requires a well-planned program of support, frequently including external public relations and some form of reward for the recognized employees. Selection criteria, fairness in judgment, and the involvement of other employees as judges or award presenters are keys to success in making these employee-recognition programs work. Management's involvement in these programs and respect for the employees and their achievements are also critical factors.

Employee-Interest Promotions

Employee-interest promotions help motivate employees and increase the marketing exposures for your establishment. An employee-interest promotion begins by identifying a hobby or a special interest of an employee. One example is that of a chef whose hobby is driving race cars. The hotel where he worked successfully placed a number of human-interest stories in the media about the "fastest chef in town," featuring the employee and his hobby. Management then displayed the news clippings and photos of the chef and his autos in a number of high-traffic employee areas within the property. Employee-interest promotion possibilities are limitless, but they should be used sparingly or their internal value may dissipate.

Employee Community Service Recognition

Another effective employee program is recognizing employees' efforts in their local communities. Many employees do volunteer work, make special efforts on behalf of charities, or make unique contributions to their communities. Identifying and providing public recognition for these employees and their service efforts benefits both your establishment and the employees. These are "win-win" promotions. Examples include employees who walk, run, or rock for contributions to charity; employees who perform volunteer work for people who are sick, disabled, or elderly; and employees who help save lives as volunteer fire fighters or rescue-squad personnel.

Clubs

Clubs for specific consumer groups are another marketing device that can work for you. Regardless of your sector of the hospitality industry, you can create a "club" concept to promote business. A few examples follow.

VIP Clubs

Just as employee recognition programs identify employees who are important to you, VIP clubs recognize segments of customers who are "very important people" to you. Examples of such concepts are numerous and include: Hertz #1 Club; Hertz Platinum Service; and the various airline frequent-traveler clubs such as United's Red Carpet Club, Delta's Crown Room Club, and American's Admiral's Club. The lodging sector also uses a variety of VIP concepts and promotions.

Today's VIP-club concepts are sophisticated and require a variety of skills, such as building direct-mail lists, publishing special magazines, and completing merchandising programs. VIP clubs can also exist *within* a lodging or food and beverage facility. It can be a concept as simple as designating upgraded rooms or floors for VIPs or sectioning off an area of the dining room for VIPs. Recognition, appreciation, and appeal to the repeat user are the motivators behind such VIP club concepts. Key factors for a VIP club concept include the following:

- Recognition of frequent users of the product or service
- Perceivable benefits to membership
- Special services
- Exclusive items or services for members only
- Membership symbols (membership cards, wall plaques, etc.)
- Emphasis on taking problems out of the travel experience
- Simplifying the product or service purchase

Administrators/Secretaries Appreciation Programs

Administrators and secretaries are important intermediaries in the hospitality industry. They are often in direct contact with the customer and, more important, are often decision-makers. Hotels have been leaders in recognizing this and developing special-appreciation club concepts. For example, one such club concept created by a hotel chain offers incentive awards to secretaries in appreciation for various levels of business directed to their establishments. The concept is well thought out and exemplifies how to organize a productive secretaries program. Here's a sketch of how it works.

The establishment assigns an individual to identify secretaries who are providing reservations on a regular basis. A list is developed, and those secretaries are invited to join the "club." The club provides:

- A quarterly appreciation luncheon.
- Flowers on each club member's birthday.
- Free weekends for certain volumes of room nights.
- Free trips for even larger volumes.

While this is an oversimplified explanation, the concept is "business is appreciated and, more important, so are you." It's no wonder that the chains' highest percentage of repeat business comes from its appreciation programs/clubs. (It is always good practice to determine the client company's policy with respect to any such incentive reward program.)

The building of lists, enrolling of members, personal letters, gestures of appreciation, incentive gifts, and all other aspects of appreciation clubs are designed to build repeat business through loyal intermediaries and friends.

Salesperson Appreciation Clubs

Special club or VIP concepts are particularly applicable to the commercial transient salesperson. These individuals form the loyal core or base for many hospitality establishments as a result of a heavy, consistent travel pattern. Building loyalty to your product or service with this market segment can be very beneficial. The club or VIP concept for salespersons assumes many different forms; however, these forms have as a common premise the recognition that it is desirable to keep this particular customer's brand loyalty. Special rates, rooms, first-drink-free promotions, every tenth room free, free coffee and breakfast, and even free car washes have been offered as part of the special treatment for salespersons.

Meal-of-the-Month Clubs

Building a loyal or regular following in today's food and beverage market is increasingly difficult because of the many new concepts and the increase in competition. One method of ensuring a regular following is to develop a meal-of-the-month or some other dining-out club. Meal-of-the-month clubs can have a number of different appeals, ranging from price and value to a variety of themes to entertainment tie-ins. Regardless of the method selected, the idea is to use the club to build a core of regulars.

Key Terms

collateral materials—Print-based materials that assist in the marketing of products and services. Some examples include brochures, tent cards, posters, directories, maps, guides, menu inserts, flyers, and entertainment promotion pieces.

flyer—A printed announcement of a special event or promotion, usually created for quick distribution by mailing it or leaving it at a location for passersby to pick up.

placement—Where your advertising actually appears, be it a time slot on radio or television, an outdoor billboard near an airport, or a spot on a page in a specific issue of a magazine or newspaper.

stock—The type of paper or material used for printed materials; usually defined by weight, grain, or texture.

Chapter 16 Outline

Competencies

1. Explain the different types of room rates charged by hotels. (pp. 217–219)

2. Describe ranges of rates set by hotels, identify the purpose of rate strategies, and give examples of strategies based on the grid–positioning concept. (pp. 220–222)

3. Describe air carriers' rates and the factors affecting rate strategies. (pp. 223–228)

4. Explain types of rental car rates and the factors affecting rate strategies. (pp. 228–230)

5. Describe cruise ship rates. (p. 230)

16

Applying Key Marketing Methodologies: Understanding Rates and Fares

$\mathbf{A}$ RATE IS THE PRICE that is established for a service. The hospitality industry applies different rates for its services. Rates may vary for virtually every day of the week, every market segment, and every event one can think of—or create. In fact, rate is one of today's most powerful marketing tools, and consumer-attracting terminology such as "discount," "special offer," "trial," and "preferred" abounds in marketing and promotions.

One purpose of this chapter is to explain and show the relationships among various types of rates used in the hospitality industry. This chapter also discusses the concept of ranges of rates and describes some of the rate-setting strategies used by hotels, air carriers, rental car firms, and cruise lines. It also emphasizes the importance of rate management.

One key to any discussion of rates is a clear and consistent use of terminology. This is especially important to consumers, whose patience with the wording of fine-print **restrictions** placed on special offers is just about exhausted. Many professionals in the industry use rate terminology inexactly, causing confusion and undermining their own credibility. Definitions of rate-related terminology should be specific and consistent; however, rate categories and associated terms or conditions are in constant flux, even within a single hospitality business enterprise.

Hotel Rates

In hotels, standard rates are applied in common situations as noted in this section. Additional types of rates that apply in market-specific situations are also discussed.

Standard Rates

Standard hotel rates include corporate, rack, preferred, super-saver, weekend, summer, and club-level.

Corporate. In today's marketplace, the **corporate rate** is a competitive rate used to attract frequent business travelers. Depending on the quality of a hotel and its location in relation to its top competitors in the marketplace, the hotel's corporate rate should be the same as or rather close to those of its four major competitors. If an established property has the clearly superior location and product, the hotel can be the rate leader in the market. But if a hotel is new or not yet established, its corporate rate might be lower than the competition's rate in order to bring in trial business.

As hotel managers plan a hotel's rate strategy, the corporate rate should be established first. Management should strive to ensure that the corporate rate that is advertised in all automated reservations systems, on-line services, and directory listings is the most competitive corporate rate or range of rates offered. The hotel's range for its corporate rate should be based on room type, location, or other selected criteria.

Rack. A hotel's highest rate category is called the rack rate. Rack rate should be used as a positioning rate. Rack rates provide the consumer and travel intermediary with a perception of the quality level of the hotel in relationship to its competition and all other hotels in a given market. Rack rates are the standard from which other rates are discounted. In general, the broadest range is desirable for rack rates, beginning with a property's least desirable room category (at its full, non-discounted price) and topping out with its best rooms priced slightly above its nearest competitors. This broad range creates the perception of the hotel as the best hotel in the marketplace and allows for revenue maximization through controlled sale and inventory of the lowest-priced non-discounted rooms. These lowest-priced non-discounted rooms should be advertised in automated systems, directories, and on-line services and entered in the central reservations system.

Preferred. Also known as a preferred corporate rate, a **preferred rate** is a specific amount charged to a volume consumer of rooms. Preferred rates are lower than corporate rates. There may be—and should be—many different preferred rates. Usually, the higher the room volume that a company consumes, the lower the preferred rate the company is charged.

Because a hotel may have many different corporate rates, preferred rates should be referred to by the name of the company or organization to which each rate has been provided, such as the "IBM rate," the "3M rate," or the "Nestlé rate."

Super-Saver. The **super-saver** is a rate that should be lower than the corporate rate and used for rate resisters (people seeking lower rates) or as a discounted promotional rate to attract guests when conditions merit. The super-saver can and should be used to fill empty rooms during valley periods or days. Like rack rates, super-savers help maximize revenue by filling what would otherwise be empty (zero-revenue) rooms. This rate also should be used to win business from the competition.

The super-saver rate can be changed as needed. It can be offered to any market segment and is usually capacity-controlled—that is, applied to a limited number of rooms in the inventory. It is the responsibility of the general manager to close off this category daily or hourly if necessary.

Weekend. Weekend rates are those in effect for weekends, meaning Friday, Saturday, and Sunday. These are flat room rates (that is, the rates do not vary depending on the number of guests staying in the room). Depending on the market and local events, this room category can be closed off for any day or period. For instance, a manager may wish to close this category on Sundays in a high Sunday-arrival market, which may be the case for football weekends or other events. Weekend rates should be promotionally oriented: they should be set at fixed amounts of $59, $69, $79, or $89 (and so forth), which lend themselves to being advertised effectively.

Summer. Usually in effect from Memorial Day to Labor Day, summer rates are promoted to attract summer vacationers. These vacationers usually belong to a specific market: families. Summer rates can be either flat room rates or person rates (that is, rates that vary with the number of guests staying in the room). The rates are flexible and capacity-controlled, based on local market conditions. The category can be open or closed at the discretion of the hotel. Because it is a promotional rate, the summer rate type should be of the $59, $69, $79, or $89 (and so forth) variety.

Club-Level. This rate is assigned to rooms located on the club floors, executive floors, or concierge-attended areas. This is a premium rate that is higher than the rack or corporate rates for the same room type on a non-club-level floor. To vie with other hotels that also have club or tower floors, a hotel's rate should be competitive, but in line with the hotel's total positioning strategy.

Other Rates

The following additional rates apply to very specific markets:

- *Package plans* provide rates for a room plus other items, such as meals, amenities, or a car.

- *Contracted rates* apply to rooms contracted for a period of more than 30 days. These may be airline crew rooms, relocation rooms, or training rooms, (if not preferred rate rooms or another category).

- *Seasonal rates* incorporate premiums added or subtracted based on the desirability of the locale due to climate. These rates are usually set for in-season or peak periods, out-of-season or off-peak periods, and "shoulder" periods (the periods between peak and off-peak seasons).

- *Group rates* are based on volume or length of stay.

- *Suite rates* vary. At the lower end, a hotel can be competitive; at the upper end, the property can strive for top dollar and positioning as the best hotel.

- *Government rates* are based on the market, competition, and need for business from government-sector employees.

- *Retirees or military personnel* are often given a lower rate. This rate is applied to a limited capacity or number of rooms allocated for these market segments.

Exhibit 1   Hotel Room Rate Categories

	Standard Room	Superior Room	Deluxe Room
Rack	$155*	$125	$145
Club-Level	135	145	164
Corporate	95*	105	115
Corporate Club	115	125	135
Super-Saver	89†		

*Rate published in airline terminals and directories.
†Rate which is managed and controlled by hotel and is used to sell empty rooms in "valley" or down periods.

Ranges

Ranges of rates should be used in the following rate categories: corporate, rack, club-level, and any other category for which there is not a flat room rate. Ranges should be broad to allow for selling up or down within the range. As mentioned earlier in the discussion of the corporate rate, a hotel should publicize the low end of the range (for example, "$99 and up") in the automated reservations system, directories, and other listings in cases where the listing space does not allow the hotel to offer the full range. Ranges may relate to various criteria, such as room types, locations, and views (see Exhibit 1).

Rate Strategies

A hotel's managers must oversee and control the property's rate categories. Management must know when to open or close these categories and must effectively control or limit the number of rooms in each rate category. Managers must also understand how to take full advantage of rate ranges. They must know how to establish rates to meet current market segments' needs, as well as how to use these rates to solicit increased business from additional, desirable markets. Effective rate strategies can help managers accomplish such goals.

Examples. The following examples of rate strategies are based on the grid-positioning concept. A property's position on the grid is a function of both the strength of its market and the position of its product within the market. This grid position helps determine what actions should be taken with respect to rate strategies (see Exhibit 2).

Strategy 1: Strong Market/Strong Product

- Maximize rates in periods of strong demand (sell up and/or raise rates).
- Stay ahead of the competition in servicing accounts.
- Use the hotel's quality to win business in valley periods at competitive rates.
- Move business to days or periods of lower demand.

Exhibit 2 Competitive/Market Positioning Grid

		MARKET		
		Strong	Moderate	Weak
COMPETITIVE POSITIONING	**Strong**	1 Strong Market Strong Product	2 Moderate Market Strong Product	3 Weak Market Strong Product
	Average	4 Strong Market Average Product	5 Moderate Market Average Product	6 Weak Market Average Product
	Weak	7 Strong Market Weak Product	8 Moderate Market Weak Product	9 Weak Market Weak Product

Strategy 2: Moderate Market/Strong Product

• Strive for market share via competitive pricing.

• Capture better (rate) market segments for the future.

• Use product strength to sell up.

• Don't price the hotel out of the market.

Strategy 3: Weak Market/Strong Product

• Go after repeat business by building loyalty. (Also, "Love thy intermediary.")

• Build the base—shrink the empties. As you build your base of rooms sold, it allows you to begin selling the remaining rooms at higher prices. Go for *all* the business!

• Use several different pricing strategies that relate specifically to different market segments.

Strategy 4: Strong Market/Average Product

• Price slightly below competitors to gain market share.

• Go after the value-oriented market—that is, the segments that are more price-sensitive but that still want a high-quality facility.

- Be sure the hotel's product is sold and perceived as an acceptable alternative: not as the most expensive, but as the best.

- Capture a corporate or preferred "base"—then sell up.

Strategy 5: Moderate Market/Average Product

- Go after market share with lead promotions and rates.

- Distinguish the hotel's product in the minds of a specific market segment, and *own* that segment.

- Price the product to the public as number two, but concentrate heavily on selling corporate and super-saver rates (as a better value by stressing price).

- Give a reason to come back—provide an incentive such as "an upgrade to club floor on your next visit."

Strategy 6: Weak Market/Average Product

- Go after competitors—take advantage of their weaknesses. Win over their business via pricing.

- Go after all market segments by using short-term promotions.

- Create new market segments or reasons to stay (such as local festivals or special events, and so on).

- Shrink the product or rooms base. Seek contracted rooms (such as those for airline crews) that provide revenue and reduce the number of rooms available in the inventory. This allows you to sell remaining rooms at a higher price.

Strategy 7: Strong Market/Weak Product

- Maximize rate on high demand days.

- Promote relatively lower rates on weak demand days.

- Consider upgrading your product and raising rates.

In positions 8 and 9, rate strategy will be of little or no value, as the combination of weak product and lack of demand suggests selling the hotel. In position 8, if the market is expected to move from moderate to strong, consider upgrading the product and following position 7 strategies.

Rate Comparisons

You can keep track of your competitors' rates by reviewing their advertisements, calling their toll-free numbers, looking up their published rates on automated systems, and talking to your customers to determine if your rates are in line. One of the benefits of knowing the competition's rates is that this information enables a manager to assess his or her rate strategy and implement new strategies if required. Exhibit 3 is an example of a weekly intelligence sheet format, and Exhibit 4 shows a similar format filled in. Many hotel managers regularly chart information about their competitors' rates on a sheet such as this so they can effectively develop rate strategies.

Exhibit 3   Sample Weekly Intelligence Sheet Format

RATES 800 Tel. No.	Competitor I	Competitor II	Competitor III	Competitor IV	Your Hospitality Hotel	
Rack	$ -$	$ -$	$ -$	$ -$	$ -$	
Corporate	$	$	$	$	$ -$	-$
Corporate Club	$	$	$	$	$ -$	-$
Super-Saver	$	$	$	$	$	-$
Hotel Direct Tel. No.						
Rack	$ -$	$ -$	$ -$	$ -$	$ -$	
Corporate	$	$	$	$	$ -$	-$
Corporate Club	$	$	$	$	$ -$	-$
Super-Saver	$	$	$	$	$	
Weekend	$	$	$	$	$	

Questions

1. Are we competitively priced?
2. What are the publicized rates in airline terminals?
3. Are we positioning our hotel correctly?
4. What actions should be taken immediately?

Airfares

The principles of rate strategy for air carriers are not very different from those for hotels. Where hotels deal with occupied rooms, average rates, and rooms revenue, airlines deal with load factors (occupied seats), average revenue per passenger mile, and passenger revenues. Instead of the term "rate," airlines use the terms "fare" or "tariff." There is general consistency among airlines in their use of symbols and definitions, although frequently the fine-print **disclaimers** and restrictions vary by carrier.

Overview of Fares

It is often said—in jest—that every passenger on an aircraft pays a different fare; in truth, such a statement is not as preposterous as you might think.

Airline customers comprise a heterogeneous group, but people typically travel either for business or for pleasure. The airlines, therefore, adopt a marketing strategy that makes it very difficult for business travelers to take advantage of special holiday fares, while at the same time maintaining their competitiveness in the leisure market.

Exhibit 4   Sample Filled In Weekly Intelligence Sheet

	Competitor I	Competitor II	Competitor III	Competitor IV	Hospitality Hotel
General					
Rack	$100 -$125	$105 -$135	$110 -$140	$115 -$155	*$100 -$165
Corporate	$ 95	$ 95	$101	$103	*$ 98 -$103 -$108
Corporate Club	$105	$115	$120	$122	$118 -$123 -$128
Super-Saver	$ 85	$ 89	$ 95	$ 99	$ 88
Corporate*					
City I	$ 79	$100	$120	$135	*$ 98 -$108 -$128
City II	$115	$118	$119	$130	*$115 -$125 -$135
City III	$ 86	$ 95	$105	$105	*$ 95 -$105 -$115
City IV	$ 89	$ 98	$ 99	N/A	$ 99 -$104 -$109
Corporate*					
City V	$ 92	$ 91	$ 81	N/A	*$ 79 -$ 89 -$ 99†
City VI	$ 79	$ 86	N/A	N/A	*$ 85 -$ 95 -$105†

*Publicized rate in airline terminals.
†Not best product—Here we have better hotels with which to compete.

Generally speaking, airlines want business travelers to pay an amount at or near the so-called "full coach fare." This fare is the regular fare quoted for travel from Point A to Point B, and it has no restrictions. Full-coach fare can be purchased at any time until (close to) departure time, it is fully refundable, it allows a reservation to be changed at any time without penalty, it has no minimum or maximum stay, and it is valid for one-way or return travel (the return fare is usually double the one-way fare). You can buy a full-coach fare on one airline for your outbound flight and return on a different airline at the same full-coach fare. In short, you can do whatever you want with a full-coach fare.

For example, imagine that a sales associate working for a large firm in New York gets a call on a Monday afternoon from a potential buyer in Los Angeles interested in purchasing a large quantity of her company's product. The buyer would like meet with the sales associate on Tuesday in Los Angeles to see some samples. Thus, on Monday afternoon, the sales associate would need to arrange for a flight on Tuesday from New York to Los Angeles, with just one day advance notice. Also, she would like to come home either on the overnight flight Tuesday or first thing Wednesday morning. This sales associate would almost certainly be required to purchase a full coach-fare ticket given these circumstances, which are representative of many business travelers' plans.

Suppose on the other hand that a college student in New York wants to return home to Los Angeles for spring break. The dates of the spring break are known well in advance, and the student will stay home for about one week. This student would generally be able to take advantage of some special fares offered by the airline, since he would meet the rather common special fare restrictions of advance purchase time (usually one, two, or three weeks) and a minimum stay requirement (usually a Saturday night). The college student might pay 75 percent less than the full coach fare paid by the business traveler, even though they may end up on the same flight.

Understanding Fares

One-Way or Round Trip. Some fares are published as one-way fares, which you may use to travel in one direction. If you prefer, you can pay twice the one-way fare and travel round trip.

Many fares are published as round-trip fares. Often a round-trip fare costs less than twice a one-way fare and, indeed, often less than a single one-way fare. Round-trip fares generally have more restricted fare rules.

If you are traveling one way only, it may be less expensive to buy a round-trip fare. Remember that you may not get a refund for the unused portion of your ticket.

The Dollar Amount (Plus Tax). The dollar amount of a published fare is what is known as the base fare. This amount goes to the airline. On top of the base fare, you must pay a variety of taxes and surcharges. Most online travel products quote the fares including all taxes. The standard federal U.S. tax is eight percent. Some airports charge what are called passenger facility charges (PFC) for all passengers going through those airports. These funds are directed to airport improvements. A federal excise tax of $2 per segment is also applicable on most tickets. International travel results in additional taxes from other countries.

The Class of Service Required for Booking. To understand this very important point, we must introduce the concept of inventory control. To be profitable, an airline is not likely to allow all seats on the aircraft to be available at special fare rates, even if every passenger could meet the necessary restrictions. In other words, the airline allocates only a certain number of seats at each fare level for each flight. The number of seats allocated at each fare level depends on many factors, such as the route involved, the time of year, the usual business/leisure passenger breakdown on that route, the time of day, etc. Airlines have inventory control departments to determine how many seats are allocated at each fare on each flight. For example, in the case of the college student, if his flight of choice was already heavily booked, all of the special fares may be sold out at the time he makes a reservation, although the flight itself may still have some seats available at the full-coach fare. The student would then have to choose a different flight or elect to pay the full fare (or some fare between).

In airline reservation computer systems, the allocation of seats at different fare categories is accomplished through the use of "class-of-service" codes. Do not confuse these codes with the actual class of service (e.g., first-class, business-class, coach). While first-class and business-class do have their own class-of-service codes, many different class-of-service codes are used for the coach cabin, even though all of the passengers sit in the same place. For example, the business

Exhibit 5   Airline Service Fares and Related Symbols

A	First class discounted
B	Coach/economy discounted
Bn	Controlled inventory or limited number of seats available—night coach rate (usually after 9, 10, or 11 P.M., depending on carrier)
C	Business class: a class of service and related fare between first class and coach, aimed at the international business traveler
Cn	Night or off-peak (peak travel hours/days) business class
D	Business class discounted
F	First-class service, usually the highest fare (generally synonymous with P below)
Fn	Night/off-peak coach in first-class compartment (a lower-than-usual first-class fare that allows seating in first class)
H	Coach economy discounted
J	Business-class premium
K	Thrift: usually capacity-controlled or offered in off-peak hours; a fare lower than coach
L	Thrift discounted
M	Coach economy discounted
P	First-class premium
Q	Coach economy discounted
Qn	Night coach economy discounted
R	Supersonic
S	Standard class
T	Coach economy discounted
U	No reservation services/baggage check limitations
V	Thrift discounted
Vn	Night thrift discounted
Y	Coach economy
Yn	Night/off-peak coach in other than first-class compartment

traveler and the college student may sit next to each other in the coach cabin, even though their reservations were made with different class-of-service codes.

Generally speaking, first-class is coded as F or P, business class as C or J, and full-fare coach as Y. Most special fares (referred to as subclasses, since they are sub-classes of the coach class) are coded using other letters, such as M, B, H, K, Q, L, V, etc. Each airline typically has a hierarchical structure for the subclass codes—e.g., on one airline, the order is generally MBHVQL, where M is usually close to a full Y fare and L is usually a deeply discounted fare. However, the hierarchical structure varies from airline to airline (e.g., on another airline, M may be heavily dis-counted). Exhibit 5 provides a comprehensive sample list of codes and services.

When checking whether a particular flight is available, what you really want to know is what classes are available? If you are looking for a low fare requiring booking in Q class, you must find a flight for which Q class is available. If Q class is sold out on that flight, you will have to pay a higher fare to take that flight, or choose another flight.

The Fare Basis Code. The fare basis code provides information about the specific fare in addition to the class of service required for booking. Every published fare has a fare basis code, and this code appears on the ticket in the fare basis box. More than one fare, and thus more than one fare basis code, may exist for each class of service for booking. For example, two fares for H class may exist, one for midweek travel and one for weekend travel.

Consider a return fare across the country with fare basis code HL7LNR. The first letter H refers to the class of service for booking (H class). The L refers to low season, the 7 refers to the requirement for 7-day advance booking, the next L refers to long haul, and the NR means non-refundable. The fare would presumably be different if it were 14-days in advance or if it were high season. In that case, both the fare and the fare basis code would be different. Often you will see the letters X or W, referring to midweek or weekend travel, respectively. You will never be required to make inferences about fare rules based on fare basis codes. The fare rules are specifically spelled out, and a whole section is dedicated to fare rules. What you should understand is that every fare has a unique fare basis code and that one class-of-service booking class can have more than one fare associated with it.

The Fare Rules. An entire section of this book could be dedicated to fare rules. In simple terms, every published fare also has a published set of fare rules. These rules govern the conditions that must be met for a passenger to qualify for this fare. These conditions may include, for example, advance purchase requirements, minimum and maximum stay requirements, day-of-week restrictions, time-of-day restrictions, routing restrictions, season restrictions, change penalties, cancellation penalties, etc. See Exhibit 6 for the basics of fare rules.

In the case of the business traveler going from New York to Los Angeles, she travels at the full coach fare in seat 18A. She booked her reservation in Y class, with a fare basis code of either Y or something like Y26 or YUA. If the fare basis code is Y alone, the ticket is transferable between airlines without any hassles. Other fare basis codes beginning in Y are usually airline-specific, but may cost less than the full Y coach fare. Our college friend, on the other hand, travels with a fare code of ME721NR, with booking in M class 21 days in advance, and sits in seat 18B.

Carrier Strategies

The large number of fares shown in Exhibit 5 suggests the broad spectrum of rate strategies that air carriers use to achieve market share. These strategies range from offering all first-class services to offering all deep-discount services, with virtually every variation in between. Some carriers select a strategy for competitive reasons, others because of their market position or even based on the hour of departure per flight.

In essence, revenue management for airlines is similar to that for hotels or any other business. The bottom line on the revenue side is to maximize revenue per

Exhibit 6   Fare Rules—The Basics

Booking Code	A letter code assigned to identify the booking class for a fare. Using booking classes, the airlines control how many seats on each flight are available for each (e.g., F, P, J, C, Y, B, M, Q, V, H, L).
Penalty	The percent or dollar amount of the fare that is not refunded. Sometimes the value of the ticket can be used as a credit for future travel. Sometimes tickets are not re-saleable or refundable—there's a 100% penalty.
Res/Ticketing	The day in advance the reservation must be made (e.g., 7, 14, 21 days in advance), and when the ticket is actually issued.
Minimum Stay	A restriction on length of stay, such as, "must stay over a Saturday night" (often stated technically as "return travel valid on the 1st Sun. after 12:01 A.M.").
Maximum Stay	A restriction on length of stay, such as 30 days, 60 days, 365 days
Day/Time	Some fares are valid only on particular days of the week, or at particular times. For example, some fares are valid Mon–Thurs. Only, or from 7:00 P.M.–6:00 A.M. only.
Season	Some fares, particularly overseas fares, have an associated season (e.g., 15SEP–12DEC). For overseas travel, usually the departure date determines the season for the round-trip fare.
Blackout Days	Some fares are not valid on certain dates (e.g., over a holiday weekend).
Eff/Exp	Effective/Expires: Many seat sale fares must be purchased by a certain date.
Flt Appl	Certain fares are valid only for particular flights (e.g., nonstop only, or flight 123 only).

flight—in other words, to get the highest yield (of revenue) out of each seat or each flight. How this yield is achieved—whether by selling many seats at lower prices or fewer seats at higher prices—is fairly well defined as the selected marketing strategy of the carrier.

Other factors that affect airlines' strategies and have counterparts in hotels are labor costs, fleet and size of aircraft (analogous to the size of a hotel), and route structure (analogous to hotel location). Then there is the consumer: the consumer who is loyal to a brand or carrier responds to the price and level or quality of service based on his or her changing needs. An air traveler on a business expense account may be willing to pay for an upgrade, while that same person traveling with his or her family may consider price to override upgrade desires. When airfare wars break out, the consumer benefits. The airline that "wins" is usually the carrier with deeper pockets (that can absorb more losses). The loser is the less financially stable carrier.

Rental Car Rates

How rental car rates are presented often depends on who is applying the rates, as well as the day(s), rental period, and time of the year during which a car is rented.

The following is a general overview of the types of rental car rates and the factors affecting the rates.

- *Weekday.* Usually applied Monday through Thursday, this rate generally is a premium rate (except in the case of a weekend destination location, for which a weekend rate may be the premium rate).

- *Weekend.* This rate is usually in effect for Friday, Saturday, and Sunday. (Many define it as noon on Thursday through noon on Monday.) In most locations, a substantially discounted rate is offered on weekends.

- *Daily.* Usually one of the highest rate categories, this rate is applied if the car is rented for a 12- or 24-hour period only. (Hourly rates, if offered, are usually at a premium over daily rates.)

- *2-, 3-, 4-, or 5-day.* Rental firms often offer some form of discounted rate based on the number of days (12- or 24-hour periods) for which a car is rented.

- *Weekly.* This rate is discounted based on a 5-, 6-, or 7-day rental.

- *Monthly.* This discounted rate is applied to long-term rentals.

- *Corporate.* This rate is usually a 10- or 20-percent (or deeper) discount, based on a company's levels of use.

- *Preferred corporate.* Rental firms may offer even deeper discounts to corporations that are frequent users. Discounts of 30 percent and even more are common.

- *Class of car.* Rental rates vary based on the type of auto—popular classes are luxury, standard, compact, and subcompact. (One problem with using this rating is that not all firms' definitions of each car type are the same.)

- *Other rates.* Holiday specials, seasonal rates (in Florida, for example), and event-related rates (such as for the Super Bowl) can also be developed and offered.

Rental Car Strategies

With all the variations available in rental periods, classes of cars, special rates, and upgrades, rental car strategies are plentiful. Some firms rent luxury-class vehicles at standard-class rates or at fixed rates—"Lincolns at $59.95," for example. Others opt for straight price sells only—"$29.00 a day." Still others may use service as their marketing pitch—"No lines. We'll meet you at the baggage claim with your rental car."

There are charge-per-mile and free-unlimited-mileage marketing options as well. These strategies depend on competition and other variables such as fuel costs, days used, distance traveled, and other factors.

The location(s) and number of rental points is a strong factor in brand selection. As is true with airlines and hotels, brand loyalty in the rental car industry is a function of price and service in meeting challenging and changing consumer needs. Just as occupied seats or occupied rooms are critical to revenue production for airlines and hotels, rented units per day for rental car firms are also critical.

Whether the break-even point is achieved through volume, price, or a combination of both factors, the strategies include the same components: rate setting, rate management, and maximization of revenue.

Cruise Ship Rates

Cruise rate options and strategies depend largely on the itineraries and configuration of the specific ship. In general, cruises are priced according to the number of days/nights—for example, "5 days/4 nights." The rate is usually inclusive—that is, it includes three meals per day. In addition, the rate will vary based on a particular ship's cabin or room layout. Generally, the higher-level cabins or rooms with outside views will command maximum rates, while lower-deck, inside cabins will be the least expensive.

Key Terms

corporate rate—A discounted rate given to a company because of its volume usage.

disclaimer—Usually a statement in fine print that defines the conditions of an offer.

preferred rate—A specially discounted rate for a frequent customer—usually based on volume and set lower than the corporate rate(s).

restrictions—Limitations and requirements that must be adhered to in order to qualify for an offer; for example, "Tickets must be purchased three days in advance."

super-saver—A popular term for a deeply discounted rate or fare.

Chapter 17 Outline

Pricing Techniques
    Technique 1: Offering a Price Range
    Technique 2: Selling Up
    Technique 3: Selling Down
    Technique 4: Focusing on Revenue and
        Profit per Unit
    Technique 5: Using the Inflation Rate-
        Plus Factor
    Technique 6: Using Intuitive Judgment
        and Flexible Breakeven Analysis
    Technique 7: Rate Pyramiding
    Technique 8: Analyzing Market
        Segments

Competencies

1. Define "pricing," and explain the importance of offering consumers price ranges and choices in hospitality products and services. (pp. 233–235)

2. Explain the concept of selling up and some general circumstances under which the technique may be applied. (pp. 235–236)

3. Describe the cost-plus theory and its application in selling down. (pp. 236–237)

4. Compare the technique of focusing on revenue and profit per unit to that of emphasizing average checks/rates/percentages. (p. 237)

5. Summarize the use of the inflation rate-plus factor. (pp. 237–238)

6. Explain the importance of making intuitive judgments, and outline the concepts and steps for conducting a breakeven analysis. (pp. 238–239)

7. Describe the uses of rate pyramiding. (pp. 239–240)

8. Explain how analyzing market segments can help maximize revenue for a hospitality operation. (pp. 240–241)

17

Applying Key Marketing Methodologies: Pricing Strategies

THE GAMUT OF MARKETING TACTICS extends beyond generating revenue through sales, advertising, public relations, promotions, direct mail, and packaging. The ultimate generator of revenue and profit is pricing. Pricing is the application of rates in a selective manner to generate sales.

Once you have a base of business for your hospitality product and service, the challenge becomes how to maximize revenues and profits, build beyond the base, and gain every possible benefit from your marketing efforts. The keys to achieving success are a creative mind, a practical perspective, and a willingness to work hard at implementing ideas. Inherent in these three characteristics is a willingness to listen to new ideas and, when necessary, to discard traditional beliefs and measures of hospitality industry success.

Pricing Techniques

Pricing can be used to maximize revenue and profit. The eight techniques described in this chapter offer a broad selection of effective tools that you can use to better focus and maximize your marketing efforts.

Technique 1: Offering a Price Range

For years, Marriott and Hilton have done an outstanding job of offering a price range for their rooms. They give the consumer a choice of rates from which to select. This multi-rate structure permits the consumer to select a rate from within a range. For instance, a reservations agent might state, "We have rooms available from $119 to $159." A price-conscious consumer can ask for the $119 room. A consumer who is not interested in the cheapest rate might ask for a room at $129. Guests who are not concerned at all with rate (perhaps individual travelers on unrestricted expense accounts) may well opt for rooms at $149 or $159. Using a price range allows a hotel to sell essentially the same room at different rates.

Offering a range is the basic starting point in increasing revenue per room. A trained reservations agent can attempt to "sell up"—that is, attempt to persuade the guest to select a room at a rate above the minimum. For example, a reservations

233

agent might say, "We still have rooms available at $139 and $149" and the guest might take one of these rates. The hotel may well have sold the same room for $119 had the reservations agent not sold up. If the guest resists and says, "Don't you have any rooms at the $119 rate?" the agent could respond, "Let me check…yes, I can make a room available to you that evening for $119."

Other chains have believed that publicizing and honoring a fixed rate for single and double rooms is the strongest promise they could make to the consumer.

The following example looks at one such chain and determines the impact of selling up by using a price range instead of stating the fixed rates. (For illustrative purposes, this first example makes broad assumptions that are not intended to represent actual financial results. This example is used solely to point out the potential advantages in using ranges of rates from which consumers can select.)

Example: Chain A—Price Ranges. With 300,000 rooms, Chain A is one of the world's largest hotel chains. This example assumes that the chain's occupancy averages 70 percent, resulting in 210,000 rooms that are occupied on a nightly basis. There will be a number of nights during the year for which occupancy is 100 percent. Let's conservatively assume that selling up can occur in half of the locations only 50 times (nights) during the year. The 210,000 occupied rooms per night thus is reduced to 105,000, multiplied by 50 nights on which rooms can be sold up. Therefore:

105,000 eligible rooms × 50 potential sell-up nights = 5,250,000 sell-up room nights

What if, rather than stating a fixed single and double rate, Chain A chose to go to price ranges and trained its front desk personnel to sell up? Assume this selling-up process resulted in only $1.50 more in rate on the average room per night. Multiply $1.50 by 5,250,000 room nights. The result would mean an additional $7,875,000 each year in room revenue. Moreover, this money essentially drops to the bottom line; assuming a profit ratio of four percent of total revenue, sales would have to increase by $197 million to generate the same amount of profit.

Offering a price range is a simple technique that maximizes profits through marketing. The technique offers the consumer a choice of rates, and human nature sees to it that the low rate is not always selected. There are many methods by which to establish price ranges; for example, hotels may vary rates based on room amenities, location, view, floor, furnishings, and so forth. The important point is to offer the choice and benefit for the customer's selection.

Even if the rate range is narrow ($72–$78), you can still realize the benefits by ensuring that the low end of the range is equivalent to the fixed rate you normally would request. This helps eliminate the risk in using ranges, because the low end of the range is identical to the fixed published rate, and both are equally available and accessible to the consumer.

The way to maintain a firm promise to the consumer and still have the ability to offer a price range can be shown using Chain A in another example.

Example: Chain A—Consumer Choices. Perhaps because the chain believed in the value of the promise of charging its stated rate but recognized the need to maximize room revenues, Chain A changed its approach to room rates and began offering consumers a selection of rooms and rates.

Chain A's approach was to do away with the traditional single- and double-room classifications and stated rate. The chain decided to offer customers three choices: "special" (priced at the low end of the rate range), "standard" (priced in the middle of the rate range), and "king leisure" (the top-price rooms, all containing a king-size bed). The hotels now had some ability to maximize room revenue through the consumer's selection of accommodation.

This approach to categorizing the rooms also relates to the different needs and desires of different market segments. The "special" category appeals to older clientele, retirees, and those on restricted expense allowances; the "standard" appeals to the broader spectrum of the market; and the "king leisure" attracts executive travelers, weekenders, escape-weekend couples, and those whose height requires a larger bed. While most rooms fell into the "standard" category, this approach still offered the consumer a choice of rooms and the operator the ability to offer a price range.

Technique 2: Selling Up

Making money is seldom easy. It frequently requires hard work, sound research, and good timing. The hard work includes keeping records, analyzing data, plotting trends, identifying the right timing, and doing your homework. All of these tasks play an important role in the technique called **selling up**. As stated earlier, selling up is seeking to obtain a higher price for a room, selling a higher profit margin item, or simply seeking a premium price when demand favors the seller. Selling up has many applications; it can mean promoting a higher-priced item on a menu or offering a higher-priced vacation. The example that follows may include some ideas that can help you make money by selling up.

Example: The Well-Trained Food Server. Dimitri owned an upscale restaurant and always managed to show better profit margins and higher check averages than his competitors. His technique for achieving this exceptional performance was called "recognition, recommendation, and results," or the "3 Rs."

Dimitri trained his food service staff to recognize regular customers and those trying to impress others. He instructed his personnel first to ask which entrees interested the customer the most. Depending on the response, the food server was then to take one of three courses of action:

- If the choice of entrée was a high-priced, high-profit item, the food server was to agree with the customer's selection by saying, "An excellent choice this evening—we have had many compliments on that."

- If the choice was a mid-priced item with a relatively low profit margin, the food server's response was simply, "That is a superb dish; however, tonight I would highly recommend [name of the same entrée as in the first action above]." If customer resistance or indecision was noted due to the price of the recommendation, an interjection was then appropriate: "May I also recommend [name of an alternate mid-priced item with a high profit margin]? It is really outstanding this evening."

• The third approach was reserved for the potential high spender who just could not make up his or her mind. It was called the "Dimitri recommendation." In this situation, the food server was instructed to say, "Please take your time to make your selection. I'll be right back." Then Dimitri would appear, introduce himself, welcome his guests, and, of course, provide his personal recommendation for the menu item with the highest profit margin. Who could resist the owner's recommendation? The recognition of the opportunity to sell up and the use of the recommendation resulted in the third "R": results.

Technique 3: Selling Down

More and more travelers today are seeking the "best" value—which often translates into the best price or lowest rate. "Selling down" works to address the price-oriented guest or "rate resister." The premise is that by using a rate range and quoting a rate in the mid to upper portion of the range, you can sell down to accommodate the rate resister. For example:

> *Guest:* "What are your rates for Tuesday?"
>
> *Agent:* "We have rooms available at $139, $149, and $159."
>
> *Guest:* "That's too much. Don't you have any lower rates?"
>
> *Agent:* "Let me check. Yes, I do have a few rooms available that night at our lowest rate of $119."

The premise behind selling down is that revenue in excess of cost is desirable, even if average rate or profit margins decline. Knowing periods of weak demand for your product or service and knowing your fixed costs are essential elements in successfully applying this technique.

The **cost-plus theory** simply states that revenue in excess of the cost of the unused product or service (an airline seat, hotel room, bus seat, etc.) is desirable. The following example shows how the cost-plus theory can be put to work.

Example: Cost-Plus Theory. A 200-room budget motel owner charted his occupancy pattern and analyzed his costs per room. He discovered that for four months a year, his property never exceeded 50-percent occupancy. He further learned that his average fixed cost per room (that is, the cost to him whether the room was occupied or not) was $6. He then calculated the incremental or variable costs (costs that are incurred only when a room is occupied, such as linen laundry and utilities) at $4 per room. His total costs therefore were $10 per occupied room. The motel's single-room rate was $32 to $38 per night.

The owner recognized that for four months of the year, half his rooms were empty and costing him $6 per night. Applying the cost-plus theory, he solicited business for the four-month period with a special program. *New* customers who stayed in his motel during the slack period were offered single rooms for $20 a night, if they stayed three to six nights; $18 a night, if they stayed seven to ten nights; and $15 per night, if they stayed 11 or more nights.

The results were dramatic—occupancy went up to 68 percent for the four-month period. His average daily rate (ADR) and his profit ratio went down, but his actual profits went up. Furthermore, when the program ended, the owner was able to retain more than 40 percent of the newcomers as regular repeat guests at the standard rates. He was not only covering his costs and earning excess revenues during slow periods, he was also converting trial business into repeat business.

Technique 4: Focusing on Revenue and Profit per Unit

In the previous example, the motel owner's competitors may have turned away low-rate rooms business because it diluted the average rate. If that were the case, what actually occurred was that they lost an opportunity to generate revenue. Such an overemphasis on average checks, rate, or percentages can become counterproductive. Unless your product or service is in constant strong demand and in a strong market area, focusing instead on revenue and profit *per unit* is a technique that can help you.

The revenue and profit per unit technique maximizes total revenues and total profits per unit. In the case of a lodging facility, the unit may be the available or occupied room. In the case of a food service facility, the unit may be a seat. Focusing on revenue and profit per unit is critical where the unused unit (room, airline seat, bus seat, and so on) is a perishable item. This means that once the night is over or the plane has left or the bus has pulled out, the fixed costs per unit remain, but the opportunity to generate per-unit revenue is gone, and zero revenue and less overall profit are the results.

For example, assume that a hotel has fixed costs of $20 per room per night and an average daily rate of $89. An empty room not only produces no revenue, it costs $20. Therefore, it makes sense to sell rooms that would otherwise go unused at a discount, even though the discount reduces the ADR. Selling unused rooms in this hotel for, say, $49 results in a lower ADR, but in greater total revenue and profit.

Technique 5: Using the Inflation Rate-Plus Factor

For many years a large national chain that relied on royalty revenue from room sales was concerned about its franchisees' lack of aggressiveness in raising rates. Many of the franchisees were absentee owners; some were looking for tax write-offs, and others lacked business sense.

The chain published a directory twice a year and solicited new rates prior to printing the new directory. An analysis of the return cards from the franchisees revealed that a large group consistently raised their rates five percent every six months. Another smaller group raised their room rates only for the January directory and indicated "no change" for the June directory. When the inflation rate was very low, the chain's concern was not very intense; however, in one 12-month period, the inflation rate jumped over 12 percent and the ramifications started to become apparent. The buying power of the royalty revenue and fees based on rooms revenue began to shrink dramatically. The costs for media, personnel, supplies, and so on were increasing at double the rate of the inflow of incremental royalty fees. The company realized it needed to take action.

Using the **inflation rate-plus factor,** the chain began an intensive program to educate its franchisees that their rates should increase in proportion to the inflation rate factor for costs associated with their facilities. The *plus* concept suggested that increasing rates beyond the inflation rate factor (where demand allowed) would enhance the profit margin.

This program worked well, but timing was another factor. The chain needed the franchisees to provide rate changes 90 days in advance of directory publication, and these rates were in effect for six months. Even if the franchisees were conscientious and raised their rates, by the time the directory was published, three percent was lost to inflation (based on the 12-percent inflation factor). Also, by the time the directory rates were replaced six months later, an additional six percent would have been lost to inflation.

To help alleviate this problem, the chain's management invested in an alternate printing schedule and directory format that cut the 90-day lead-time to 30 days. In addition, the chain went from publishing two directories per year to four. Publication costs went up, but were more than covered by the increase in the incremental royalty revenues being received.

Technique 6: Using Intuitive Judgment and Flexible Breakeven Analysis

Establishing the most effective price to charge for your product or service is based on many factors. The local market and competition will, in all likelihood, prove to be dominant factors in influencing a pricing decision. However, the local market conditions and your need to break even need not overly restrict your judgment or creativity in establishing a pricing strategy. Frequently, the most important factors in selecting the optimum rate or pricing strategy will come from your own intuitive judgment about what will work best for the product or service in view of the local market and competition.

Once the market has been analyzed and the competition profiled, a breakeven analysis is another tool to assist in selecting the optimum pricing strategy. A breakeven analysis is a look at the relationship between total sales and total expenses for an establishment, be it a lodging facility, airplane, or restaurant. Often depicted on a simple graph, such as that shown in Exhibit 1, the analysis demonstrates the effects of changing the levels of total sales in terms of dollars or volumes. The vertical (Y) axis represents revenue. The horizontal (X) axis represents volume in units sold, which can be expressed as occupancy, occupied seats, and so on.

Total costs at the various levels of volume are plotted with a straight line that crosses the Y-axis at the level of fixed costs. In the simplest terms, total costs are a combination of fixed costs (costs that are incurred whether sales occur or not) and variable costs (costs that are incurred only when sales are made). Therefore, at zero sales, total costs equal fixed costs ($18,000 in Exhibit 1); at any level of sales beyond zero, total costs equal fixed costs plus the number of units sold times the variable cost per unit. Total revenue is also entered as a straight line starting at zero on both axes (since, unlike fixed costs that are incurred regardless of sales, revenue is only received as sales are made; that is, zero units sold means zero revenue). The point at which these lines cross represents the breakeven point, the point at which sales are adequate to cover costs. Any point above the total cost line represents profits; any point below the total cost line represents losses. In the sample shown in

Exhibit 1   Sample Breakeven Chart

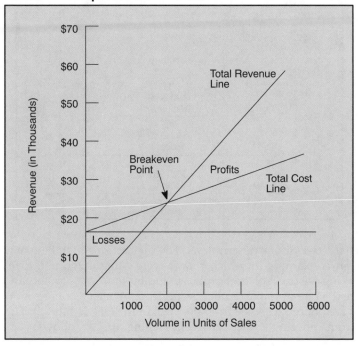

Exhibit 1, the breakeven point can be stated either in dollar volume ($24,000) or in unit volume (2,400 units).

Breakeven charts are useful tools, although they are not always precise. There are also two mathematical equations that can be used to calculate the breakeven points for units or sales.

The breakeven point in units is determined by first subtracting the variable cost per unit from the selling price per unit. The result is then divided into the total fixed costs:

$$\text{Breakeven point in units} = \frac{\text{Total fixed costs}}{\text{Selling price per unit} - \text{variable cost per unit}}$$

To determine the breakeven point in sales, multiply the breakeven point in units by the selling price:

$$\text{Breakeven point in sales} = \text{Breakeven point in units} \times \text{Selling price}$$

With the tools of the basic breakeven chart and the unit and sales equations, you can use the flexible breakeven analysis to establish profit objectives and the required sales revenue to meet these objectives.

Technique 7: Rate Pyramiding

This technique is a hybrid of Technique 1, offering a price range, and Technique 2, selling up. **Rate pyramiding** is segmenting or identifying the product or service by

Exhibit 2   Rate Pyramid

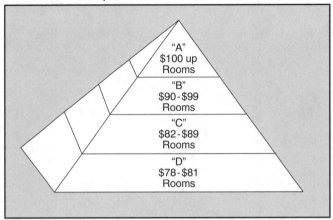

different characteristics or descriptions. The distinctions may be like those in the earlier Chain A example in which rooms were categorized as "special," "standard," or "king leisure," or as simple as "mountain view" or "ocean view." For each category, a rate or range of rates is specified. When customers inquire about a room, they are offered a choice from the "pyramid" (see Exhibit 2). The technique then goes from "offering a price range" to "selling up," as follows:

> *Front desk clerk:* "Welcome to the Clifton Hotel, Mr. Jones."
>
> *Mr. Jones:* "What are your rates?"
>
> *Front desk clerk:* "Our rates range from $78 for an economy room, from $82 for a standard room, from $90 for a deluxe room, and $100 and up for a suite."
>
> *Mr. Jones:* "I'd like an economy room, please."
>
> *Front desk clerk:* "Mr. Jones, we only have an $80 economy room available; however, we do have a very nice $82 standard room that I think you would like. It is in a better location and has a better view of the city."

If Mr. Jones opts for the $82 standard room, he has been "pyramided" up $4 from the $78 economy room he wanted. If he opts for the $80 economy room, he has still been sold up $2. Many people will not ask for an economy room simply because they do not want the cheapest room; usually they do not want the most expensive, either. By offering a pyramid rate structure, you capitalize on this tendency and can directly affect your revenue potential.

Technique 8: Analyzing Market Segments

Another way to view pricing or revenue generation is by the type of business. The mix or types of guests in a facility are not all the same in terms of their needs, desires, and level of expenditures. On one hand, kids may stay free, eat hot dogs, or not eat on your premises at all. On the other hand, a man attending a group meeting may eat a banquet meal, drink in your bar, and buy gifts for his children and spouse in your gift shop. Given a choice of to whom you should sell your room, the decision becomes clearer.

Marriott has been a leader in food and beverage sales in its hotels. While it is true that Marriott creates restaurant concepts that appeal to the local market, it is also true that Marriott's mix of business is heavily oriented toward groups, executives, and corporate meetings. The result of this orientation is that it produces higher revenues throughout the properties.

You do not have to be as sophisticated as Marriott to analyze your market segments and go after the revenue producers. For example, take the case of a local restaurant called Nick's. The restaurant appeals to a broad spectrum of consumers, ranging from families, to office workers, to couples dining out. Nick's faced a choice—a local office supply company wanted to book the banquet room for Friday evening for 15 people for a sales award dinner. At the same time, the River City boys' baseball champions requested the room for 23 boys and 2 adult coaches for a dinner.

Nick's selected the office supply company with only 15 people instead of the baseball champions with the party of 25. The restaurant's analysis revealed that while both groups selected the same item (at the same cost) from the banquet menu, the office supply group was expected to purchase enough alcoholic beverages to more than offset the reduced food revenue from 10 fewer people. The message is simple: Whether you're Marriott or Nick's, go after the high-volume/high-profit producers.

🔑 Key Terms

cost-plus theory—The recognition of the need to price or sell a product or service in periods of low demand by discounting the price beyond fixed and variable cost levels to stimulate sales.

inflation rate-plus factor—A method for increasing rates or prices that is based on the premise that increases in rates should be at the inflation rate plus a percentage target.

rate pyramiding—The concept of offering a variety of rates and/or ranges from which consumers may select; also includes the opportunity to sell up.

selling up—Seeking to obtain a higher price for a room, sell a higher profit margin item, or obtain a premium price when demand favors the seller.

Chapter 18 Outline

Market Mix
     Example: The Church Convention
Pricing
     Example: The Park, the Plaza, and the
        Palace
Yield Management
Revenue Maximization in Practice

Competencies

1. Describe how market mix is used to maximize revenue. (pp. 243–245)

2. Give examples of how pricing strategies are used to maximize revenue. (pp. 245–246)

3. Describe how yield management is used to maximize revenue. (pp. 246–248)

4. Identify objectives, strategies, and key tactics of revenue maximization. (pp. 248–250)

18

Applying Key Marketing Methodologies: Revenue Maximization

Revenue maximization consists of the total management of revenue production. It involves the selection and use of marketing tools to bring in the desired market mix. It also involves researching your market and competition and developing correct pricing for each market segment. And it requires the application of yield management to set rates according to changes in demand and supply patterns. The smooth management of all three processes results in **revenue maximization.**

Market Mix + Pricing + Yield Management = Revenue Maximization

Market Mix

Market mix is the combination of different guest categories that a hotel tries to attract. Before you can manage yield (defined later in the chapter) or set prices, you need to determine the targeted market mix that provides you maximum revenue and profit potential. Research has shown that there are different levels of rate resistance and different on-premises incremental spending patterns for different segments of the market. For example, executives on unrestricted expense accounts or attending corporate group meetings are likely to pay higher room rates and spend more in high-profit areas (the bar, gift shops, etc.) than government employees or those on restricted expense accounts. The same spending differences can be found among leisure travelers. For example, incentive groups usually produce higher revenues than individuals traveling with small children (see Exhibit 1).

Guidelines for determining marketing priorities and sales objectives may be as simple as targeting only certain market segments in the high-potential categories or as complex as tracking and modeling revenue and profitability by industry category. The principle is the same: seek the highest revenue-producing market segments with the greatest overall profit potential. An example of the use of the "market mix" principle to maximize revenue is discussed in the following section.

Example: The Church Convention

Two 400-room hotels in the same market, both having rack rates of $150, know their city is likely to sell out during a large three-day church convention. Hotel A

Exhibit 1   Revenue and Profit Segmentation

Market Segments with High Revenue/Profit Potential

- Executives with unrestricted expense accounts
- Corporate group-meeting attendees
- Selected association group-meeting attendees

Market Segments with Medium Revenue/Profit Potential

- Couples without children, business travel
- Couples without children, pleasure travel
- Selected association group-meeting attendees

Market Segments with Low Revenue/Profit Potential

- Executives/business travelers with restricted expense accounts
- Rooms-only weekenders
- Families with children
- Government, military, and education market segments

---

believes a rate of $130 for a double room and $110 for a single is acceptable, projecting that 60 percent of its rooms will achieve double occupancy, or a rate of $130. Hotel A likes the idea of selling out during the convention, and it commits to a church group nine months out. Hotel A revenue projection is as follows:

$$3 \text{ days} \times (400 \text{ rooms} \times 60\%) \times \$130 \text{ per room} = \$93,600$$
$$3 \text{ days} \times (400 \text{ rooms} \times 40\%) \times \$110 \text{ per person} = \$52,800$$
$$\text{Total Room Revenue:} \qquad \$146,400$$

Historic trends have shown that this particular church group will not generate much in-house food and beverage revenue. Let's assume in-house food and beverage revenue (all food, as this is a non-alcoholic group) has been estimated at a per diem of $15 or:

$$240 \text{ rooms} \times 2 \text{ people} \times 3 \text{ days} \times \$15 = \$21,600$$
$$160 \text{ rooms} \times 1 \text{ person} \times 3 \text{ days} \times \$15 = \$7,200$$
$$\text{Total Food \& Beverage Revenue:} \qquad \$28,800$$

Thus, Hotel A estimates that this church group will generate total revenue of $175,200. Let's look at how the other 400-room hotel approaches the same week of the church convention.

Hotel B reviews the same research and knows it too can sell out. However, Hotel B believes in revenue maximization. It knows that 200 of its rooms that particular week, like most other weeks, are projected to be occupied with executives at the average corporate and concierge level rates of $140. The sales department has a commitment from a small corporate group for 50 rooms per day over the three-day period, at $105 per room plus meal functions. Since Hotel A and two other competitors usually sell their rooms to individual executive travelers and/or high-rate incentive groups and have committed 50 percent of their rooms to the church group convention, Hotel B believes it will capture another 100 rooms at the full corporate rate of $135. Finally, knowing a citywide sellout will occur, it believes it can get the full rack rate of $150 for 25 rooms and can sell its remaining rooms to church-group overflow guests at $110 at the last moment, thereby having a room revenue mix as follows:

$$200 \text{ rooms} \times 3 \text{ nights} \times \$140 = \$84,000$$
$$50 \text{ rooms} \times 3 \text{ nights} \times \$105 = \$15,750$$
$$100 \text{ rooms} \times 3 \text{ nights} \times \$135 = \$40,500$$
$$25 \text{ rooms} \times 3 \text{ nights} \times \$150 = \$11,250$$
$$25 \text{ rooms} \times 3 \text{ nights} \times \$110 = \$8,250$$
$$\text{Total Room Revenue:} \qquad \$159,750$$

Hotel B knows that its executive-segment guests spend an average of $28 on food and $7 on beverages and that the small corporate group has committed to a food and beverage budget of $50 per person per day, including its cocktail reception. Food and beverage revenue is therefore estimated to be as follows:

$$325 \text{ people} \times \$35 \times 3 \text{ days} = \$34,125$$
$$50 \text{ people} \times \$50 \times 3 \text{ days} = \$7,500$$
$$25 \text{ people} \times \$15 \times 3 \text{ days} = \$1,125$$
$$\text{Total Food \& Beverage Revenue:} \quad \$42,750$$

As you can see, Hotel B, by opting not to seek a sellout nine months in advance and by not participating in the church convention business, has a total revenue of $202,500, far in excess of Hotel A's $175,200.

There are many more examples that clearly demonstrate how managing the market mix maximizes revenue, and which demonstrate the importance of planning ahead, knowing your competition, and understanding the real value of market segments.

Pricing

Another component of revenue maximization is pricing. As one of the key elements in revenue maximization, pricing involves setting rates using strategy and flexibility.

Have you ever wondered what might be the "best" hotel in a city you have never traveled to, or how you would find out which hotel is the best? You might look at a directory of hotels or a publication like *Hotel & Travel Index,* scan the listing looking for the highest rates, and assume that the hotel with the highest rack rate listed must be the best. What if you saw that that same "best" hotel had a corporate or weekend rate that was competitive with the corporate or weekend rate of a hotel with a lower rack rate? You might conclude that the "best" hotel also has the best deal, or that the other hotel has a high corporate or weekend rate in comparison to its own rack rate. Let's look at a rate example in the following section.

Example: The Park, the Plaza, and the Palace

The Park, the Plaza, and the Palace are hotels located in the same city. The Park has a listed rack rate of $150 to $170, the Plaza has a listed rack rate of $145 to $175, and the Palace has a listed rack rate of $155 to $200.

You might assume that the Palace must be the best hotel in town—its rooms cost up to $200, and its minimum rack rate is $5 more than the Park's minimum rack rate and $10 more than the Plaza's minimum rack rate. You call the three hotels' reservations departments and find out that the Park's *corporate rate* is $138, the Plaza's corporate rate is $135, and the Palace's corporate rate is $138 to $153. The Palace also tells you it has rooms available at $138 the night you desire to stay. The Palace wins both the pricing perception strategy and value strategy in this case—you could have a $200 room at the Palace versus a $170 or $175 room at the Park or Plaza.

Using the same city and same hotels, let's compare weekend pricing strategies. This particular city runs about 50 percent occupancy on weekends. The motels and "middle tier" hotels charge anywhere from $49 to $79 for a weekend room. Our three upscale competitors have taken a different approach, seeking to maximize revenue and maintain their position as the "best." The Park states weekend rates of $109 and complimentary continental breakfast for two in its all-day restaurant. The Plaza advertises the same rate and complimentary continental breakfast for two in its all-day restaurant. The Palace advertises somewhat differently, with three weekend packages: (1) a room only, at $109 (plus continental breakfast in the lobby lounge); (2) a concierge-level king room with in-room continental breakfast for two at $119; and (3) a suite (based on availability) with a king bed, welcoming champagne or beverage, and an in-room complete breakfast for two at $129. The Palace is offering the same price/value as its competitors in package one, and an option for privacy and prestige in packages two and three. With a hotel that has a concierge level, suites, and empty rooms, why not up-sell, keep your positioning, and yet remain price-competitive in your own segment of the market? The Palace understands the psychology of the market. For those seeking privacy and prestige, a $10 or even $20 premium will bring many takers. Not having these options simply eliminates the opportunity to up-sell or meet the needs of a portion of the weekend market. Think about the consumer perception strategy: Would you say your hotel has a "weekend room rate of $109 and two coupons for breakfast in the all-day restaurant," or would you say either "we have a concierge-level king room and breakfast in the room for $119," or "we have a suite and breakfast served in the room for $129"? Using your empty suites and concierge- or club-level rooms to up-sell and keep your image and value perception is not only a good pricing strategy—it is a revenue maximization strategy.

Yield Management

Yield management is a tool used to increase revenue by establishing prices based on supply and demand and the competitive dynamics of the market. In essence, when demand is strong and trending toward exceeding supply, prices are increased. Conversely, when demand is trending downward and supply exceeds demand, prices are decreased. The objective is to achieve the maximum yield, given the supply and demand scenario. The **yield** measurement is a comparison of actual revenue achieved to the theoretical total potential revenue. The definition and calculation of the total potential revenue often varies by chain or hotel.

The principle of yield management can be applied to demand trends that have been determined hourly, daily, weekly, or even months or years in advance. For example, rates can be raised for a period when future demand is forecasted to be strong, and rates can be lowered during weak demand periods in order to bring in room revenue by taking market share.

Instead of measuring occupancy or rate, the focus in yield management is on *revenue per room*, not unlike revenue per rental in the rental car industry or revenue per passenger in the airline industry. Although the term "yield management" originated in the airline industry, hotels and resorts were applying the principle of yield management long before there were airlines. Historically, resort managers knew that "in season" the property would sell out because demand was so strong. Accordingly, many resorts charged only their highest rates when they were in season. Thus, one component of yield management—the relationship of rate to demand—was in practice.

In fact, to a large degree, the forecasting element of yield management was also in place—if you desired a room next "season," you were going to be quoted an "in-season" rate. And some resorts would use rate categories, selling their water-view rooms for the higher rates or their beachfront rooms for a premium, with in-season versus off-season rates for both. So before the first jet airplane ever took off, another component of yield management—variable rates/pricing—was being practiced. Granted, the hospitality industry was still focusing on occupancy and average rate as their performance measures when the yield management concept emerged in the airline industry and spread into the hospitality and rent-a-car industries.

The application of yield management in the hospitality industry blossomed in the mid-1980s. By the late 1980s, the concept of a multi-dimensional model incorporating market mix, pricing strategies, and yield management proved to be a better methodology for maximizing revenue than a single principle or application. Yield management had matured from a measuring tool for judging performance to a science and methodology unto itself. Regardless of the school of thought, yield management was a tool for the 1990s that would continue to emerge in virtually every major hotel chain in the hospitality industry as a standard procedure.

In the hospitality industry, management of **room categories,** discounts, and length of stay all help determine yield. Components of yield management also include variables such as the **booking pace** for groups (the rate at which the group's room block is filling up) and the transient sales trend/forecast (the rate at which individual reservations are being made). These factors, plus cancellations and other influences, help shape the actual forecast. The forecast then suggests the strategy for rate quotes and availability. This total interactive process is the product of yield management.

While hotel chains and major hotels and resorts guard their specific yield management procedures, some of the key yield management premises and components are as follows:

1. Use rate ranges. A **rate range** allows you to sell up or down.

2 Develop "room categories" (for example, deluxe, standard, and views). Room categories allow you to **close** or **open** room categories in order to increase either rates or occupancy.

3. Maintain rack-rate positioning. Set your published rack rates high enough to allow yourself the flexibility to discount when needed and to "max out" when demand is strong.

4. Develop rate categories. Have rate categories for as many valid reasons or segments as you can identify. This allows you to meet everyone's needs within your own rate-range parameters.

5. Establish guidelines. Be sure you have in place clear and enforceable rate-control guidelines in all areas where rates are provided—reservations, sales, front desk, catering, etc. Make sure your signals for closing or opening up rates are understood by all. Better yet, automate the rate categories.

6. Conduct a review meeting daily. A daily review meeting allows you to check to make sure that all assumptions regarding demand (and supply) are correct and that everyone understands the status for the day, week, month, and the future months.

7. Contact the Central Reservations Office (CRO) daily. This (contact) allows you to determine if all changes to your rate strategy have been communicated to all shifts and are clearly in place.

These seven keys will help ensure that yield management works for you.

Revenue Maximization in Practice

To maximize your hotel's revenue, you must first understand market mix, pricing, and yield management. But you must also be able to implement these concepts. The objectives and strategies in the following checklists will help you put revenue maximization into practice.

Objectives

- Select the optimum market-mix targets.
- Develop pricing strategies and related rate ranges.
- Plan for the sale of all empty rooms.
- Aim to sell all rooms at the maximum rates demand will allow.
- Control and manage the type and nature of group business and transient business.
- Provide for hourly, daily, weekly, monthly, quarterly, and yearly management of room rates, room reservations, room sales, and catering functions.

Strategies

- Adjust your corporate rates to be competitive with your top four competitors.

- Tell everyone about your new rates. Communicate!

- Establish rack rates—both top-end and low-end rates—to increase revenue. Publish the low-end rate.

- Shop your competitors daily via direct calls to their hotels. Call your competitors' "800" numbers or call through the airline terminals.

- Publish your corporate rate and list it wherever you can (at airline terminals, in directories, and so on).

- Establish a super-saver rate and appropriate room allocations, timing, etc.

- Establish a task force to implement your rate strategy and provide: (1) ongoing training, (2) daily management responsibility, (3) checks and balances, and (4) measurement.

- Price your product appropriately. *This is your most important management responsibility.*

While these objectives and strategies are overall steps to revenue maximization, there are many tactical steps that must be taken on a daily, weekly, and monthly basis to ensure that the goal of revenue maximization is achieved. These key tactics are as follows:

Key Tactics

- Develop a 365-day calendar that clearly states the selling tactic (up or down) for each day.

- Be sure all room rates are available during low occupancy periods (no "closed out" rate categories).

- Be sure discounted room rates are not available during forecasted high-occupancy periods.

- Consider implementing a "minimum stay" requirement for extremely high-demand periods (for example, during citywide sellouts).

- Hold a review meeting each morning to be sure everyone in sales, reservations, catering, convention services, and the front-desk area is informed of the day's revenue maximization game plan:

  — Review the prior day's revenue performance and compare it to budget and forecast.

  — Review the month-to-date revenue and year-to-date results.

  — Review your competitive intelligence (rate surveys, groups booked, etc.).

  — Review the day's, week's, and month's occupancy forecasts.

  — Review the group room blocks and related trends (cut-offs, pace, etc.) and make adjustments.

— Review future valley periods and/or peaks in demand.

— Review the impact of all new business from all sources in the forecast.

— Make appropriate adjustments to the rate strategy for that day, that week, the month ahead, and any period in the future that will be affected by changes in the demand pattern.

- Communicate daily with the Central Reservations Office (CRO) to ensure that all the property-level rate changes the CRO desires have been implemented.

- On a daily basis, communicate any rate strategy changes to all other selling functions (regional sales offices, contracted agents, automated systems, representatives, and so on).

By following these tactics, you will have achieved effective management of market mix, the best selection of pricing strategies, the highest yield, and—ultimately—the maximum revenue.

Key Terms

booking pace—The rate at which a group's room block is filling up.

close—To end the sale of a room category or rate.

open—To begin the sale of a room category or rate.

rate range—The dollar range (lowest to highest) charged by hotels for different categories of rooms.

revenue maximization—Achieving the highest potential revenue through management of market mix, pricing strategies, and yield management.

room category—A grouping of rooms that has been determined by type (standard, deluxe, etc.) or location (view, beach-front, and so on).

yield—The comparison of actual revenue achieved to the theoretical total potential revenue.

Chapter 19 Outline

Revenue and Profit Production Ideas
Methods to Distinguish Your Property
Ten Keys to Positive Consumer Reaction
Five Steps to More Competitive Marketing

Competencies

1. Describe several revenue and profit production ideas. (pp. 253–256)

2. Explain how to distinguish an establishment from its competitors. (pp. 256–258)

3. Give ten examples of how to secure positive consumer reaction. (pp. 258–261)

4. Explain five steps you can take to have more competitive marketing. (p. 261)

19

Practical Steps to Maximize Marketing

YOU DON'T HAVE TO USE sophisticated techniques to produce effective marketing results. There are many practical steps to increasing revenues and profits that include marketing and capitalizing on what already exists within your hotel, restaurant, or customer base. This chapter discusses methods that will distinguish your establishment from its competition. The reaction your customers have to you will be based in large part on how you treat them; this chapter also discusses ten traits that will help customers have a positive reaction to your establishment. Finally, this chapter will guide you through five quick steps that you can take to make your establishment more competitive.

Revenue and Profit Production Ideas

Some of the following ideas may prove useful in bringing additional revenues to your property.

Merchandise and Earn Money. One sure-fire way to bring in additional revenue is to take advantage of your **in-house profit centers.** These centers are ideal spots to offer additional merchandise and services for sale. Two major steps in recognizing the potential of in-house profit centers are to:

- View your establishment as a place through which consumers pass.

- Recognize that even the smallest service you can provide—and from which you can profit—will help you meet some need of the consumer.

A hotel traditionally has revenue and profit centers in the major areas of rooms and food and beverage; some also have banquet sales and gift shops. View each area as a profit center with target markets, sales goals, and profit margin objectives. Try to identify other profit centers within the property. Are there game rooms, lobby displays (space leased from the hotel for display purposes), a health club, a barber/beauty shop, or a lobby bar? Does the property have an infrequently used storage room that should be cleaned out and used to generate revenue and profit? Would a coin-operated copy center be useful? How about secretarial services? Laundromat? Book stand? Wall-art display sales? Do restaurant restrooms lend themselves to vending for necessity items? Examine all these possibilities as well as other opportunities at your establishment that can generate the maximum amount of revenue and profit per room. Apply your creative marketing ability to "sell that guest" when he or she is on your premises.

Restaurants frequently have an old display case with mints, gum, and cigars visible through dirty glass. This is sometimes their only method of increasing revenue through sales at the cashier's stand. However, much more can be done to generate small amounts of additional revenue and profit from a customer who is already purchasing. Ask yourself the following questions: Are the items in the display case presented in an attractive manner to encourage sales? Are there one or two desserts or specialty items that can be packaged and sold to the departing customer? Are there any items that appeal to children? (Even if children are not your clientele, many parents will buy on a whim.) Would a dessert cart improve the merchandising and volume of dessert sales? Do you have enough customers and space to put in a gift shop?

The answers to these questions will help you maximize merchandising with items that fulfill the customer's needs while he or she is in "your house." Make sure you monitor sales and set goals for each profit-making opportunity.

Reduce Guilt and Earn Money. Research has shown that humans have guilt complexes. You can help your guests resolve feelings of guilt and earn money for yourself at the same time. For a long time, the telephone company, postal service, and greeting card companies have suggested, "How nice it would be to call home," or "Aren't you rotten for not thinking of Grandma and sending her a card or a letter?" So, why shouldn't hospitality establishments—through marketing—simply say, "Remember your spouse and children: try our gift stand."

One large hotel chain with mostly male guests tripled its gift-shop sales by tapping into the guilt of businessmen away from home. The chain stocked its gift shops with items for women and children that fit into a suitcase or travel bag, and redistributed its shelf space from 80 percent men's items to 80 percent women's and children's items. Sales of these items, such as jewelry and sturdy high-markup children's toys, helped the male guests feel better by reducing their guilt about being away from home. For the hotel, it meant sizable additional revenues and profits. In addition, the female guests found the women's items attractive and also made purchases from the gift shop. The merchandising was skillful, and the marketing message was subtle. The in-room material simply stated, "We have a well-stocked gift shop, including a fine selection of women's and children's items. It is open from 6 a.m. to 1 a.m." Not coincidentally, the gift shop remained open 30 minutes after the bar and lounge closed. The gift shop was located between the bar and the elevator. A small poster-picture of a child with a tear in his eye was visible through the glass window of the gift shop. The caption, "Did You Remember Me, Daddy?" was clearly visible even to the blurry eye. The period one hour before the gift shop closed was the period of highest volume revenue and profit for gift-shop sales.

Make a Kid Happy and Earn Money. Do you have electronic games or a game room? A game room may make not only children happy, but their parents as well by providing something for the children to do. This revenue- and profit-generating opportunity can be marketed through in-room merchandising. One entrepreneurial hotel owner goes one step further by providing a free game token to all children. Other hotels put electronic games in the guestrooms that are hooked up to the establishment's in-room movie system. They then charge by the hour for the use of them.

Invest $0 and Earn Money. If you have the space, there are many ways to invest nothing but still make money. Consider the game room as one opportunity. You can make a deal with a reliable distributor to set up your game room in the space you provide and collect a percentage of the profits. The same concept applies to vending, although the percentages may be lower. Earlier we mentioned dressing up your property with a display of artwork or glassware. Other possibilities include flower carts, plant displays, and paperback racks. You can collect a percentage of the sales of these items as well. By setting up deals with these types of outside businesses or vendors, you may be able to meet the needs of your customers, enhance your property, and generate additional revenues and profits with little or no investment!

Stay Healthy and Earn Money. Keeping in shape has become a major psychological goal of our population. Take advantage of this fact. If your property has the space (one large room, a rooftop, or a parking-lot perimeter), consider the possibilities of an exercise room, sauna, or jogging course. Some hotels charge guests for using these amenities, but even if you don't charge guests for using, say, your exercise room, that does not mean you cannot earn money through promotions and tie-ins to these health-oriented amenities. In-room materials can promote a "health cocktail of the month" or a "special high-protein dinner." One hotel's promotion program lays out the jogging course and tells the guest to pick up his or her "time card" which when given to the hostess in the lounge, will give them their second health cocktail free. In addition, the hotel has three menu items (good profit margins on all three) promoted as the "lo-cal," "high-pro," and "dieter's delight." The results have been excellent—guests are satisfied because their needs are being recognized, and the hotel is realizing increased beverage sales and food profits.

Redirect Your Cash Flow and Earn Money. You can improve your earnings and simplify your banking by improving your cash management program. Avoid keeping cash on the premises—for one thing, it's hazardous. Checking accounts *cost* money (for checks, fees, services, etc.)—they don't *earn* money. Savings accounts and interest-bearing checking accounts earn money but *can* lose to inflation, if inflation is high. Most people cannot tie up their cash flow in long-term savings certificates. So what other options are available? Money-market funds are one place to look. Interest rates generally exceed most local rates offered by savings and loans institutions, and liquidity (the ability to use your cash when needed) is the same as a checking account. Most money-market funds also provide free checks. Consider this approach: Use an interest bearing account (where allowed) for general disbursements, and use a money-market fund to channel your cash on a regular basis. Consider the results to your bottom line. (A list of the money-market funds and prevailing rates is published daily in the *Wall Street Journal* and other newspapers. Money-market funds also represent a good resting place for advance deposits—why not earn interest on someone else's money?)

Increase Productivity and Earn Money. Improving the productivity of your salespeople can increase your profits. There are two opposite approaches to increasing your salespeople's productivity. Approach one is a "see-what-happens" approach called "Let Someone Go" or "Don't Fill It." It often applies when there is a sizable staff involved. Someone leaves your sales staff or is released by you. You then need to evaluate what happens to your overall sales (and, more important, your overall profits) if you do not fill the position. A number of things can happen, such as a decrease in costs per sale, an increase in productivity per remaining salesperson, or the worst—a decline in sales, which is greater than the total cost of the person who left the operation.

Approach two, called "Bring Someone In, " adds a salesperson to the staff but sets a reasonable production target that the salesperson has to meet; this target may equal total costs for the new salesperson times nine or ten, or some other specific dollar amount in sales.

A variation on the "Bring Someone In" approach is to offer an attractive incentive to travel agents producing a specific multiple of the incentive cost in sales for your product or service. The advantage to this alternative is that you have no additional overhead, yet you have effectively extended your sales force. One hotel chain offered an expensive sports car to the travel agency that produced the greatest sales increase over the base figure (four times the recovery cost of the car). The results were dramatic—agency sales quadrupled and the winning firm produced enough additional sales to pay for a fleet of vehicles!

Methods to Distinguish Your Property

Increasing revenue and profits from your operations may involve more than applying a marketing strategy. Frequently you may need to make operational, physical, or attitudinal changes. Let's briefly look at some ideas that may help you distinguish your operations, products, or services.

There are a number of marketing methods that can add to the *marketing attractiveness* of what you offer. The following suggestions may not work for all, but they might help you think of other ideas to improve the marketability of your hospitality product or service.

Make Something Perfect. Offering a good selection (in price and variety) in your food and beverage operation or restaurant will help you meet broad customer needs. However, you should also identify at least two items that you can offer to perfection. You should be able to build a reputation as the best place to have the items. These "signature items" can help you attract repeat visitors. The perfection of an item can be measured in any of the following characteristics:

- Quality
- Preparation
- Presentation
- Promotion
- Perception as a real value

A signature item may be a specialty dish, main entrée, or unique dessert. For a signature item to be successful it must have broad appeal and be consistently perfect. *Consistency* in the preparation and presentation of a signature item is critical.

Do Something Unique. If you can find something unique to offer guests in your establishment, your guests will not only purchase it—they'll talk about it to their friends and acquaintances. Find some way to make some of your services or products stand out from your competition. This method of distinguishing your operation can take on many forms. For example, one Midwest hotel's restaurant/lounge offers a unique "English Bloody Mary." The drink is served in a large, frosted bowl-shaped glass, dressed with a salt coating, and garnished with a celery stick and parsley. In addition, a four-ounce cold beer chaser is set next to the mildly spicy drink. Tent cards advertise this unique beverage and well-trained servers encourage guests to buy it. The pricing is two-tiered: $2.25 for the English Bloody Mary and the first beer chaser; refills of the four-ounce chaser, which are served by alert and well-trained servers carrying small 16-ounce frosted pitchers of cold brew, are priced at $1.50. Needless to say, many patrons end up spending six or seven dollars on their English Bloody Mary, because they buy many four-ounce chasers to go with their one large, well-presented specialty drink. This beverage offering has developed its own following, thus encouraging repeat business. It is also an excellent trial item for the new patron. The result is higher profits, more volume, and a unique identity for the restaurant.

The Up-Front Signals. What is first perceived is believed. Applying this phrase can help you market your products/services and add revenue to your bottom line. A hotel in the western United States has taken this "up-front signals" method to heart and to the bank—here's how.

The hotel (we'll call it Classic Hotel) was a first-class hotel, but it was more than 40 years old. The owners were concerned about competition from a new Hilton high-rise with a magnificent black-glass exterior. The new Hilton looked good—it had marketability from the outside appearance; however, the older hotel's service levels and quality were better. How could the older facility distinguish itself and retain its status? It needed to give an immediate "up-front" perception to potential customers that was equal to, or better than, the "black-glass special" without spending millions. A consultant came up with a practical and inexpensive "up-front signal." He suggested that the owners of the older brownish stone building add a door-to-street gold-colored canopy and an appropriately plush sidewalk covering. The consultant also suggested a few additional investments. One was to add the word "The" before the hotel's name on the canopy in script writing: *The* Classic Hotel. Next he helped the owners recruit a local college basketball player (over six feet, four inches tall) to work in a luxurious doorman's suit and top hat (also gold and brown) from 4 p.m. to 9 p.m. Finally, to recover these investments, he suggested that the older hotel *raise its rates* slightly above the new Hilton's. The owners agreed. Here are the results.

First, the canopy and tall doorman were the most visible sights when coming down Main Street. So eye-alluring were the canopy and doorman that the "black-glass special" just faded into the skyscape. First-class guests coming to this western city received only one reply when they asked about the best place to stay—"The Classic Hotel is the classiest place in town, and it is only one or two dollars more a night than the Hilton." (This same concept has worked well for a number of restaurants trying to upgrade their images.)

Inside Signals. Improving the marketability of your product or service to the consumer doesn't have to involve the outside wrapper or packaging. There are a number of highly visible interior areas where simply changing the lighting or adding a mirror can work wonders. For example, a major luxury hotel chain discovered it had an operational problem: occasionally its elevators gave slow service during high-occupancy periods. In addition, the windows at the end of the corridors where the elevators were located, looked out onto the hotel's heating and ventilation equipment. It was physically impossible to add elevators. The solution to keeping the guests occupied during their wait was very simple. The hotel installed full-length mirrors on the walls near the elevators. The mirrors provided a perfect distraction for the guests, who could look at themselves and check their appearance. With this simple ploy the hotel diverted attention from a potential annoyance and enhanced the appearance of its interior. Complaints virtually ceased and other hotels in the chain with similar elevator problems soon adopted the idea. The guests' dissatisfaction turned into satisfaction when they viewed themselves in those wonderful mirrors by the elevators!

Another general manager knew his guestrooms were not due for refurbishing but that their appearance was not competitive with the guestrooms of other properties. His approach was to compensate through substitution. He decided to set aside about 20 percent of his rooms for female travelers, and another large percentage for men only. In the rooms for women, he added a fresh flower in a clearly visible bureau-top vase, new and softer-color towels, new shower curtains of a different color, a skirt hanger, and a new double dead-bolt lock. In the rooms for men, he placed a current issue of *Sports Illustrated, Time, Newsweek,* or *U.S. News,* the latest edition of a newspaper, and a complimentary pen and pencil set. While the hotel incurred small costs, it regained guest satisfaction and business stayed. The hotel's slightly worn rooms remained competitive. In essence, his inside signals were compensating for the aging-guestrooms problem.

The "Can-of-Paint" Technique. The least expensive way to change the appearance of something old or dirty is to paint it. The "can-of-paint" technique can work for you! Walk around the outside of your property. Look for the most visible aging signals. It may be a dirt-stained wall near the lobby entrance, striping on the parking lot surface, or deteriorating signs. Invest in a "can of paint"—it's a signal to consumers that you have changed from dirty or old to fresh, clean, and well kept.

Ten Keys to Positive Consumer Reaction

There are signals or keys that can help bring new consumers to you and then bring them back as repeat visitors. Let's look at ten keys for repeat business, greater marketability, and improving the consumer's perception of the product or service you order.

Key 1: The Fresh and New Signal. "Fresh" and "new" are positive signs to most consumers. Whether it is the can of paint or the replacement of tablecloths, napkins, towels, uniforms, or menus, you need signals that clearly convey that your product or service is fresh or new. Take a good look at your facility or operation and identify what you can do to provide the strongest "fresh and new" signal to your market.

Key 2: The Neat and Clean Test. Your product or service need not be brand new to convey positive signals. Cleanliness is another very strong desire on the part of the lodger, diner, or traveler. Rooms (especially bathrooms), lounges, restaurant floors, and even airline seats should pass your cleanliness inspection. Even new facilities will lose out if they are sloppy or dirty. Guests rank cleanliness consistently high when they are surveyed about hotels, restaurants, and public travel-oriented facilities. Check out your establishment:

- Are the lounges cleaned before and after meeting breaks or large volumes of traffic?
- Are the carpets clean and vacuumed?
- Is everyone a member of the "paper patrol"? (This means that if discarded paper is on the floor or room-service trays are in the hallways, do all staff members—including you—understand it is their job to pick it up or move it from the consumer's view?)

Key 3: Efficiency. For many travelers, time is of the essence. Fast check-in and check-out and an impression of efficiency at the front desk are essential to ensure a positive customer reaction. While it is important that front-desk personnel display warm, friendly attitudes, pleasant faces are no substitute for efficiency to the busy executive. Your employees can smile all they want, but if the customer has been waiting for ten minutes, you can bet he or she won't be smiling back. An efficient check-in and check-out, coupled with that smile, will be the winning combination for pleasing your customers.

Key 4: Reliability. The obvious place to start with reliability is ensuring that the customer's reservation is there and correct when he or she arrives. However, this is certainly not where reliability should end. Some other key reliability factors include, but are not limited to:

- A television that works.
- Adequate guestroom lighting (especially in work or reading areas).
- Towels and tissues.
- An accurate and prompt message service system.

Reliability means that when room service says, "It will be up in 15 minutes," the tray arrives in 10 to 12 minutes—not 30 or 45 minutes. Reliability means that when someone calls a guest, the message is taken and delivered. Reliability is a combination of all these factors that gives the guest a comfortable feeling that "this place works."

Key 5: Acceptability. People like to be accepted. Does your operation convey acceptance or do your guests feel as though they are processed? Are they viewed as outsiders instead of guests? Does the word "welcome" still exist in the vocabulary of all your guest-contact personnel? Are the employees also acceptable to your customers? Rude attitudes, shabby appearances, and so on can take a perfectly reliable operation and turn it into a very unacceptable environment for your customers. Make sure your customers feel accepted.

Key 6: Empathy. Not all of your customers will arrive at the front desk in a good mood. Be sure your personnel are trained to deal with difficult guest attitudes and are capable of recognizing those who might have just been through a trying experience. The importance of empathy and making sure your guests feel accepted can be related in the following true story.

I was invited to give a presentation at a distant resort area. Having had other commitments, it was necessary for me to take a very late flight, and there was no time to shave or clean up. Arriving at the resort after a six-hour flight, unshaven and having had the two drinks on board, I wanted to check in quickly and get some rest before the early morning presentation. Unfortunately, my suitcase had been lost by the airline. By the time the lost-bag forms were completed, it was after 1 a.m. when I entered the hotel. Trying to check in at the front desk proved to be an equally trying experience in this first-class resort.

A night auditor, sitting behind the front desk sorting through index cards, peered at me over his bifocals. The look was easily readable: "If I ignore him, maybe he'll leave." After all, I was unshaven and had no suitcase. Finally the auditor decided to take on his role as front desk agent and came to the desk, but he continued to sort his little cards and mumbled, "I'll be with you in a minute. I want to finish this batch." To say the least, I was not feeling particularly "accepted" at this point. After a brief exchange, in which I indicated that I would appreciate an efficient check-in, the night auditor asked, "Do you have a reservation?" My response was, "Yes, it was guaranteed by both my host (the resort's owner) and my American Express card." The auditor's response was, "I don't see it—are you sure you had a reservation for the 29th?" By now, a full ten minutes had passed and still no registration card, no key, no room—the night auditor had made things even worse by moving from no "acceptability" to no "reliability."

I won't go into the details of how Mr. Night Auditor learned empathy or how to hustle, but I will tell you he is no longer with that resort!

Key 7: Uniqueness. Because you so often hear the expression, "They are all about the same," wouldn't offering some uniqueness make sense? It does not have to be totally different (like a double-decker London bus for a limo), but you should have something that tells your market, "This is the place that has great food," or "hustling personnel," or "a good piano bar," or "the six-foot, four-inch doorman." Offering customers something that can be identified with you will give your product or service a recognizable edge.

Key 8: Class. Class has many definitions. One of the most applicable to the service industry is *the ability to function with grace under pressure.* The handling of an irritated executive by an experienced front desk agent can be a demonstration in class for all to observe. Class is also a feeling within the property that comes from the employees' overall esprit de corps. Class is *not* an arrogant general manager or director of food and beverage who is unable to extend a helping hand to a lower-level employee. Class is an attitude that you and your employees convey to customers when you offer your product or service. If you have class, your customers will know it and react positively.

Key 9: Beat-the-System Offer. Survey after survey indicates that most people do not like a regimented environment, or what "the system" offers. One technique in obtaining positive customer reactions is to make sure that your customers have at least one opportunity to "beat the system" (your system) during their visits with you. The opportunity may be nothing more than free after-dinner mints or the second drink on the house, or a discount.

Key 10: Value. Value is *quality at a fair price.* Just as most people want to believe they have "beat the system," no one wants to feel cheated. Over-pricing, poor-quality products, and inadequate service levels are "rip-off" signals that destroy the opportunity to offer consumers the strongest reason to be your customer—value. Today, more than ever, the public is demanding quality at a fair price, yet finding it increasingly difficult to obtain. Offer value and you will be successful. You will have given the customer the strongest possible reason to do business with you, and that signal will result in repeated purchases of your product or service.

Five Steps to More Competitive Marketing

The following five steps can help you market your property more successfully:

1. Go out and look at your strongest competitor's operation. That means looking at more than the rates and facility. Look at the competitor's staff—their level of desire, competency, enthusiasm, courteousness, and thoughtfulness. Set some stringent performance objectives.
2. Make more sales calls—even if it's only one more. Make going after revenue and customers the number one priority.
3. Make deals. Today, you need to make deals to maximize revenue. Unless every room is occupied, you are losing revenue.
4. Change strategy. There are a lot of ways to beat your competition, so don't hesitate to change strategy if it makes sense. If it doesn't cost you anything to offer it, do so. Even if it does cost you something, it might be less costly than losing the business. For example, shop your competition and find out the rates they are quoting in your valley periods, and then adjust your rates accordingly. Go after and steal the business.
5. Select and inspect. Check the sales file daily and discuss it with the responsible employee. Every day, observe the front desk and check-in and the cashier at check-out. Be sure your guests are being taken care of properly. You work hard to sell them; make sure others are working hard to keep them coming back.

Key Terms

in-house profit center—Any area of an establishment that generates revenue.

Chapter 20 Outline

Preparation Methods
Presentation Components
Marketing Budget Checklist

Competencies

1. Provide a guide to preparing a marketing budget. (p. 263)

2. Describe the various methods used to establish budget parameters. (pp. 263–264)

3. Delineate the major components of a marketing budget. (pp. 264–265)

20

The Marketing Budget

T HE MARKETING BUDGET SHOULD BE VIEWED as the document that quantifies the cost of your strategies and presents the monetary resources and related expenses in the best possible manner. The budget should help all understand your overall strategy and the role of each marketing tool in the plan. It is usually beneficial to approach preparing the budget in a number of different ways to provide a reality check on the overall budget plan. The following sections describe some of the methods you can use.

Preparation Methods

Percent of Sales—Industry Averages. Most industry sectors have *averages* expressed as *percent of sales*. The average is the percent of sales for the total marketing budget; for example, companies in the industry spend on average 15 percent on marketing. Also, in many industry sectors, the same percent allocations may be available for some of the marketing tools/categories, such as advertising at 5 percent, sales at 7 percent, etc. Use the **percent of sales—industry averages** method to compare with your own averages. If you are higher overall or in a category, delineate the reasons (e.g., new product introductions, desire to raise awareness levels, adding sales offices, etc.). Analyze the overall percentage comparison, excluding those exceptions mentioned above, and see if you are in line with the averages.

Task Method. This approach begins by looking at the objectives (e.g., revenue/ sales increases desired, etc.) and the factors making up the cost of the *tasks* (marketing tools) needed to achieve success. For example, the new product launches will cost X, the incremental and existing sales effort will cost Y, and so on. The sum to accomplish all base-level and incremental-level tasks is the overall marketing budget. (Compare this total to the industry average to ascertain how aggressive your spending is in relationship to the "norm.")

Competitive Method. In the **competitive method,** you select your closest leading competitors (those most like your company or the industry sector leaders) and compare your marketing budget to theirs, both individually and on an average/ composite basis.

Zero-Base Method. This is a broad concept that can help you prioritize where you want to spend your limited resources. With **zero-base budgeting**, no expenditure is justified just because it was made last year. Each expense is re-analyzed and justified annually to determine if it will yield better results than spending the same amount in another way. A note of caution, however: frequently there are vital functions that must be maintained at certain minimum levels; for example, a sales force or reservation system must retain certain expenses that relate to those functions. Use extreme caution in applying zero-base budgeting to these functions. Some marketers subdivide the marketing budget into a "vital core" of expenses and "all other" categories and apply the zero-base concept to only the "all other" category. Some consider this a violation of the principle of zero-base budgeting, while to others it is simply common sense. You are the best qualified to determine which approach is most applicable for your business.

In all methods, you should seek to analyze and calculate the **payback** or "revenue generation" attributable to the expense category. For example, if you are adding $100,000 in incremental sales personnel and your ratio (multiple of per-salesperson-cost in sales or **revenue generation** expected per person) is 20, then you should be factoring in $2 million in incremental sales (revenue) into the overall budget. Normally, marketing programs should be judged in total only on their ability to cover variable expenses and contribute to fixed overhead. Other useful comparisons include indexing the budget to previous years and related company sales. This simply helps to determine a general "efficiency" factor. Note, however, that this comparison could be misleading without detailing the various factors that impacted each year's (previous and current) marketing budgets.

Presentation Components

Marketing Objectives. At the outset, delineate the overall key marketing objectives, such as percent revenue/sales growth, market share expectations, customer retention goals, customer satisfaction index target, brand awareness objectives: etc. Also, be sure to include a "mandated" new or an incremental objective: for example, six major new product launches. Divide the objectives into a logical (to the audience) format: for example, short-term objectives and longer term or immediate—1 year and next 2 years. Another method is to present "existing" marketing programs and "new" programs and build to the total. Irrespective of method, you must provide the rationale for all increases or decreases if comparing to prior years. Also, compare your marketing expenditures "trend line" to that of the industry sector, closest competitors, and competitive average/composite.

Budget Overview. A **budget overview** is normally a one-page summary of the major expenditure categories and marketing mix (tools). This delineation should be expressed both in dollars and percentages of the total budget. Included would be items such as media (TV, newspaper, direct mail, electronic marketing, outdoor, radio, etc.); production expense for the media; sales (personal selling); promotions, merchandising, public relations, marketing research, branding/packaging-related expenses; agency fees and other costs; overhead; and any extraordinary items related to a new endeavor, such as acquisition integration expenses, etc.

Marketing Calendar. This is a reference tool that provides a visual summary of how and when media expenditures will take place week-by-week. Usually, it references "media" expenses, breaking them down by geography (for example, national television, spot markets, etc.) and by media weights by week (for example,

GRPs/TRPs). Marketing **calendars** can also be used for promotions and events in the same manner. These are referred to as the promotions or events calendars.

Program Plan Summaries. **Program plan summaries** are summations of the major program plans or marketing tools desired to be highlighted in the overall presentation (for example, new advertising creation, new electronic marketing site, new image/branding campaign, new distribution system, new call center, etc.).

Comments/Notes. It is always good practice to provide a bullet point commentary or note on items that have impact on the marketing budget. Such items include sales office lease escalator clauses, changes in commission structures, media cost increases, inflation-specific items, union contract settlements, etc. Noting these items helps explain variances or abnormalities.

One final point: when you prepare marketing budget presentations, always take into account your audience. Lenders may and usually do have a different perspective than your directors or management. Tailor your marketing budget presentation to each audience, be accurate, and be prepared. The following budget checklist can be helpful in this effort.

Marketing Budget Checklist

- How does your ratio/percentage compare to the industry sector average percentage? How does it compare to your closest competitors?

- What has been the historic trend in your spending ratio/percentage compared to the industry and your competitors?

- Are your objectives quantified and linked to the budget allocations?

- Have you considered preparing and submitting an incremental spending budget tied to incremental results?

- Have you identified expense increases (and decreases) that appear abnormal?

- Has the mix of expense allocations (by marketing tools/functions) been charged on a dollar and percent basis within your budget plan? Why?

- Is your budget plan summary presented with both dollar and percent changes.

- Have you prepared appropriate summations for media, promotions, events (calendars), etc.?

- How does your overall budget index against (compare with) previous budgets? Can you readily delineate the rationale/reasons behind the changes?

- Have you prepared separate documents for all major new programs and major changes?

☞ Key Terms

budget overview—A one-page summary of the major expenditure categories and marketing mix (tools).

calendar—A reference tool that provides a visual summary of how and when media expenditures will take place week-by-week.

competitive method—An approach to preparing a marketing budget in which you select your closest leading competitors and compare your marketing budget to theirs, both individually and on an average/composite basis.

payback—The revenue generated that is attributable to the marketing expense category. If you add $100,000 in incremental sales personnel (cost), for example, and your ratio (multiple) of per-sales-person cost in sales (revenue) generation expected per person is 20, then you should factor in $2 million in incremental sales into the overall budget.

percent of sales—industry averages—A budget preparation method in which you can compare your overall marketing budget with the average of marketing budgets in the industry as a whole. It is an effective tool to ascertain if you are in line with industry averages.

program plan summaries—Summations of the major program plans or marketing tools the budget planner wishes to highlight in the overall budget presentation.

revenue generation—The dollar value attributable to a specific marketing budget category. See also payback.

task method—A budget preparation approach that begins with determining marketing objectives (increase in sales and revenue, for example) and then factoring in the cost of the new tasks required to reach the objectives.

zero-base budgeting—A budget preparation method that does not rely on historical expenditures or allocations. Each expense under consideration is re-analyzed and justified annually to determine if it will yield better results than spending the same amount in another way.

Chapter 21 Outline

The Marketing Plan
    Marketing Plan Outline and
      Instructions
    Competitive/Market Positioning Grid
Work Plan Example

Competencies

1. List the elements of a marketing plan and summarize steps for putting one together. (pp. 269–276)

2. Describe and use the competitive/market positioning grid. (pp. 276–277)

21

The Total Hotel/Unit Marketing Plan

Your hotel's marketing plan is its blueprint for gaining market share and financial success. Completing it requires detailed analyses of your product, market, and competition. Once completed, it should be periodically reviewed, assessed, and—when appropriate—adjusted to account for changing circumstances.

This chapter provides instructions, sample forms, and an actual workable marketing plan for an individual hotel or unit. The chapter's purpose is to walk you through the complete process of preparing an annual marketing plan.

The Marketing Plan

One of the best ways to begin creating a marketing plan is to establish a timetable for completion of key plan components. Here is an example:

Marketing Plan Timetable

July 15	Instructions issued
September 1	Completion of mission statement
	Objectives and strategies
	Competitive/market analysis
September 15	Preliminary expense budget summary
	Completion of preliminary advertising plan
October 1	Final detailed budget
	Completed advertising plan
November 15	Summary work plan by segment
	First-quarter chronological plan
January 15	Second-quarter chronological plan
April 15	Third-quarter chronological plan
July 15	Fourth-quarter chronological plan

Marketing Plan Outline and Instructions

The first step in creating a marketing plan is to set forth all the items and information required to produce a complete plan. In the pages that follow, an actual outline of a marketing plan is reproduced. Included are step-by-step instructions and definitions of what is to be completed and presented.

Exhibit 1   Sample Statement of Objectives and Strategies

OBJECTIVE 1: BUSINESS MIX

Increase the group segment from 35 percent to 40 percent of the hotel's business mix.

Strategies

- Raise group room allotment to 250 rooms Monday to Thursday nights.
- Raise sales goal for staff.
- Increase number of sales trips to New York and Washington, D.C.
- Increase advertising and direct mail to corporate group meetings planners.

OBJECTIVE 2: PRICING PHILOSOPHY

Become the price leader in the city, maintaining a $10 margin over the competition. Achieve an AT of $82.

Strategies

- Increase rates $2 every two months or as needed to maintain the number 1 position.
- Conduct a monthly rate survey.
- Maintain a $60 average rate for packages June to September; $64 October to December.
- Raise suite prices 10 percent in January.
- Do not book groups below $50 average rate on weekends without approval of general manager.

MARKETING PLAN

OUTLINE AND INSTRUCTIONS

I. Mission Statement—due September 1

Provide a concise mission statement for your hotel that includes the following:

a. Desired position and perception in the marketplace

b. Targeted **business mix** (transient percentage versus group percentage)

c. Overall revenue goals such as revenue per available room (RevPAR), average daily rate (ADR), occupancy, gross operating profit, and other measures significant to your hotel

II. Objectives and Strategies—due September 1

Using brief statements, list the key objectives (what you wish to achieve, quantified by dollar amounts or percentages if volume-related) that, when achieved, will result in the fulfillment of the mission statement. For each objective, list the strategies or action steps you will implement to achieve the objective. (See Exhibit 1 for a sample excerpt from a list of objectives and strategies.) Objectives should address, but not be limited to:

a. *Business Mix.* Identify the objective and strategies planned to achieve the group/transient business mix goal you have set.

Exhibit 2   Sample Rate Survey

	Hospitality Hotel	Hilton	Marriott	Holiday Inn	Sheraton	Radisson
Single Rack Rate	105/115/125	95/105/115	89/99/119	79/89	85/95/105	89/99
Corporate Rate	95/105 S/D	85/95 S/D	80/90 S/D	69/79 S/D	75/85 S/D	79/89 S/D
Preferred Corporate Rate	85/95 S/D	80/90 S/D	75/85 S/D	65/75 S/D	70/80 S/D	74/84 S/D
Secretary's	85/95 S/D	80/90 S/D	75/85 S/D	NA	70/80 S/D	NA
Club Level Executive Room Tech. Room	$20 Extra	$15 Extra	$15 Extra	NA	$15 Extra	NA
Government Rate	$72	$68	$65	$60	$60	$60
Weekend Room Only	$79	$69	$69	$59	$59	$59
Weekend Package Room/Breakfast for 2	$85	$75	$75	NA	NA	NA
Suite Range	$175-$375	$160-$380	$175-$425	$125/$150	$150/$175	$125/$175

b. *Pricing Philosophy.* State your objective pertaining to room rate and positioning. List strategies for achieving your targeted average daily rate. Include a competitive rate survey (such as the example in Exhibit 2) in the appendix to the marketing plan.

c. *Transient Market.* State your objective for weekday/weekend transient rooms mix. List major strategies planned to achieve desired results. List major strategies for travel industry sales and corporate transient sales.

d. *Group Market.* State your objectives for group business as they pertain to group room nights, rate, and revenue. List your strategies. Include a summary of your group room-night targets by market segment (including travel industry sales) in the appendix, using the Group Rooms Market Mix form shown in Exhibit 3. Also include a list of sales staff market assignments.

e. *Low Occupancy Periods.* Provide specific strategies aimed at boosting occupancy levels during low occupancy periods, be they weekends, summer, off-season, holidays, etc. Include results expected.

f. *Community Awareness.* List strategies planned to increase your hotel's visibility and enhance its reputation in the marketplace. In the appendix, include a list of professional and civic organization memberships maintained by the management staff.

III. Competitive/Market Analysis—due September 1

In this section of the marketing plan, give a very brief overview of market conditions and trends, and then identify your hotel's position in the marketplace as it relates to your competitors. Be concise.

Exhibit 3   Group Rooms Market Mix Form

Group Rooms Market Mix **(trends and forecast)**			Hotel: _____ No: _____	

Market	20XX Total		20XX Total		20XX Total		20XX Total		20XX Total	
	Total	%	Total	%	Total	%	Total	%	Total	%
Corporate										
State/Regional Association										
National Association										
Travel Agent										
Motor Coach										
Sports										
Government										
Total (%)		100		100		100		100		100

a. *Economic Conditions.* Describe how the prevailing local economic conditions will affect your transient and group business. Information should include average occupancy for the marketplace during the past 12 months (if available).

b. *Opportunities/Concerns.* List any known or anticipated changes in your marketplace that would positively or negatively affect your hotel during this plan year.

c. *Business Trends.* Briefly describe any trends exhibited during the past 2½ years with regard to transient demands (weekday and weekend), business mix, and valley periods. Complete the Group Rooms Market Mix form (Exhibit 3) for this past period and include it in the appendix.

d. *Product and Competitive Analysis.* Complete a fact sheet on your hotel and your three major competitors. Market your strengths and develop strategies to overcome your property's weaknesses.

Exhibit 4   Competitive/Market Positioning Grid

		MARKET		
		Strong	Moderate	Weak
COMPETITIVE POSITIONING	Strong	1	2	3
	Moderate	4	5	6
	Weak	7	8	9

e. *Competitive/Market Positioning Grid.* Using the form shown in Exhibit 4, denote your hotel's position by placing an "X" in the most appropriate box. Do the same for your three major competitors on separate grids. (This form is discussed later in the chapter.)

IV. Appendix—due September 1

a. *Marketing Budget Estimates.* Using the summary form shown in Exhibit 5, outline your actual expenses for the past year, your estimated expenses for the current year, and your projections for the plan year ahead.

b. *Room Rate Survey.* Complete a rate survey of your competitors using the sample format shown in Exhibit 2.

c. *Business Mix Trends.* Record the desired transient rooms mix versus group market mix by month for future measurement against actual performance.

d. *Transient Market Segment Prioritization.* List all transient market segments you will address in the plan year and prioritize them according to their profitability to your hotel.

e. *Group Market Segment Prioritization.* List all group market segments you will address in the plan year and prioritize them according to their profitability in your hotel (see Exhibit 6).

f. *Sales Staff Market Assignments.* List how market solicitation responsibilities have been assigned within the sales department (see Exhibit 7).

Exhibit 5   Marketing Expense Budget Form

**Marketing Expense Budget
Summary and Estimate**

Hotel: _____ No. _____

Account	Last Year	Current Year	Plan Year
Direct Sales (Includes Travel, Telephone, Dues/Subscriptions, Professional Fees, Entertainment)	$_____ / ___%	$_____ / ___%	$_____ / ___%
Public Relations (Includes Professional Fees for Public Relations Only)	$_____ / ___%	$_____ / ___%	$_____ / ___%
Sales Promotions (Includes Direct Mail and Postage)	$_____ / ___%	$_____ / ___%	$_____ / ___%
Collateral Materials (Includes Costs for Photo Shoots, Brochures, and Other Sales Collateral)	$_____ / ___%	$_____ / ___%	$_____ / ___%
Payroll (Includes Salaries, Wages, and Benefits)	$_____ / ___%	$_____ / ___%	$_____ / ___%
Office Supplies	$_____ / ___%	$_____ / ___%	$_____ / ___%
Miscellaneous	$_____ / ___%	$_____ / ___%	$_____ / ___%
Advertising			
a. National Media and Production:		$_____ / ___%	
b. Local Media and Production:		$_____ / ___%	
c. White/Yellow Pages Listings:		$_____ / ___%	
(a.b.c.) Sub-Total:		$_____ / ___%	
Total:		$_____ / ___%	

V. Preliminary Budget and Advertising Plan—due September 15

A first cut at the budget and advertising plan should be completed by mid-September.

VI. Final Detailed Budget and Advertising Plan—due October 1

Final budget and advertising plan should be agreed to in order to allow optimum time to prepare advertising and purchase media.

VII. Summary Work Plan by Segment—due November 15

Using brief statements, for each market—including travel industry sales and corporate transient sales—outline your specific planned activities under the categories of:

Exhibit 6   Group Market Segment Prioritization

HOSPITALITY HOTEL		
Segment A	**Segment B**	**Segment C**
Local corporate	National associations	Fraternities/sororities
State associations	Motorcoach tours	Military reunions
Corporate transient (RSVP)	Sports teams	Social rooms
Weekend packages	Relocation/long-term stays	Airline crews
	Government	Special events
	Travel agents	

Exhibit 7   Market Assignments and Goals

HOSPITALITY HOTEL	
Sales Manager:	Jim Smith
Primary markets:	Washington, D.C. national associations
Primary accounts:	All major associations
Secondary markets:	Government groups; Baltimore corporations
Secondary accounts:	IBM; Ernst & Whinney; Star Shipping Lines; Baltimore Port Authority
Geographic area:	Washington, D.C.; Maryland; Virginia (Washington NSO)
Room nights:	250 per week
Outside calls:	8 per week
Steam leads:	1 per week
In-house entertainment:	3 per week

Note: Use this format, but include *all* salespeople on one or two pages.

a. Direct sales and promotions (familiarization trips, trade shows, etc.)

b. Direct mail (local and regional only)

c. Advertising

d. Public relations

Activities are to be tied to a targeted month and assigned to a salesperson. Ongoing activities are not to be listed. All work plans are to follow the sample format.

VIII. Quarterly Chronological Plans (first quarter due November 15)

The **chronological work plan** for January–March will be due by November 15. Activities should be listed in the date order by month (see the sample in Exhibit 8). The chronological plan for April–June is due January 15.

Exhibit 8   Sample Chronological Work Plan

HOSPITALITY HOTEL, HEAVENLY, MARYLAND
JULY 20XX

Week One: Monday, June 27–Friday, July 1

Association sales calls in Washington, D.C. (two days)	J. Smith
Summertime government rate mailer to Annapolis	M. Patton
Local sales calls in Towson with G.M.	B. Wallace
Begin to prepare for August corporate phone blitz	D. Carney

Week Two: Monday, July 4–Friday, July 8

Attend Meeting World in New York City	P. Johnson
RSVP Quarterly Newsletter mailed	B. Wallace
Research reunion leads from VFW magazine	J. Smith
Update DVSAE list	M. Patton

Week Three: Monday, July 11–Friday, July 15

Sales calls on state associations (two days)	M. Patton
Brainstorming session on marketing plan	All staff
Deliver mailer for wedding rooms to local country clubs	B. Wallace
Attend counselor selling class in Houston	J. Smith

Week Four: Monday, July 18–Friday, July 22

Local sales calls in Reistertown	B. Wallace
Follow-up calls to summertime government rate mailer	M. Patton
Sales calls in Philadelphia (two days)	P. Johnson
Finalize lists for August phone blitz	D. Carney

Competitive/Market Positioning Grid

A property's operating success is a major factor in determining an appropriate future action plan for that property. The operating success of a lodging facility is a function of both the potential of the market sector in which it is located and its competitive positioning within that market sector.

In order to develop an action plan, use the grid shown earlier in Exhibit 4 to relate the market sector potential to an estimate of the competitive position of each property within its market sector. The horizontal axis of the grid denotes the potential of the market sector, while the vertical axis represents the competitive position of the specific property within that market sector. Ranking on both axes ranges from strong to weak. Competitive position is a function of both quantitative and qualitative considerations, such as the following:

- Amount and quality of competition
- Advantages of location, access, image, facilities, size, rate, etc.
- Ability to meet the needs of available market segments

Fill out these grids for each property. If your property or that of any of your competitors is undergoing renovation or changes that will affect your positioning during the plan year, complete another grid for the future positioning. Obviously, there is a meaning to the position on the grid where a particular property is placed. A hotel in position 1, 2, or 3 is the best show in town, or there is no discernable difference between the number 1 and number 2 competitors. A hotel in position 4, 5, or 6 is not number 1 or number 2 in town. It is of average quality. A hotel in position 7, 8, or 9 is of relatively poor quality when compared to its competition. This hotel is in a discernibly disadvantageous position.

For each hotel, complete four positioning grids, one for each of the four major markets:

- Business Travel—Group

- Business Travel—Transient

- Leisure Travel—Weekend

- Leisure Travel—Vacation

Consider your property's position for each of these consumer targets. For example, a number 1 position means you have the best hotel in a strong market; that is, you have the best hotel in (for example) an 80-percent occupancy market. A number 3 position means you have a weak market—say, an occupancy market of 40 percent.

To use the grid shown in Exhibit 4, denote your hotel's position on the grid by placing an "X" in the most appropriate box. Do the same on separate forms for each of your three major competitors. Once this is done, you can develop and use strategies that are appropriate for your positioning.

Work Plan Example

The following is an example of a work plan for group business from the corporate market.

Action Plans

	Responsibility	Due Date

Direct Sales and Promotions

1. Schedule sales solicitation trips to call on key accounts in:

New York	Smith	Jan./Sept.
Dallas/Fort Worth	Carney	February
Detroit	Patton	March
Boston	Patton	April
St. Louis	Wallace	May
Kansas City	Carney	June
Minneapolis	Marshall	September
San Francisco/San Jose	Smith	October

Action Plans *(continued)*

	Responsibility	Due Date

Direct Sales and Promotions

2. Attend national business-related meetings for:

	Responsibility	Due Date
Meeting Planners International	Smith	June/Dec.
Dialogue in Dallas	Carney	February
Dialogue in Chicago	Smith	June
Dialogue in New York	Smith	September
Meeting World in New York	Smith	July
Participate in Midwest Business Travel Association Annual Meeting	Patton	May

3. Participate in the following blitzes:

	Responsibility	Due Date
Boston	Patton	April
St. Louis	Wallace	May
Minneapolis	Marshall	September
San Francisco/San Jose	Smith	October
Host a Friends-of-the-Family account appreciation function	Staff	May
St. Louis corporate executives fam trip	Wallace	March

Direct Mail

		Responsibility	Due Date
1.	Include all Illinois corporate clients in quarterly activity schedule mailing	Staff	December March June September December
2.	Schedule a mailing to all corporate accounts promoting our "meetings package" to generate business for July, August, November, and December	Staff	April October
3.	Develop a meetings brochure and mail to Chicago-area corporate accounts not currently on file	Wallace	March

Advertising (local/regional media only)

	Responsibility	Due Date
Heavy emphasis to be placed on advertising to the corporate group market. The following publications have been selected for local/regional placement: Chicago Tribune/Business Section Crain's Chicago Business	Carney	Ongoing

Public Relations

		Responsibility	Due Date
1.	Releases to St. Louis media on Corporate Executive's Fam trip	Carney	March
2.	Releases to trade publications on meetings package	Carney Carney	April October

Action Plans *(continued)*

	Responsibility	Due Date
Advertising (local/regional media only)		
3. Releases to local media on Friends-of-the-Family party	Carney	May
4. General releases on newsworthy events relating to corporate meetings in the hotel	Carney	Ongoing

Key Terms

business mix—The major market segments from which your guests come; for instance, 30 percent group, 60 percent transient, and 10 percent leisure.

chronological work plan—A listing of action steps to be taken in date order, with identification of responsibility.

Chapter 22 Outline

Zero-Base Budgeting
Research and Required Information
    Market Segmentation, Needs
        Identification, and Measurement
        of Customer Perceptions
    Facts About the Competition
    External Facts
    Internal Facts
    Other Hospitality Industry Sector
        Applications
Marketing Plan
    Analysis of Research and Information
    Objectives
    Marketing Program
    Marketing Appropriations
    Sales Goals
    Action Programs
    Communication of Assigned
        Responsibilities
    Monitoring of Action Program

Competencies

1. Define zero-base budgeting, identify the four major types of information required to complete a marketing plan, and summarize how this information is obtained. (pp. 281–288)

2. Describe the structure of a marketing plan and summarize tips for putting one together. (pp. 288–293)

22

The Total Corporate/ Multi-Unit Marketing Plan

YOU CANNOT DEVELOP an effective marketing plan without knowing your consumers and knowing which marketing tools to use to sell to consumers. The purpose of this chapter is to provide you with an outline for your marketing plan that ties together the research and application phases of marketing.

The issues and strategies addressed in this chapter can be applied, with some modification, to all sectors of the hospitality industry.

With few exceptions, there are rarely sufficient financial resources to support all of the programs and tools a marketer desires. Many marketers approach their marketing plans in a traditional fashion—they sit down with last year's plan and apply additional dollars, or cut out certain programs as a result of budgetary constraints. Those who do approach a marketing plan in this way ignore the basic premise of marketing—researching and knowing the consumer. They may feel comfortable "ball-parking" marketing budget allocations because they have become familiar with their guest markets over time.

To develop a truly effective marketing plan and make the best use of financial resources, you need to know your **consumers' needs** *today*. You also need to know to which direction their needs are moving. You must know the consumers' habits, preferences, and perceptions of your products or services as well as how consumers perceive your **competition**. You must know your problem areas, whether they are markets, cities, specific properties, or people. Finally, you must identify your strengths and related opportunities. Don't commit one marketing dollar until you have exhaustive knowledge of all these areas. For planning purposes, begin with the zero-base budgeting concept.

Zero-Base Budgeting

Zero-base budgeting is a broad concept that can help you prioritize where you want to spend your limited resources. With zero-base budgeting, no expenditure is justified just because it was made last year. Every expense is re-analyzed and justified annually to determine if it will yield better results than spending the same amount in another way.

One note of caution: frequently there are vital expenses that *must* be maintained at certain minimum levels. For example, a property with a sales force or reservation system must retain certain expenses that relate to those functions and should use extreme caution in applying zero-base budgeting. Some marketers subdivide the marketing budget into a "vital core" of expenses and "all other" categories and apply the concept only to the "all other" category. Some consider this a violation of the principle of zero-base budgeting, while to others it is simply common sense. You are the best qualified to determine which approach is most applicable to your property.

Research and Required Information

The first step in developing a complete marketing plan is to research and gather required information. Required research and information can be divided into four major areas:

• Market segmentation, needs identification, and measurement of customer perceptions

• Facts about your competition

• External facts

• Internal facts

Market Segmentation, Needs Identification, and Measurement of Customer Perceptions

You may already know a great deal about your market and its segments, based on internal customer-origin analysis, your customer data base, or external marketing information you purchased. To update your knowledge and make the most of your marketing expenditures, use the following nine-step process:

1. Identify the geographic markets that yield the greatest number of travelers (both business and pleasure) to the areas in which your facilities are located.

2. Using the major geographic markets identified in step 1 for research sampling, determine the proper segmentation of the total market. Some common market segments in the lodging industry are:

   • Individuals attending a group meeting or convention.

   • Individuals traveling for business with a relatively unrestricted expense account.

   • Individuals traveling for business with a restricted expense account.

   • Individual pleasure travelers without children.

   • Families traveling for pleasure.

   • Couples or families interested only in the essentials of lodging (no-frills).

   • Couples or families seeking to avoid the service, tipping, high costs, semi-rigidity, etc., of hotels, motels, and resorts.

   • Banquet and local restaurant customers.

Common intermediary market segments include:

- Meeting planners.
- Travel agents.
- Traffic departments of major corporations.
- Secretaries.
- VIP clubs.
- Wholesalers.
- Airlines.
- Car rental companies.
- Reservations services organizations.

3. During the segmentation process, *roughly* determine the demographic characteristics of each segment, including the segment's approximate size and trend. With respect to "trend," you should be looking for which direction each segment is heading—is the segment increasing or decreasing as a percentage of your business? Is the segment itself growing or declining? (Research techniques are available to more accurately and specifically determine the demographics, but the costs of extensive research may outweigh its value. An approximate demographic definition should be adequate.) Then select appropriate media to promote your product or service to these segments.

4. Evaluate the travel in each of the demographic segments you want to reach. A national probability sample will give you a fairly accurate assessment of these trends. When you add the results of this sampling technique to your in-house demographic data, you can project meaningful trends for your targeted segments. These will probably be sufficient for your initial efforts in **marketing planning.**

5. Decide which segments you want to pursue and which you do not want to pursue. In making these decisions, consider such facts as:

- Suitability of your existing facilities to meet the needs of these segments.
- Each segment's trend—is it growing or shrinking?
- The profitability of the segment.

For the most part, such decisions will not change your marketing approach. However, for certain segments peripheral to your current business mix, these decisions will be very important, and you will need more information. Defer the marketing decision on whether to pursue the peripheral segments until you get a better idea of the suitability of your property to the defined needs of these segments. (Step 7 helps determine your property's suitability.)

6. Identify in detail the specific needs of each of the segments you hope to reach. Determine what factors, products, or services are most and least important to customers in each segment. Trained interviewers can glean this information from focus groups. (Step 9 helps further measure customer perceptions

through focus groups.) A **focus group** is a small representative sample of your customer base or potential customer base. The group is subjected to a structured interview or series of questions; responses are then analyzed to glean marketing information.

7. Analyze how well your existing products and services meet the needs of each segment. Does your property fall short in providing the products or services required by each segment? Can your existing facilities and services be adapted to meet the needs of each segment? Remember to be objective when analyzing your facilities, products, and services. **Customer perceptions** of your facilities and services often differ from yours. At this point, you may eliminate additional segments from your potential market if your facilities don't meet the needs of those segments. (Note: Even though your property may not fulfill the exact needs of a segment, your property may still do so better than any competitor. This will be determined in step 9. If so, you may still want to pursue that segment.)

8. Identify all major companies that serve your total market. To do this, you will have to analyze the companies based in your market, the type of offices they have (i.e., corporate headquarters, regional offices, district offices, and so on), and their major suppliers/visitors and where they come from (their origin points).

9. Conduct focus group interviews with customers from each **market segment** to measure their perceptions of both your products/services and those of all competitors serving the lodging industry. This should be done in several steps:

    *   Determine which properties are preferred by customers in the segment. What property characteristics do customers in that segment prefer? How do segment customers perceive each property? Which properties relate best to customers in the segment and why?

    *   Determine customer perceptions of other (non-preferred) properties. What characteristics are seen as positive and negative?

    *   Determine how each property is perceived to meet the most important need of the segment (as identified in step 6).

    Make sure your property is considered equally with other competitors. You want an objective measurement of how customers in different market segments view each of their lodging options.

    The perceptions customers have of each lodging competitor are the result of the quality of the property's facilities and operations and of its advertising and promotion schemes. Likewise, the solutions to making any changes in your image will lie equally in operations, facilities, and marketing.

The information obtained through research may not be entirely new to you. However, information on how you compare to your competition will probably be more objective than you have obtained before and, therefore, should be more useful to you. For example: Where does your property have a real advantage over your competition? What are your property's weak spots? What are your competitors' weak spots? Into which new segments can you expand your market? Which segments (if any) absolutely don't want your products or services?

With the nine-step process, you have identified the following information:

- Your market's segments, as classified by needs plus rough demographics

- The size of each market segment and its growth trends—which segments are growing and which are shrinking

- The specific needs of each segment and the relative importance of these needs

- An objective measurement of how well your firm and product or service is perceived to fulfill these needs in relation to your competition

- An identification of which lodging companies best relate to each segment and why

With this information you will be able to more accurately position your property in the marketplace.

Facts About the Competition

You may tend to dismiss the effects of competition on your business. However, when you ignore the competition, you may overlook several variables that affect marketing planning. Focusing solely on your present strengths is also short-sighted in situations involving increased competition, especially in a given market segment.

Although you regard all the things you do as important, consumers may not always agree with you. They see you as a bed, a courteous (or discourteous) employee, a smoothly handled (or fouled-up) reservation, and so on. They often have different priorities than you. Furthermore, consumers in different segments have different priorities. Price, service level, and an overall good experience (lodging, food and beverage, and service) are extremely important. It is important to know how you stack up against your competitors in these areas.

To evaluate your competition, you need the following information: market share data, competitive marketing strategies and practices, and occupancy detail by city.

Market Share Data. Market share data provides a long-range overview of how your property is faring in relation to your major competitors. Often, accurate figures on the size of the total market are unavailable; however, you can get a fairly useful measurement by comparing your own figures (e.g., occupancy and rate figures) against the total of all your major competitors or against a smaller select group of competitors. This can be accomplished on a local, regional, and national level by subscribing to and participating in various industry services such as Smith Travel Data Research, by reviewing market reports issued by industry accounting firms, and by contacting convention and visitors bureaus for information.

Competitive Marketing Strategies and Practices. Be aware of your competitors' current marketing programs when formulating your own marketing strategies.

The most effective way to get information about your competitors' marketing programs is to clip all of their advertising from magazines and newspapers for a period of several months. A clipping service can do this for you, or your advertising agency may be able to help.

It is also useful to get a fix on other media and methods used for competitors' marketing activities, including:

- Radio and TV.
- Outdoor and airport advertising.
- Direct mail.
- Direct solicitation.
- Travel agent solicitation.
- Publicity.
- Sales promotion.

This information will be more difficult to obtain, but there may be ways to learn more about these areas. Most advertising agencies subscribe to syndicated services that supply this data. You may also obtain market information on your own from advertising sales representatives and other individuals who work for the various media outlets (magazines, radio stations, etc.).

The information you gather about competitors' marketing programs doesn't have to be precise or detailed. Try to get enough information to answer the following questions:

- What segments are your competitors pursuing?
- What are their strategies in terms of image-building?
- What media or marketing methods are they using?
- How successful do their marketing programs seem to be?

After gathering this information over a period of time, you will be able to detect shifts in competitive marketing strategies.

Occupancy Detail by City. Compare your property's occupancy data and trends to those of each competitive hotel or motel in your major metropolitan area. Occupancy data should include all major competitors, including hotels and motels that meet recreational and family travel needs as well as business-oriented hotels.

External Facts

External data on market industry trends and travel patterns will be useful when you are ready to develop your own marketing strategies.

Trends in the Overall Travel and Lodging Market. Look for a broad overview of major segment trends, such as signs of growth or decline in pleasure travel versus business travel and/or any other information you can obtain regarding growth trends of the other market segments. This information will be very general, but will help you determine a marketing **strategy.**

Feeder City Data. Feeder city data can be very beneficial when you plan advertising and may already be available to you. It will be included in the total marketing program. **Feeder cities** are the cities from where your business originates. Convention and visitors bureaus, airport authorities, and rental car agencies are just a few of the sources you can explore for this data. There may be differences in feeder city data for pleasure and for business travel. You must consider both markets.

It may seem overly ambitious to try to gather information in this category. Nonetheless, it may prove beneficial to gather information regarding when certain types of group customers historically have met, when certain industries put their salespeople on the road, and other similar information. Concentrate on areas that may help determine specific strategies that can plug holes in your sales patterns.

Internal Facts

Marketing Expenditures. Look at your marketing costs objectively. Marketing cost should be defined as "that amount necessary to procure the sale." Using this definition, include as part of your marketing costs all the following expenses and reductions to income:

* Salesperson salaries and administrative expenses

* Advertising expenditures

* Public relations expenditures

* Travel relations expenditures

* Coupon discounts

* Reservation systems expenses

* Credit card fees you pay to credit card companies

* Others

This definition may not conform to a uniform system of accounts, but it will give you a clearer picture of your actual marketing costs. When you combine an overview of expenditures with a trend analysis, you should be able to more objectively determine the proper allocation of funds needed to carry out the marketing strategies you develop.

Trends in Your Mix of Business. Measure trends in your property's room sales in the following segments:

* Family and pleasure

* Commercial (salespeople, trade, etc.)

* Executives

* Groups (corporate and association)

This information—for a single hotel, on a geographical area basis, or chain-wide—will tell you what is really happening when sales go up or down. You need to know how effective your efforts are in building business in a particular segment.

When you have a decrease in sales, you need to know in what segment the problem lies so that you may take immediate, focused corrective action.

In short, trends in room sales are your monitoring system—the indicator of what is happening and how effective you are in your marketing planning and execution.

Other Hospitality Industry Sector Applications

The marketing planning process outlined in this chapter can be directly applied, with some tailoring, to other hospitality industry sectors. The four major types of research and information required apply to restaurant chains, airlines, car rental firms, cruise companies, and any other major entity serving the away-from-home market. The steps and questions listed within each research phase are, to some extent, applicable to your market and product or service. How you apply these, answer the questions, and analyze the data is up to you. The better your effort, the better your marketing and competitive edge.

Marketing Plan

Now that you have examined the first part of the total marketing plan structure, asked the right questions, and obtained factual answers, you can start the actual marketing plan. The following outline displays the next phase of the total marketing plan.

MARKETING PLAN STRUCTURE

- Analysis of research and information
- Objectives
- Marketing program
- Marketing appropriations (the marketing budget)
- Sales goals
- Action programs
- Communication of assigned responsibilities
- Monitoring of action program

In the marketing plan, you analyze what you have learned about your business and translate it into **action programs.** By combining all of your research into one document, you force yourself to see:

- How (and whether) everything you are doing actually fits together.
- Whether it is logical and sound.
- Whether, in total, it is possible to accomplish with the manpower and money available.

You also clearly establish guidelines for handling day-to-day matters in a manner consistent with your longer range objectives.

Analysis of Research and Information

The following questions identify specific areas to target in the marketing program. Information needed to answer the questions will come from the market segmentation, needs identification, and customer perceptions research discussed earlier.

Customer Needs, Preferences, and Perceptions

1. Which market segments relate best to your products or services?

2. In which areas of need are your products or services perceived to be strong by current market segments? In which areas are they weak?

3. In which areas of need do your strengths (as perceived by the segment) correspond to the first priority needs of the segment?

4. In each weak area (as perceived by the market segment), are there operational factors that contribute to the perceived weakness, or is it purely an image or awareness problem?

5. In each market segment with which you presently best identify, who are your major competitors and what are their major strengths and weaknesses (as perceived by the segment)?

6. Are your main markets presently within the segments that best identify with your product or service? Are there any areas of need in which your competition is perceived as doing a superior job?

7. Which market segments relate least to your product or service? Is this a result of your past marketing programs being focused in other directions, or does it stem from an inaccurate or inadequate awareness of the product or service itself?

8. In each market segment where you see an opportunity to broaden your market, who are your major competitors and what are their major strengths and weaknesses (as perceived by the segment)?

Competitive Trends

1. How has your property fared against competitive lodging chains in recent years?

2. What are the primary marketing directions of your major competitors?

3. What are the major competitive threats facing your property now and in the near future?

Immediate Problems

What are the immediate problems that must be corrected this year? The following list suggests examples of problems that must be addressed immediately:

- Sales problems at a specific property

- Declining business volumes in particular market segments

- Quality and service problems
- Pricing problems
- New competitive lodging facilities that are expected to have an adverse effect on a particular market or property
- Existing marketing strategies that are unsuccessful

Long-Range Major Problems

What are the major marketing problems you face that must be solved to achieve greater success over the next five years? For example:

- Change of image required
- Industry-wide declining business volumes in particular market segments
- Increasing success of a particular competitor (in hotel facility design, in quality and service, in marketing, in overall results, or in combinations of these items)
- Changes in preferences and needs of a particular market segment
- Pricing
- Adverse trends or yields in marketing expenditures

Opportunities and Alternatives

1. What are the major weaknesses of your competitors that you would exploit more fully?

2. What unsatisfied needs have been identified in your present market segments? Is it possible to provide a service or product that will satisfy this need?

3. What market segments peripheral to your current marketing thrust offer opportunities for you to broaden your market?

Objectives

What are the overall **objectives** of your marketing program? These objectives should be determined on the basis of your research and information analysis. Objectives should correspond to the following areas:

- Identification of customer preferences and the desire to change customers' perceptions of your product or service
- Changes in marketing direction desired after comparing your present markets with shifts in the total market
- Defensive or offensive marketing moves dictated by competitive successes and new competitive directions
- Immediate problem-solving
- Long-range problem-solving
- Taking advantage of opportunities open to your property

In order to make the marketing program as effective as possible, restrict the number of marketing objectives to the major items of the highest priority. The whole purpose of marketing planning is to "separate the wheat from the chaff" and to focus on those areas that will yield the greatest results. Attempting to focus on everything will result in more work, greater expenditures, minimal results, and frustration for all. By separating priority from non-priority objectives, you can achieve positive results; hence, it is desirable to limit the number of objectives you establish.

Marketing Program

This section suggests an approach to developing your total marketing program for the next several years, with emphasis on the first year. This section, like the whole marketing plan, should be updated each year.

Overall Strategy. First, state the proposition. That is, define, in general terms, what you are trying to provide and sell to your markets. The proposition should be the promise that can be made to have the strongest appeal to the customers' self-interests. It should be based on the information gathered during the research steps of this marketing planning process. It must be truthful, possible to achieve, and unique. It must clearly distinguish you over the competition.

You may need a different proposition for each market segment. If so, make sure there are no inconsistencies among the propositions.

Next, clarify the platform. Your marketing platform is the list of benefits to the customer and advantages over the competition that your property provides. Spell out, item by item, all the claims you plan to make to your customers. This is not another general statement; it is the detail that supports the proposition. Your promotion and advertising will be based on the platform.

Media Strategy. Use your established objectives to identify precise target markets at which to aim the media. Establish specific advertising, public relations, and direct mail programs, and clearly determine the intent of the program, media selection, dates, and dollars for each.

Each of the advertising, public relations, and direct mail programs should be compared with previous media programs. Program changes should be made on the basis of how the new program will achieve the desired objectives and results better than did the old program. Also, compare your media programs to those of your competitors and address any obvious deficiencies.

Selling Strategy. Specific strategies should be developed for sales and promotion to associations, commercial groups, individual commercial travelers, travel agents, and other market segments. Development of selling strategies must be accomplished at two levels:

- *Corporate level.* Identify activities that will be carried out by your national sales departments' marketing staffs. Also identify overall sales strategies to be implemented by individual or regional sales teams (where applicable).

- *Property level.* Develop specific sales targets and strategies for each property. (Again, identify a few major strategies rather than attempting all the possible ways of building sales.)

Compare these sales strategies with competitors' sales programs and correct any obvious deficiencies. Strategies should also be compared with previous strategies to determine if there are sufficient differences to achieve your desired changes.

You must also identify new staffing requirements and the difference in cost from the preceding programs.

Operations Changes. Identify the changes in operations or procedures required to achieve the desired marketing objectives and establish timing costs.

Marketing Appropriations

Amount. Determine how much funding is needed to achieve the agreed-upon marketing objectives and supporting programs. What is the difference between the amount needed and available funds? Ultimately, a final amount should be determined. If incremental funding is used, keep in mind that there should be an expected offset in incremental revenue.

Allocation. Determine the allocation of available funds among the various functions of marketing: advertising, publicity, sales force, travel agents' commissions, discount coupons, pre-opening campaigns, and research. Use zero-base budgeting, wherein all expenditures must be fully analyzed and their justifications verified each year. This approach may help in re-allocating resources from year to year into areas where they will do the most good.

Since there rarely will be sufficient funds available to execute all the programs needed, available funds should be apportioned according to costs and benefits.

Justification. The justification for the marketing budget is the research and analysis you conduct. If you have approached the marketing planning process in an analytical and pragmatic way, then you will have a strong argument for your budget. If management does not allocate sufficient funds to achieve the necessary results, or if these funds are not efficiently spent, then you must accept something less than the desired objectives.

Sales Goals

Sales goals can be both macro and micro in nature, but they should always be quantified. You may be looking at a sales increase measured in dollars, or you may want to increase your sales percentage as measured against the entire chain's average. The following is a list of questions that can help you identify sales goals:

1. What is the total sales goal for all properties (as a group)? This may be expressed as revenue or in terms of a percentage increase.
2. What is the revenue-per-available-room goal?
3. What is the average occupancy goal for all properties?
4. What is the average room rate goal for all properties?

Exhibit 1   Marketing Program Organization Chart

Item	Target Date	Approved Expenditure	Responsibility
Media Plan			
Selling Plan			

5. What are the goals for room sales in each major business segment? Determine the percent for each segment.

Family and pleasure _____ %

Commercial (sales/trade) _____ %

Executive _____ %

Groups (corporate and associations) _____ %

6. How much additional sales will be generated this year (over last year) for the increase in marketing expenditures over those of last year? Estimate the increase in dollars.

Action Programs

List, in chronological order, all the specific strategies that were allocated available marketing funds. Identify specific target dates, budgeted-approved expenditures, and responsibility. Exhibit 1 shows one way of organizing this information.

Communication of Assigned Responsibilities

Proper steps must be taken to ensure that the most important aspects of this plan, particularly the action program, are clearly communicated to those individuals responsible for program implementation.

Monitoring of Action Program

To properly monitor progress on the action program, institute an adequate follow-up process. The appendix to this chapter presents a simple worksheet to help you allocate the marketing budget by expenditure and by market segment. The worksheet can be modified and applied at the individual property level.

The first attempt at completing a marketing planning process of this nature is always the most difficult. Updating and scheduling periodic research will provide you with an ongoing flow of relevant and applicable information. You must be careful to make sound judgments at stages before the research is completed. However, depending on management's judgment, knowledge, and expertise, some of the data may have immediate application and be beneficial to your marketing programs.

🔑 Key Terms

action program—A list of actions that must be taken to fulfill the marketing plan. It includes target dates, approved expenditures (as differentiated from unapproved estimated costs), and the person(s) responsible for implementing each action.

competition—Any business concern, product, or concept that competes for customers in your market.

consumer needs—Those products and services required by customers in your market, which they are prepared to purchase from you or your competitors.

customer perceptions—The ways in which the customer, in his or her own mind, looks at a product. They include the customer's image of the product. Customer perceptions often differ from management's beliefs and perceptions.

feeder cities—Principal cities within a geographic region that tend to "feed" travel to each other. For example, in the western region of the United States, travel from Los Angeles feeds Palm Springs, Las Vegas, Phoenix, and San Francisco, and vice versa.

focus group—A marketing research technique that combines personal-opinion solicitation in the form of group discussion with a structured set of questions.

market segment—A portion of the total market wherein all of those particular customers have something in common. There are many ways of segmenting a market; the most widely used is by demographics—e.g., sex, age, income, education, etc.

marketing planning—The organized process of studying the market, identifying and measuring its trends, developing objectives and supporting programs, and using the available facts in combination with the experienced judgments of the marketing team. The process includes the development of targets (timing, costs, results expected) and the monitoring of actual achievement against those targets. The purpose of marketing planning is the achievement of maximum desired results through the efficient application of effort and resources.

objectives—What you want to achieve with your marketing efforts. Example: By next year, increase our business in the pleasure travel market by 10 percent.

strategy—How you plan to achieve the objectives you have set. For example: To increase our business in the pleasure travel market by 10 percent within the next 12 months, we will: (1) increase outdoor advertising and (2) shift some of our advertising to family magazines.

zero-base budgeting—A budgeting concept in which no expenditure is justified just because it was expended last year. Every expense is re-analyzed and justified each year on the basis that it will yield more favorable results than spending the same amount in another way.

Chapter Appendix

	MARKET SEGMENTS											
	Pleasure						Business					
	Int'l	Resort	Family	Singles	Weekend		Other	Group		Execu-tives	Commercial		Other
					Family Escape	Children's Escape		Comp.	Assoc.		Exp. Acct.	Per Diem	
National Advertising Consumer Trade Sports Directories Yellow Pages Airport Display													
Local Advertising													
Production Advertisements & Commercials Agency Fees Agency Travel													
National Public Relations Fees Expenses T.V. Participations													
National Direct Mail Mailings Listings													
Brochures													
Research (Advertising & Marketing)													
Projects/Internal Promotion/Mini Markets													
Advertising Administration													
Local Public Relations													
Local Tie-Ins & Contests													
Direct Selling Local Sales Departments National Sales Departments Special Intermediary													
Trade Shows (Exhibitions)													
Familiarization Trips													
Promotional Parties													
Department													
TOTAL													

Chapter 23 Outline

Federal Laws
  The Sherman Act
  The Clayton Act
  The Federal Trade Commission Act
  The Robinson–Patman Act (Section II
    of the Clayton Act)
Laws and Competitive Marketing

Competencies

1. Describe the major federal acts and
   laws that impact marketing.
   (pp. 297–298)

2. Delineate what you cannot do with
   respect to marketing strategies and
   pricing. (pp. 298–299)

3. Identify unfair competitive practices.
   (p. 298)

4. Discuss the concept of anti–trust.
   (p. 298)

23

Marketing and the Law

THERE ARE LITERALLY VOLUMES OF LAWS at the federal, state, and local levels that have direct bearing on marketing tools and strategies. Rule number one for anyone in marketing is to check the law or, better yet, to run it by the legal department. Be sure your external agencies/suppliers run any materials, promotions, advertising, pricing data, mailings, etc., by their legal departments as well. Also, remember to give legal reviewers an adequate amount of time to review your marketing offering/strategies. Don't print it, post it, advertise it, or give it to anyone unless it has cleared legal.

Federal Laws

Numerous laws govern virtually every aspect of marketing. For example, at the federal level there are major "acts" and entities, such as the FTC, Justice Department, etc., that focus on marketing practices. Let's look at just a few of these.

The Sherman Act

The **Sherman Act**, in general, prohibits "every contract, combination, or conspiracy" in restraint of trade, and monopolizing (or attempting to monopolize) any part of trade or commerce.

The Clayton Act

The **Clayton Act** contains basic prohibitions against: (1) exclusive dealing agreements and tying agreements with dealers and customers; (2) corporate mergers and acquisitions that may have adverse competitive effects; and (3) individuals serving at the same time as directors of competing corporations.

The Federal Trade Commission Act

The **Federal Trade Commission Act** is used to supplement the Sherman and Clayton Acts and prohibits "unfair methods of competition in or affecting commerce, and unfair deceptive acts or practices in or affecting commerce."

The Robinson-Patman Act (Section II of the Clayton Act)

This law generally prohibits discrimination in prices or services between two purchasers, which injures competition. Under the **Robinson-Patman Act** buyers can also be held liable. You cannot offer a different price to one buyer than you do to another, if the two are purchasing substantially the same product or service, during the same period of time, in the same quantity. This does not prohibit you from meeting a competitive price.

Laws and Competitive Marketing

The laws also are very specific about what you can and cannot do with respect to your competitors. You cannot **denigrate** your competitors' products or services. You cannot make fraudulent demands for samples. You cannot have friends call and clog the competitors' phone lines. You cannot sell your products/services at cost or below in an attempt to force your competitor out of business.

The greatest danger in **anti-trust** law is **contact** with competitors. Any kind of agreement or understanding with a competitor, formal or informal, oral or written, expressed or implied, in regard to prices, terms, conditions of sale, volume of production, limitations of production or sales or of territories, allocations of customers or product markets or limitation of quality, is illegal under one or more of the acts described above.

Violations of these laws have severe penalties for the individual and the company. Individuals can be sent to federal prison. These above-referenced acts/laws are not all the laws your marketing strategies must comply with. There are numerous state and local laws with respect to virtually every marketing strategy. Here are just a few of the areas governed by laws:

- Product **liability** (includes **fraud**, deceit, misrepresentation, design defect, breach of warranty, product safety, etc.). Product safety is monitored by the Consumer Product Safety Commission.

- Packaging/labeling law—promotional strategy and compliance

- Warranty compliance

- Patent protection

- Your trademark as part of your package

- Anti-trust issues related to the channels of distribution

- Laws with respect to physical—handling relationships

- Sales laws

- Direct marketing legal compliance (includes privacy, high-pressure tactics, telemarketing, copyright, obscenity, "infomercials," etc.)

- Franchise legal compliance (includes disclosure statements, terminations, trademark licensing issues, anti-trust issues, etc.)

- Tie-ins and co-ops and coercion

- Pricing policy (includes price fixing, competitors, price discrimination, etc.)

- Promotional policies (includes time frames, access, coupons, mail fraud, label and advertisement issues, etc.)

- Traditional advertising (includes copyright protection, photographs, releases, film, headline compliance, "sale," "new," inclusion/exclusion, disclaimers, conditions, rules, "trial," "examination," wording, use of flags, use of money/ currency, demonstrations, claims, comparisons, endorsements, etc.)

- Personal promotions (includes door-to-door sales, product demonstrations, cancellations, multilevel marketing schemes, pyramiding, referral sales agreements, bait and switch advertising, etc.)

- Credit/financing (includes truth in lending, disclosure laws, security interest, late fees, credit card purchases, damages, cash discounts, billing, prescreening, discrimination, credit reporting/checking, clear wording/contract terms, electronic fund transfers, fraudulent use, etc.)

- Collecting debts (includes dunning, telephone practices, prohibited practices, methods, etc.)

- Contracts (includes contractual relationships, terms, clauses, trade secrets, signatures, computer hardware and software agreements, employment contracts, contracts related to confidentiality, product and character licensing agreements, character copyrights, computer fraud, etc.)

Laws change every day; some are amended, others are replaced, new laws are approved, and even new court interpretations are made of existing laws. Before you launch your marketing program, be sure you are in compliance with the law. The best check is to run every element of your program through the legal review process. Also, be sure to use the laws to your benefit as marketing tool. Establish a monitoring system of your key competitors' activities, and make sure they are competing not only fairly but in compliance with the law.

☞ Key Terms

anti-trust—A U.S. federal law prohibiting the establishment of trusts, business monopolies, or cartels. The law specifically prohibits "contact" with competitors with regard to prices, terms, conditions of sale, volume of production, limitations of production or sales or of territories, allocations of customers or product markets, or limitation of quality, etc.

Clayton Act—A U.S. federal law prohibiting exclusive dealing agreements and tying agreements with dealers and customers, corporate mergers and acquisitions that may have adverse competitive effects, and individuals serving at the same time as directors of competing corporations.

contact—As regards anti-trust law, any business-oriented meeting of individuals for the purpose of manipulating or controlling competition.

denigrate—To disparage the character or reputation of a competitor or competitor's products with the purpose of elevating the character and reputation of your own.

Federal Trade Commission Act—A U.S. federal law supplementing the Sherman Act and prohibiting unfair methods of competition in or affecting commerce and unfair deceptive acts or practices in or affecting commerce.

fraud—Intentional deception or misrepresentation of a product's or service's features, capabilities, quality, etc.

liability—The legally bound responsibility of a company to make good any loss or damage that occurs in a transaction.

Robinson-Patman Act—A U.S. federal law that prohibits discrimination in prices or services between two purchasers, which injures competition. The law prohibits sellers from offering a different price to one buyer over another, if the two are purchasing substantially the same product or service, during the same time period, in the same quantity.

Sherman Act—A U.S. federal law prohibiting all contracts, combinations, or conspiracy for the purpose of restraining trade. This law also prohibits monopolizing or attempting to monopolize any part of trade or commerce.

Chapter 24 Outline

Research
Operations

Competencies

1. Explain how research supports a property's overall marketing effort. (pp. 303–304)

2. Describe how operations can meet the expectations of guests, and summarize ways to handle guest complaints. (pp. 304–307)

24

Marketing, Operations, and Research

Using every available marketing tool and sticking to an organized marketing plan are not enough to guarantee success in the hospitality industry. Marketing tools and plans cannot be fully effective unless they are: (1) based on sound research and (2) supported by your operations team. This chapter focuses on the relationship between research, marketing, operations, and the guest.

Research

Research can, and should, play a major role in both operations and marketing. Research does not provide strategies, but it does identify issues that both marketing and operations need to address. Research supports the overall marketing effort by identifying:

- *What* is currently happening within the market (customer perceptions, needs, etc.).

- *Which* competitors are having an effect on the market (competitive strategy assessment).

- *What* is likely to happen to the market (environmental forecast).

- *How* the property or brand is performing within the market against the competition (see Exhibit 1).

In a very real sense, research provides balance and support to both marketing and operations.

Research results should be factual parameters within which marketing, operations, and development can function. These results identify key market and industry trends, competitive strategies, and implications upon which marketing strategies may be developed.

Research should also be used to objectively measure property performance, strategy execution, guest preferences, and guest responses to the property's marketing strategies. Once you've measured these variables, you can evaluate the effectiveness of the property's overall marketing plan—how well marketing selected its strategies and how well operations fulfilled the expectations created by those strategies.

Research provides the basis upon which to rank, grade, and compare your property and your competition. Regardless of how the "scorecard" reads (share of

303

Exhibit 1   Focal Points of Research

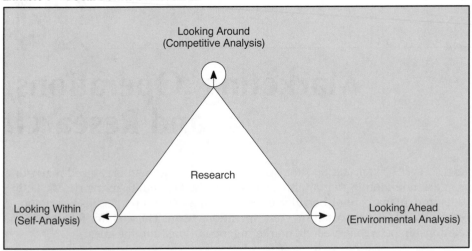

market, occupancy, average rate, covers, check averages, etc.), these results reflect guest reactions to the marketing message or promise and to operations' fulfillment of that message. Analysis of guest needs and preferences must go beyond the research identification stage to convey an accurate assessment of guest expectations to both marketing and operations.

Operations

A marketing plan is developed based on the guest needs and expectations that were identified by research. A marketing plan cannot be executed successfully until operations delivers a product or service that meets guest needs and expectations as promised in the marketing. In order to ensure **customer satisfaction**, operations *must* meet guest needs by providing a level of service or product that matches the marketing message and related pricing.

Given the assumption that research, marketing, and operations act as a team, a number of practical steps can be taken to see that guest expectations are satisfactorily met. One useful tool that can be easily adapted to the hospitality industry-lodging sector is an operations checklist. An operations checklist is based on the **guest's perspective,** not necessarily on the viewpoints of the property's marketing and operations staff members.

Operations Checklist (from the guest's perspective)

Preliminary Guest-Contact Points

_____   Advertising Display Boards—Are they clean and up-to-date? Do they show the correct telephone number and clear directions to the property?

_____ Limousine/shuttle/courtesy transportation—Are the vehicles clean and well-maintained? Is the service convenient for guests? Do the vehicles leave on schedule?

_____ Drivers/valets—Do drivers/valets have a clean, professional appearance? Do they have a sales-oriented, positive, friendly attitude?

_____ Facility Exterior—Are the buildings and outside areas clean and well maintained? Are bushes and other landscaping well maintained and free of debris? Are walkways well lit, clean, and obstacle-free? Are parking and exterior areas secure and well-lit?

Major Guest-Contact Points (Front Desk/Lobby)

_____ Front Desk—Is the area clean and well maintained? Does it project a feeling of activity? Are promotional materials visible and readily available without cluttering the counter?

_____ Front Desk Employees—Do front desk employees greet guests in a friendly, positive manner? Do employees efficiently help guests check in and check out? Do employees ask if departing guests would like to make future reservations?

_____ Telephone Operators—Are operators courteous and well trained? Is there an adequate staff? Do operators consistently answer the phone within three rings?

_____ Bellstaff—Are bellpersons courteous and helpful? Do they "hustle" to provide service to guests? Are they informative and sales-oriented without seeming too talkative?

_____ Restrooms—Do restrooms near the public areas have adequate supplies? Are the floors cleaned before and after meeting breaks? Are the counters wiped before and after breaks?

Food and Beverage Areas

_____ Breakfast Service—Is service fast? Do employees always offer coffee refills? Is a morning paper available? Do employees demonstrate friendly, courteous attitudes?

_____ Food and Beverage Employees—Do all food and beverage employees convey a friendly and helpful attitude toward guests? Does each employee have a clean, professional appearance? Are employees well trained and efficient?

_____ Food Quality/Presentation—Does the food convey value, quality, and quantity? Is the presentation of the food attractive?

_____ Menus and Promotional Materials—Are menus and promotional materials on the tables or quickly presented to the guest? Are they up-to-date and accurate? Are they clean?

_____   Floors/Windows—Are floors clean and dry? Are they free of obstacles and safety hazards? Are windows and window treatments clean and well-maintained?

_____   Tabletops—Are all utensils, linens, and glassware clean and in their proper places? Is anything missing from the table set-up? Are tables and chairs clean and well-maintained?

_____   Check Presentation—Is the customer's check quickly presented when requested? Is the customer told how and whom to pay at that time?

Other Areas

_____   Gift Shop—Is the gift shop well stocked with current issues of reading material? Do available items meet travelers' needs, such as toiletries or gifts for spouses and children? If credit cards are accepted, is this information adequately displayed?

_____   Recreational Amenities Areas—Are recreational facilities and amenities clearly promoted? Are directions to the facilities clearly visible? Are recreation areas clean and well maintained? Are plenty of towels available in the pool area? Are supplies, such as rackets and balls, available for sports and game areas?

These checklist items are what the guest sees or experiences; the manner in which they are presented determines the guest's perception of your operation. Successfully addressing each of the checklist items should result in customer satisfaction with the marketing message and the property. *Always remember the customer's perspective!*

Recognizing that it is impossible to always meet every guest's needs, both marketing and operations personnel should be thoroughly trained to handle problems if they occur. Complaints and problems often indicate areas in which the operation is not fulfilling the marketing message. Some key questions to answer include the following.

- Does your property have clear refund procedures and guidelines for dealing with dissatisfied guests? Do employees understand these policies and procedures?

- Is there a guest comment card and/or a number or person a guest can call to have a complaint resolved?

- Are employees trained to respond to and take care of guest complaints immediately?

- Are employees trained to notify a manager or supervisor about all guest complaints?

Having a well-trained staff and procedures for handling guest complaints can help keep customers satisfied and result in repeat business. One way to ensure that procedures work is to develop a "listen and tell" system. Simply stated, each employee is trained to listen to guest comments and conversations for clues to guest dissatisfaction, such as, "The light bulb doesn't work," or "The faucet leaks." The employee then passes the information along to the appropriate person or department to promptly correct the problem—before the guest returns to his or her room, if possible. This approach reduces the need to placate the complainer and results in a satisfied guest.

Marketing does not drive operations nor does operations drive marketing—the guest drives both. Research is one way to determine guest needs and the best way to meet those needs. Marketing cannot work without researched information and operational fulfillment. Marketing, research, and operations form a dependent, mutually beneficial support system with research as a base, marketing as the means of communication, and operations as fulfillment; the result is customer satisfaction.

Key Terms

customer satisfaction—Meeting the identified needs of each guest with a level of service and product quality that matches or exceeds the expectations created by your property's marketing message and related pricing.

guest perspective—How the guest views your products or services.

Chapter 25 Outline

Automation
> The Relationship to Marketers and
> Consumers
> Reservations Systems
> Property Management Systems
> Marketing Information Systems
> Travel Purchasing Systems and
> Beyond

Competencies

1. Summarize the history of automation
   in the hospitality industry and
   describe automation applications and
   trends. (pp. 309–314)

   Note: This chapter presents
   speculation about the future. Although
   the speculation is based largely on
   current factual information, it is
   nonetheless speculation. For that
   reason, it is presented strictly for your
   information and enjoyment. The test
   materials for the course include no
   questions on this chapter.

25

Travel Purchasing Systems: Automation and Beyond

THE HOSPITALITY BUSINESS is not driven by operations or marketing, but rather by consumers. As a result of automation, consumers have come to expect ever more from marketing. The advances in computer applications in travel transactions, the purchase of travel, reservations services, front office systems, guest histories and relations, customer services, and research analysis are all changing the game called marketing in our industry. In fact, these computer applications will, in all likelihood, cause a marketing revolution in the hospitality industry. This chapter reviews these automation trends and predicts what the future will hold.

Automation

The hospitality industry is no exception to worldwide industrial trends when it comes to **automation:** the replacement of manual or personally performed functions by automated equipment such as computers. Granted, the hospitality industry is one of the last to be engulfed by automation, but, just as computer-driven assembly lines and robotics transformed the automobile and other heavy-manufacturing industries, automation is likely to have a dramatic impact on the hospitality industry. In fact, the impact will be in the very area that opponents of automation claimed to be sacred in the service industries: the people-contact areas. Automation will have some of its greatest impacts on the hospitality industry in the expediting of consumer purchasing decisions, changing consumer purchasing behavior, and providing new services to travelers.

Traditionally, automation was narrowly perceived as a tool for producing and analyzing budgets, reports, statistics, and accounts. Starting with these largely financial applications, computers began to creep into other areas of application such as sales reporting, rooms inventory control, and timekeeping. As telecommunications and computer technology grew, so did reservations systems and their ability to handle transactions. This, in turn, led to further inroads by computers, as computers were used to analyze the captured reservations data, thus providing marketing information. Further applications of automation and computer technology resulted in front-office systems that provided such marketing data as customer histories, patterns of use, and preferences. It became very clear that automation had entered the world of marketing in the hospitality industry.

The Relationship to Marketers and Consumers

These technological advances in computers, system development, and telecommunications continue to produce many different relationships among automated equipment (such as computers), marketers, and consumers. For marketers, automation has provided the valuable tools of **guest histories,** customer preferences, demographic and psychographic profiles, and the resulting improvement of services and delivery of such services to consumers. For consumers, their purchasing behavior has been affected by 800 numbers, central reservations offices, pricing based on statistical analyses of supply-and-demand periods/ratios, and a host of conveniences made possible by automation. These conveniences include the presentation of multiple choices instantly displayed on CRTs, express/automated ticket purchasing, express check-in and check-out, automatic traveler's check- and cash-dispensing machines linked nationwide, and one-stop trip purchasing, to name just a few. Today, consumers can simply dial an 800 number or even access their own CRTs and do all their travel/trip purchasing with one call—hotel room, car rental, airline ticket, events tickets, etc. How these conveniences are delivered to the marketplace and which industry players are alert enough to fully embrace and employ these automated conveniences are things to watch for as the hospitality industry makes exciting advances in the years ahead. Those businesses that recognize the automation trends and invest and adjust should be successful. Failure to recognize these trends will likely result in losing touch with consumers and losing sales. Think about it. Today, consumers opt for the convenience of an automated teller or transaction machine (**ATM**) to access their cash. Why shouldn't they expect the same convenience when checking in or out of a hotel, buying an airline ticket, or renting a car?

Reservations Systems

Airline, car rental, and hotel reservations systems all have evolved into performing much broader functions than their original function of enabling a consumer to make a purchase or a rental. Today, airline systems have become travel purchasing systems with immense capabilities. Car rental systems have evolved into highly sophisticated data banks that can generate everything from car-preference to purchase-preference histories. Hotel reservations systems have turned into marketing and information management systems that store guest history and preference records.

Before we look at specific reservations systems as they have evolved into travel purchasing systems, let's put reservations systems into perspective. Basically, reservations systems have become collectors or gathering points of vast amounts of consumer, product, and marketing data. Exhibit 1 depicts reservations systems in this collector or gathering role.

One of the first phases in the evolution of reservations systems was simply the *purchase facilitator* phase, which is often associated with an 800 number and a central reservations facility. The second phase was an expansionary one that might be termed the *data collector* phase. The third evolutionary phase was the organized

Exhibit 1   Reservations Systems as Collectors

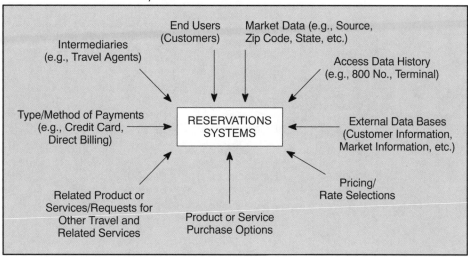

process of recasting this data into usable marketing and operations data—what is often referred to as the *management information* phase.

Many expansions of reservations-system capabilities paralleled the development of computer hardware and software. Today, one could argue that the ability to interface external data bases with reservations systems, thus providing data back to consumers, is the fourth phase of system development. The instantaneous or simultaneous relationship of data in all transaction outlets and locations may be thought of as another key phase or breakthrough—call it phase five. These five phases are shown in Exhibit 2. Regardless of terminology or the number of phases involved, these developments were, and are, major changes to what was originally simple purchase-facilitating systems.

There are many different reservations systems in the travel industry. Historically the Westron hotel-related system was one of the pioneers. Its capabilities were often used as a model for the development of many other hotel reservations systems. Holiday Corp. developed the Holidex system, Hilton the Hiltron system. The rental car industry has the "Wizard of Avis" and the "Hertz System." For years airline reservations systems were dominated by American Airlines' Sabre system and United's Apollo system.

Property Management Systems

Just as automation has influenced the purchasing process, so too is it influencing how the product or service is operated. **Property management systems, front office systems,** and back-of-the-house automation can be complex subjects in themselves. This section is intended to simply relate the relationship of property management systems to marketing. There are dozens of property management systems and firms in the business and dozens of hardware and software suppliers. Our concern is their significance to marketing and consumers.

Exhibit 2   Major Phases of Development and Growth of Reservations Systems

Marketing directly benefits through applications of data that come from property management systems. Revenue maximization can be the big payoff from having a property management system with related software technology that can provide accurate forecasting. The ability to make rate adjustments daily, even hourly, based on historic profiles is one of the benefits of such systems. Knowing when to sell up or when to discount can be invaluable to maximizing revenue. Other benefits include better rooms inventory control, more accurate management of room blocks, and yield management capabilities.

The importance of automation to marketing and consumers also includes better service through guest histories and related recognition programs. Today, a consumer often can count on the same room, same seat, and same car preference as a result of guest or user history and preference systems. Property management systems have also enhanced the ability of hotels to offer express check-in, express check-out, and even automated check-in and check-out. This same technology has allowed for automated airline ticketing and car rentals.

To understand the significance of all this technology to hospitality marketing, marketers must closely monitor consumer acceptance and use of automation and understand how automation has changed consumer behavior. If consumers put a high value on any particular aspect of hospitality automation, marketing and operations must respond. Banks that didn't offer 24-hour access through automatic teller machines found that their customers deserted them, despite their fine "personal" service, for banks that offered this convenience. Hoteliers, especially those of the old school, will need to open their minds and be flexible in their attitudes about automation in order to keep up with and serve their customers. Customers and their desires are the true driving forces today in the hospitality industry.

Marketing Information Systems

Automation has also spurred numerous applications of data and information for marketing purposes. Today, the sales department in a hotel can act with some sophistication in profiling customer behavior, analyzing meetings patterns, prioritizing accounts, and generating leads. Marketing can assess promotions by tracking patterns of consumer response, identifying geographic and demographic segments, and pinpointing the types of consumers who responded and why, where, and how they actually responded.

Selection of media based on key feeder market data, and selection of a creative approach based on identifiable potential customer likes and dislikes, is now at our fingertips and demanding to be used and applied. Marketing partners such as travel agents and tour operators can be selected and evaluated based on automated records of performance, market preferences, and even demographic and psychographic clientele profiles. The influence of automation continues in virtually every aspect of marketing from research sampling to media selection.

The elements of a marketing information system include key group trends such as location preference and history, frequency of use, type and number of rooms, and spending patterns. For corporate accounts, these can be categorized by dollar volume, market, size, or other measurement. Promotional programs and travel agency productivity can also be included as part of the detailed data output. Again, the purpose of all these applications is simply to be better in marketing your product or service and, most important of all, to keep up with and understand how to reach consumers.

Travel Purchasing Systems and Beyond

All the pieces are identified and the major players are emerging for what many believe will be a revolution in the marketing of travel. The technological developments in hardware and software have evolved to a remarkable level of sophistication.

Let's take another look at the origin of today's travel purchasing systems. In the 1960s, airlines created reservation systems and in the 1970s began aggressively installing them in travel agencies. Rental car and hotel reservations capabilities were added to make the systems multi-product/service in nature. When the U.S. government deregulated the air carriers in the 1980s, most airlines decided to treat their reservations systems as separate businesses and spun them off into new companies. This was followed by the merger or acquisition of systems as the airline industry sorted out and consolidated. In the 1990s, through interlinks and networking, the airline reservations systems became global in nature.

The Galileo reservations system had its origin in the United Airlines' Apollo reservations system. Galileo and Sabre (a reservations system that originated with American Airlines) have more than half of the market share of CRTs today. There are a variety of ways hotel chains link and participate in these various global systems. One common way is in the form of an agreement directly with the system or through a "switching" service/company.

Today, system enhancements include everything from quicker/instant information access to video displays to interlinks with on-line services to personal computers. On-going technical enhancements in inventory control and various marketing programs are constantly changing the delivery capabilities of these systems. MSN, America Online, etc., all include travel information services that allow subscribers to check airline schedules, view resort facilities, check visa requirements, and book their own travel arrangements. The amount and type of information available to today's traveler is virtually unlimited.

Naturally, marketing your product or service through these global distribution systems, networks, and services means access to the consumer and potential gains in market share. If you are not participating, you are simply not visible to the electronic consumer or travel intermediary.

Going beyond the traditional boundaries of airline-reservations-system automation has become a reality. The linking of consumer-related services, hospitality industry services, home banking systems, and even manufactured travel-related products is not only technologically feasible but in progress today. Because of the interest of hardware suppliers and software services, the world's technology experts are dreaming up ideas on how to enhance the purchase and marketing of the hospitality industry's products and services. Today you can sit in your home, office, or car and—via a PC, laptop, or hand-held computer—select everything from your airline seat to the view desired from your resort room. You can press a button and receive your e-ticket or access code, traveler's checks, etc.

Today's technology is revolutionizing travel marketing and purchasing. Advancements in technology and consumer demand all point to a total TPS (Travel Purchasing System). The total system will encompass more than can be imagined, as the technologies of reservations systems, automated banking, fiber-optics, and telecommunications are linked with new microprocessing technologies to form a super TPS capable of providing everything from your seat assignment to your travel advance, your room access code to your car access code. The future of travel automation is now.

Key Terms

ATM—Automated teller, transaction, or ticketing machine.

automation—The computerization of manual functions.

front office systems—The computerization of front office functions, including items such as rooms management, housekeeping, rooms availability, rates, etc.

guest history—A record of a guest's purchase patterns and preferences.

property management systems (PMS)—Computer systems that help managers with a variety of management tasks, including rooms inventory control, guest histories, and rate management.

Chapter 26 Outline

The Historic Foundations of Corporate
   Marketing Strategies
     Internally Driven Forces
     Externally Driven Forces
Corporate Strategies
Strategic Assessment
The New Paradigm

Competencies

1. Explain the historic foundations of corporate marketing strategies. (pp. 317–318)

2. Describe how internal and external forces help shape corporate marketing strategies. (pp. 318–323)

3. Describe the forces likely to have a significant impact on the hospitality industry and hospitality marketing in the future. (pp. 323–325)

Note: This chapter presents speculation about the future. Although the speculation is based largely on current factual information, it is nonetheless speculation. For that reason, it is presented strictly for your information and enjoyment. The test materials for the course include no questions on this chapter.

26

The New Paradigm

U NDERSTANDING CORPORATE MARKETING STRATEGIES in the hospitality industry requires an insight into both internal (within the industry itself) and external (sociodemographic and psychographic) factors affecting these strategies. During the twentieth century many external trends and internal industry occurrences helped shape corporate marketing strategies. As we move into the twenty-first century, new driving forces will influence hospitality corporations' overall marketing strategies. This chapter will discuss the historic twentieth-century forces that will continue to influence the future and provide a strategic assessment of the trends shaping the twenty-first century and the implications of those trends for marketing in the hospitality industry.

The Historic Foundations of Corporate Marketing Strategies

A brief historical review is essential to understanding the evolution of most corporate marketing strategies in the hospitality industry. Historically, the hotel was a lodging property that served the person traveling to urban centers. In the 1950s one of the first alternative corporate strategies to hotels was the invention of the roadside lodging property—or "motel"—by Kemmons Wilson: Holiday Inn. Thus, two major product segments emerged in the hospitality industry: the hotel, a downtown product, and the motel, a highway or roadside product. One was geared for business travelers; the other was aimed at the family market. With this development came the beginning of large-scale market segmentation in the hospitality industry.

In the early decades of the twentieth century, Marriott, Howard Johnson's, and other companies grew from root beer stands, ice cream shops, and coffee shops into legitimate restaurant companies. The evolutionary strategy that took both Willard Marriott and Howard Johnson from one simple, small food establishment into the full gamut of food service facilities continued until it manifested itself in the next logical service to travelers—providing beds. This became the multiple-product strategy: providing multiple services with integrated, generally related products to consumers.

As these early hospitality entrepreneurs began to succeed, demand for their concepts outstripped their resources for expansion. The answer for bringing more of their products and services to the market was quickly found in another pioneering corporate strategy called **franchising**, an expansionary strategy. The phenomenal growth of Holiday Inn best exemplifies franchising in its heyday. One need only look at other franchising companies within the hospitality industry such as McDonald's, Burger King, and Wendy's to see how successful franchising is as a strategy for growth.

These basic market segmentation, multiple product, and expansionary strategies nurtured growth in the hospitality industry throughout the twentieth century. These three strategies are the foundation of today's corporate marketing strategies. Internally driven forces and externally driven forces made these strategies dynamic rather than static.

Internally Driven Forces

The early strategies of today's hospitality corporations were internally driven. Simply stated, the driving force of entrepreneurs was the desire to see their businesses grow, and new ideas were the principal corporate strategies. This occurred during a time—the 1950s and 1960s—in which quantitative units and growth rates were the only buzz words known in hospitality companies. In fact, not until the early 1970s did "strategic planning" even become a part of the vocabulary of hospitality corporations. This internal strategic drive resulted in further market and product segmentation. It took on different meanings for different companies. For Holiday Inn it meant locations that were at logical stopping points along the highway. Later, for Hilton and others, it meant entering the marketplace with an "inn" product and expanding this product through franchising. For the hospitality industry as a whole, it meant the birth and development of what would one day be known as the age of brand proliferation—the 1980s. Ramada Inns, Quality Inns, Sheraton Inns, and Hilton Inns emerged, along with larger companies such as Sheraton Hotels, Hilton Hotels, and InterContinental Hotels.

It is evident that a dual strategic thrust existed—internally driven product diversification and externally demanded market segmentation. However, in the 1950s and early 1960s the motivator or cause was internal, and growth in the number of units was the game.

Externally Driven Forces

Long before John Naisbitt wrote or even conceived of *Megatrends*, major external forces were in place that would have a lasting impact on the strategies of corporations in the hospitality industry. These external forces were large enough to influence and shape corporate strategy as it relates to markets, products, quality, levels of services, pricing strategies, and so on. Those who stayed in step with these trends would become the industry leaders and growth companies of the 1980s. Key external forces can be succinctly listed:

- Population trends (growth, mix, and movement)

- Growth of affluence (wealth, discretionary income, etc.)

- Emergence of classes (low, middle, upper-middle, upper)

- Development of transportation systems (interstates, airports, "hub" airports, etc.)

- Tier qualitative segmentation of values, tastes, and psychographics
- Internationalism of commerce: global perspective versus national isolationism

What is significant is not the importance of each of these external forces, but the fact that components of each (a wealthier America, an older population, the emergence of "yuppies," etc.) were strong enough to cause the emergence of everything from today's supply of luxury accommodations to a surge in the budget motel lodging segment. In the late 1980s and early 1990s, the hospitality industry lived up to its label as a dynamic industry. The savings and loan crisis, real estate reevaluations, the falling away of weak companies, and constant changes of ownership (not just of properties, but of entire chains), and the growth of REITs (real estate investment trusts) were prevalent throughout the last decades of the twentieth century.

Corporate Strategies

As you have read, there is no single overriding factor that determines a hospitality corporation's marketing strategies. Rather, multiple internally driven and externally driven forces combine with a company's historic roots to determine its strategies today. There are as many ways to categorize strategies as there are corporate strategists in the industry. The perspective presented in this section is based on the author's participation in planning processes within several of the companies used as examples and from 25 years of study and observation of other corporations in the industry. The first strategy categorization might simply be termed *horizontal expansion.*

Corporate Strategy I: Horizontal Expansion. The hospitality industry encompasses food, beverage, lodging, and travel-related services. Therefore, horizontal expansion simply means expanding from one line of hospitality product or service (for example, food) to another (for example, lodging). For instance, Marriott now encompasses many hospitality services: food, lodging, retirement communities, etc. Holiday Inn now offers multiple lodging brands. Other hotel chains now include restaurants, resorts, and gaming and casino operations.

Corporate Strategy II: Geographic Expansion. At first, hospitality companies developed within a relatively small radius of their origin. For example, Marriott was known primarily as a Washington, D.C.-area company until the late 1970s. But its rapid growth in lodging west of the Mississippi helped it develop into a national brand in the 1980s. Holiday Inn was a mid-south company, Ramada a southwestern company, La Quinta a Texas company. A combination of factors—market growth opportunities, sales of franchises, and the unit-growth mentality of the 1960s and 1970s—caused many local and regional hospitality firms to emerge with national—and ultimately international—status. The same is true of restaurant firms, such as Denny's, Wendy's, Burger King, and Arby's. For airlines, mergers and route system expansions created regional and then national carriers. Southern, Mohawk, Northeast, and Hughes AirWest all were absorbed into larger carriers, while Eastern, Pan Am, and others disappeared as brands.

Corporate Strategy III: Product Hybridization. Perhaps because of Holiday Inn's phenomenal growth and the entry of other motel developers into the marketplace, it wasn't long before traditional high-rise hotel companies began developing and franchising low-rise "inns." Hilton Inns and Sheraton Inns are two examples of **product hybrids** (variations on base products) that developed in the late 1960s and early 1970s. Product hybrids also were natural strategies for companies that began simply as motels: soon there were high-rise motels called Holiday Inns, Ramada Inns, and Marriott Inns. Motel product hybrids continued to appear as high-rise and mid-rise facilities offering more services than the traditional motel.

Corporate Strategy IV: Specialization. Just as Holiday Inn began with the idea of offering families affordable accommodations, other entrants into the marketplace began as specialists categorized by price or service levels. For example, Motel 6, Days Inns, La Quinta, and Budget Inns began with a specialized product offering limited facilities—essentially guestrooms only. In the food segment of the industry came fast-food, salad bars, pizza parlors, specialty restaurants, steak houses, and seafood eateries. Specialization also went upscale in both pricing and services offered. Today there are all-suite companies such as Embassy Suites and a plethora of luxury-only hotel chains. Interestingly, some of these specialized products and services were the result of what is perhaps one of the most commented-on corporate strategies: product "tiering."

Corporate Strategy V: Product Tiering. Product tiering was an initial corporate response to growth limitations and the aging of corporations' prevalent products. The limitations of growth could have resulted from market saturation or could have occurred when the actual economics of the original concept no longer worked or were not as lucrative as an alternative approach. Ramada developed a three-tiered approach in the early 1980s: Ramada Inns, Ramada Hotels, and Ramada Renaissance Hotels. Each of these product tiers reflected different pricing, different levels of service, and operational variations. Holiday Inns, Holiday Inn Hotels, and Holiday Inn Crowne Plazas represented Holiday Inn's original product tiering. Other companies soon followed with various forms of product tiering, manifested in an upscale movement from inn to hotel to super hotel. Product tiering also influenced companies such as Marriott, which de-emphasized inns and franchising and opted to go in other directions with hotels and mega-hotels (1,000 rooms or more) called Marriott Marquis. Marriott Marquis was followed by a low-rise lodging product, Courtyards by Marriott, and extended-stay and all-suite products. Radisson, Choice Hotels International, Hyatt, and other lodging chains all developed types of facilities with varying levels of services, amenities, and pricing structures. This was simply the lodging industry's response to the mega-forces of population growth and demographic, economic, and psychographic segmentation. Product tiering was rampant in the industry by the early 1980s and continued to expand in the 1990s.

Corporate Strategy VI: Product Branding. Product branding is one of the more recent corporate strategies. This is a result in part of the proliferation of tiering and the subsequent consumer and franchise confusion it caused. The confusion was the result of a considerable amount of product re-labeling mixed in with some genuine product tiering. An establishment looked like a motel and smelled like a motel, but often had another name. As a result of this confusion and of an even stronger force or marketplace dynamic known as consumer awareness, product branding emerged. Ironically, this occurred as the hospitality industry, one of the world's oldest industries, was just entering the era of brand identification. The focus of product branding is to clearly define what a product or service is, in terms of level and quality of service, location, price, and other key consumer-oriented factors such as the psychographic appeal of "prestige" or "thrift."

There are a number of clear examples of today's product branding. To understand these, one might think of a hospitality corporation as analogous to General Motors. For example, Holiday Inn has followed the General Motors product branding concept and now offers multiple brands, such as Crowne Plaza, Holiday Inn, and Holiday Inn Express—everything from a Chevrolet to a Cadillac. Marriott has adopted a similar strategy, with Marriott Hotels, Marriott Resorts, Marriott Marquis, Courtyards by Marriott, etc. Other companies have elected to develop what might be analogous to the Porsche or Jaguar concept: one product of high quality—one brand, no variations. Examples of hospitality corporations with one-brand strategies include Four Seasons, Ritz-Carlton, and Westin, to name a few. These brands may change ownership, but their labels and names depict a very specific product positioning.

Corporate Strategy VII: Non-Franchising. Usually, firms do not franchise in order to keep greater control over the quality, ownership, and management of their properties. Often these firms are strong enough financially that franchising is unnecessary. Examples of lodging chains that do not franchise are few. Four Seasons, Westin Hotels, and Motel 6 are such examples.

Corporate Strategy VIII: Franchising. Franchising companies are more prevalent in the hospitality industry than non-franchising companies. Holiday Inn, Radisson, and Choice Hotels International are examples of lodging firms that are large franchisers. McDonald's, Burger King, Wendy's, Dunkin' Donuts, and Arby's are leading franchisers in the fast-food area. Today it is possible to purchase a franchise for virtually everything from a travel agency to a destination resort.

Corporate Strategy IX: Brand Collection. During the late 1980s and the 1990s "brand collectors" emerged. These were companies primarily driven by investors who took advantage of the relatively low prices needed to acquire chains or brands that had growth potential through global franchising. Companies such as Cendant (owner of the Howard Johnson, Ramada, and Days Inn brands) and Choice Hotels International (owner of Quality Inns, Comfort Inns, and Comfort Suites brands), Hilton, with Hilton, Embassy Suites, Doubletree, etc., and Starwood with Westin, Sheraton, W Hotels, etc. are now among the largest in the industry.

Corporate Strategy X: Management Contract Companies. Another byproduct of the lodging industry sort-out of the late 1980s and early 1990s was the growth of large **management contract** companies. These are firms that specialize in managing hotels and motels for owners such as banks, insurance companies, trusts, pension funds, partnerships, or individuals. Today, there are mega-management companies such as the one formed by the recent merger of Meristar and Interstate (now Interstate in name), the chains that manage properties, and hundreds of smaller management companies.

Corporate Strategy XI: Vertical and Horizontal Integration. Vertical and horizontal integration are corporate strategies that involve a hospitality company in more than one component of the hospitality business. One example is the Carlson Company and its subsidiaries. Carlson is the parent of the Radisson hotel chain, and its line of hospitality products includes the world's second largest travel agency group, a cruise ship company, and a restaurant company, among others. Unlike the period before 1980, when integration in the hospitality industry meant a firm owned hotels and restaurants or an airline and a hotel chain, deregulation has provided hospitality companies the opportunity to gain competitive edges by owning or investing in multiple components of the industry.

Corporate Strategy XII: Singleness. Some hospitality firms have chosen to develop just one product or service, forgoing product segmentation, tiering, and vertical and horizontal integration strategies. Four Seasons, for example, has opted for a single product of all first-class hotels with ownership and management control. La Quinta is following this strategy at the value-priced segment.

Corporate Strategy XIII: Value-Related Products and Services. Residence Inns and Embassy Suites exemplify lodging concepts developed to respond to specific value and psychographic trends among consumers. As the sophistication of the consumer continues to develop and is expressed in new product and service demands and desires, corporations will identify and satisfy these demands and desires with appropriate and timely strategies. Other examples of value-related products and services include the variety of credit cards and credit services, such as gold cards and platinum cards; the variety of air travel options, such as all-first-class fares and budget fares; and new airline brands.

Corporate Strategy XIV: Global Positioning. The oceans, political ideologies, and other traditional trade barriers no longer seem insurmountable hurdles for the hospitality industry. Six Continents, Carlson, Marriott, Cendant, Accor, Choice Hotels International, and others have products throughout the world. The signs of fast-food chains can be seen in most international cities and airports. As the brands originating in the United States expanded globally, foreign brands also entered the market—Meridian, Trusthouse Forte, Nikko, and others. Investment reasons, risk levels, growth strategies, and reasons for expansion all vary by corporation and by market. These are influenced by many different social, economic, and political trends and events. These corporations' perspectives are as varied as the products, services, and markets they serve.

Corporate Strategy Implications. The once relatively simple family-driven businesses and single-branded lodging concepts that made up the hospitality industry in the first two-thirds of the twentieth century have given way to much more complex business concepts and multiple branding. Some businesses with family origins grew enormously, such as Marriott, while others were acquired or merged, such as Stouffer (whose hotels and resorts now bear the Renaissance brand). The global ownership of physical assets, brand switching, short-term management contracts, changes of ownership, brand collection, global brand expansion through franchising and joint ventures, and vertically integrated travel and hospitality companies are all changing the dynamics of the industry and accelerating its pace of change.

To the consumer, the hospitality industry gets more confusing, as his or her favorite hotel switches brands, changes management, or is replaced with a new concept or product. To the marketing professional, it's more challenging to bring in new customers and retain existing customers because of internally driven industry dynamics. But there is yet more challenge for today's hospitality marketers, in the form of new externally driven forces or trends to which marketers must respond. Let's briefly look at some of the key strategic trends that will impact the hospitality industry in the future and the marketing implications of these trends.

Strategic Assessment

Earlier in the chapter we listed a number of key internal and external forces that shaped the hospitality industry and influenced marketing during the twentieth century. As we look to the future, there are forces that are likely to have a significant impact on both the industry and the marketing of it in the twenty-first century. They are:

- Globalization.

- Technology.

- Competency.

- Behavioral pendulums.

- Consolidation.

- Vertical and horizontal integration.

- Branding.

There are many other important marketing forces to assess in the years ahead, such as global distribution systems, networks, communications media, and emerging market segments. However, the forces just listed appear to be the major trends, or **megatrends,** right now. But the hospitality industry currently is one of the most dynamic industries on earth and we're in a period of rapid change. In other words, a new megatrend could develop at any time.

Globalization. The marketplace is becoming increasingly more global. As business investment and business and related travel flow across every region of the globe, multinational and cultural positioning will be essential to attracting market share in the hospitality industry. Linkages and networks to major origin markets—the geographical areas where large numbers of travelers come from—will be necessary for a hospitality company to remain competitive in the world marketplace. As new businesses and business investment flow to new regions, leisure travel will also develop in these regions. Economic growth in Asia, the Pacific Basin, Latin America, and China will provide impetus to a more diverse travel market. Understanding these regions and knowing how to market on a multinational and culturally diverse basis will be essential for marketing success.

Technology. Integrating the latest technologies into a company's business practices is an all-encompassing survival strategy. Marketing as well as operations must keep pace with technological developments to not only remain competitive, but—more importantly—to meet the changing needs of consumers. New technologies that reduce costs and provide consumer conveniences should receive the highest priority. Implementing these technologies will allow marketing to attract consumers and gain market share. In addition, as globalization accelerates, being "plugged in" to the right global distribution systems will be a competitive advantage. Providing the technologically "latest" in guest conveniences, security, and safety will be key marketing advantages as well. The implications and stakes are immense in the technological area. Technology that facilitates the purchase process, and having the technology customers desire in guest amenities and services, are not just operational niceties but marketing necessities in the twenty-first century.

Competency. Finding, attracting, and retaining competent employees may turn out to be one of the greatest challenges of this decade. The service industry will be especially challenged as new employees seek higher paying industries, and many others find that they are not prepared to work in a global multicultural environment. The need for multi-lingual staff is accelerating, as is the need for competent hourly wage staff. The decline of service (and related impact on sales) is directly related to the competency levels, training, and attitudes of all guest/customer contact personnel.

Behavioral Pendulums. The prolonged recession of the late 1980s, economic uncertainties of the early 1990s, and terrorism of the 2000s, forced career changes, and new ways of doing business—combined with the resultant human psychological consequences of stress—have caused deep behavioral changes in consumers that are likely to remain, not only in North America, but wherever in the world economic or political turmoil occurs. Unless we enter into a new age of global wealth, the overriding concept of "value" will remain with us throughout our marketing lives. Value in good economic times will weigh more heavily toward quality; in times of economic uncertainty, value will be price-oriented. For marketers, the key will be knowing when and where to change the marketing message to be in line with the direction of as many behavioral pendulums across the globe as possible.

One common denominator is the need for speed and convenience. More and more travelers are stressed out and time constrained. In fact, it has been said that timely service and convenience are now the redefining aspect of "value." Value now equals quality at a fair price, but moreover, timely service and ease/convenience of purchase transaction. This new ingredient also needs to be a focal point for marketing and operations.

Consolidation. Whether through mergers and acquisitions or through affiliations and agreements, consolidating with other companies may prove essential for a hospitality company's survival. Establishing a marketing relationship with the components of the industry that can help you either distribute your product/service or provide you with brand presence will be a necessity. The big are likely to get bigger and the specialized likely to get better. Whether a company is big or specialized, it will rely more on its booking sources (suppliers of customers—e.g., travel agents) and preferred consumers (key corporate accounts). The farther you reach, the more likely you will be able to attract market share from the growing international feeder markets—those economically emerging areas that are now beginning to generate more travelers. The bottom line is that "critical mass" in both product and promotions will be advantageous—that is, the larger you are the more marketing clout you will have in the marketplace.

Vertical and Horizontal Integration. Vertical and horizontal integration has taken on a new meaning in the twenty-first century. Marketing survival is now more closely connected to agreements, coalitions, mergers, joint ventures, acquisitions, and expanded distribution channels. This is all driven not just by economies of scale, but, more importantly, by the consumer's expectations of "single-source conveniences." Consumers will prefer one-stop shopping or one-call or one on-line service to handle all of their air, hotel, and car rental arrangements, rather than making three separate trips or calls. Survival will necessitate developing the right affiliations with other suppliers within the travel industry, stretching marketing expenditures through extensive co-ops (joint marketing or service offerings with travel partners, such as an American Airlines/Hyatt Resorts package offer), and building other affiliations that extend your brand presence and build customer loyalty.

Branding. Branding has become and will continue to be increasingly important as consumers seek to sort through the plethora of new market entrants around the globe. Brands that are clearly identified, have a distinct positioning, and are consistent in multiple global markets will emerge as the winners. Developing a global brand image with universal appeal will be another key to successful marketing.

The New Paradigm

Under the new paradigm, marketing takes on new meaning. Under the new paradigm, "urgency" or "critical" are replaced with "immediacy" and "act now." Customers will expect immediate action. Loyalty is replaced with "you've got one chance to keep me as a customer." Brand loyalty will be won by performance—this time and every time. Competitiveness now means providing what is most convenient and best for the customer. Today, marketers must be proactive and react immediately to survive. Fundamental change must occur on demand. Understanding multifunctional marketing tools and selecting the correct ones will be critical to winning. There will be little room for mistakes and defects, and few second chances. Individual marketing superstars will be replaced by all-star teams (and teamwork) whose focus will shift from being "just good enough to win" to "continually improving so as to never lose." Most important of all, the ability to change, to adapt to the new, and to understand the diverse will form the basis for success.

Key Terms

franchising—The method of growing a brand through selling the rights to use the brand name and related services.

management contract—A contract to provide management for a hotel, motel, or other facility for which fees are paid to the management company.

megatrend—A massive qualitative or quantitative trend that has a substantial impact on an enterprise or society.

product branding—Labeling a product with a name by which it is marketed and identified, such as Embassy Suites or Residence Inns.

product hybrid—A variation on a base product, such as a high-rise inn or motel.

product tiering—A variation in degree of a company's product quality or level of services, such as Ramada Inn, Ramada Hotel, and Ramada Renaissance Hotel.

vertical and horizontal integration—The interrelationship between two or more hospitality industry products or services performed or offered by the same firm.

Bibliography

Abbey, James R., and Milton T. Astroff. *Convention Sales and Service*. Dubuque, Iowa: Wm. C. Brown Co., 1983.

American Hotel & Motel Association and School of Hotel, Restaurant, and Institutional Management. *Commercial Lodging Market, Phase Two*. East Lansing, Mich.: Michigan State University, 1968.

Arnold, David. *The Handbook of Brand Management*. Reading, Mass.: Addison-Wesley, 1992.

Aronin, Robert A. "U.S. Travel Industry." Unpublished Manuscript, 1976.

Berrigan, John, and Carl Finkbeiner. *Segmentation Marketing: New Methods for Capturing Business Markets*. New York: HarperBusiness, 1992.

Berry, Leonard L., and A. Parasuraman. *Marketing Services: Competing Through Quality*. New York: Free Press, 1991.

Bogart, Leo. *Strategy in Advertising*. New York: Harcourt, Brace and World, 1967.

Boyd, Harper, William and Massy. *Marketing Management*. New York: Harcourt Brace Jovanovich, 1972.

Chase, Cochrane, and Kenneth L. Barasch. *Marketing Problem Solver*. Radnor, Pa.: Chilton Book Company, 1977.

Clancy, Kevin J., and Robert S. Shulman. *The Marketing Revolution: A Radical Manifesto for Dominating the Marketplace*. New York: HarperBusiness, 1991.

Coffman, C. DeWitt. *Hospitality for Sale*. East Lansing, Mich.: Educational Institute of the American Hotel & Motel Association, 1980.

Drucker, Peter. *Management—Tasks, Responsibilities, Practices*. New York: Heineman, 1974.

Feig, Barry. *The New Products Workshop: Hands-On Tools for Developing Winners*. New York: McGraw-Hill, 1993.

Hayden, Catherine. *The Handbook of Strategic Expertise*. New York: Free Press, 1986.

Holloway, Robert, and Robert Hancock, eds. *The Environment of Marketing Behavior*, 2nd ed. New York: John Wiley and Sons, 1969.

Kotler, Philip. *Marketing Management*. Englewood Cliffs, N.J.: Prentice Hall, 1972.

Lele, Miland M. *Creating Strategic Leverage*. New York: Wiley, 1992.

Levitt, Theodore. *The Marketing Imagination*. New York: Free Press, 1986.

Linneman, Robert E., and John L. Stanton, Jr. *Making Niche Marketing Work: How to Grow Bigger by Acting Smaller*. New York: McGraw-Hill, 1991.

Lodish, Leonard M. *The Advertising & Promotion Challenge: Vaguely Right or Precisely Wrong?* New York: Oxford, 1986.

Lundberg, Ronald E. *The Hotel and Restaurant Business*, 3d ed. Boston: CBI Publishing, 1979.

Magrath, Allan J. *The 6 Imperatives of Marketing: Lessons from the World's Best Companies*. New York: AMACOM, 1992.

McIntosh, Robert. *Tourism—Principles, Practices, Philosophies*. Columbus, Ohio: Grid, 1972.

McKay, Edward S. *The Marketing Mystique*, rev. ed. New York: AMACOM, 1993.

McNeill, Daniel, and Paul Freiberger. *Fuzzy Logic: The Discovery of a Revolutionary Computer Technology and How It Is Changing Our World*. New York: Simon & Schuster, 1993.

Michalko, Michael. Thinkertoys: *A Handbook of Business Creativity for the '90's.* Berkeley, Calif.: Ten Speed Press, 1991.

Myers, James H., and Edward Tauber. *Market Structure Analysis*. Chicago: American Marketing Association, 1977.

Nykiel, R. A. "Away from Home Eating Trends." Washington, D.C.: Marriott Corporation, 1973.

———. "Cruise Market Trends." Washington, D.C.: Marriott Corporation, 1974.

———. "Factors Influencing the Domestic and International Hotel Development Process." Paper and speech to the Business and Economics Graduate Program, Industrial College of Armed Forces, Washington, D.C., 1975.

———. "The Incentive Travel Market." Washington, D.C.: Marriott Corporation, 1972.

———. "The Japanese Travel Market—Outbound." Washington, D.C.: Marriott Corporation, 1973.

——— "Market Segmentation and its Applications to Sales and Advertising." Washington, D.C.: Marriott Corporation, 1973.

———. "Marketing Planning Process." Washington, D.C.: Marriott Corporation, 1973.

———. "The Next Thirty Years—A Study of Significant Quantitative and Qualitative Trends Affecting the Business Climate and Lifestyle in America." Washington, D.C.: Marriott Corporation, 1972, 1973.

———. "The Prospects for Future Growth in International Pleasure Travel." Washington, D.C.: Marriott Corporation, 1973.

——— "A Qualitative Study of the Domestic Lodging Market Needs by Segment." Washington, D.C.: Marriott Corporation, 1973.

———. "The Vacation Market's Preferences and Needs." Washington, D.C.: Marriott Corporation, 1973.

———. "Vertical and Horizontal Integration of the Travel Business." Washington, D.C.: Marriott Corporation, 1974.

Powers, Thomas F. "The Competitive Structure of the Hotel/Motel Market." A paper presented to the Council on Hotel, Restaurant and Institutional Education, 1969.

Rapp, Stan, and Tom Collines. *MaxiMarketing: The New Direction in Advertising, Promotion, and Marketing Strategy.* New York: New American Library, 1988.

Ray, Michael, and Rochelle Myers. *Creativity in Business*. Garden City, N.J.: Doubleday, 1986.

Reis, Al, and Jack Trout. *Marketing Warfare*. New York: McGraw Hill Book Co., 1986.

————. *Positioning: The Battle For Your Mind.* New York: McGraw Hill Book Co., 1981.

———— *The 22 Immutable Laws of Marketing: Violate Them at Your Own Risk!* New York: HarperBusiness, 1993.

Russell, Thomas, and Glenn Verrill. *Otto Kleppmer's Advertising Procedure.* Englewood Cliffs, N.J.: Prentice Hall.

Schwartz, Peter. *The Art of the Long View: Planning for the Future in an Uncertain World.* New York: Doubleday Currency, 1991.

Sherlock, Paul. *Rethinking Business-to-Business Marketing.* New York: Free Press, 1991.

Summer, J. R. *Improve Your Marketing Techniques: A Guide for Hotel Managers and Caterers.* London: Northwood Books, 1985.

U.S. Government Printing Office. *Directory of National Trade Associations of Businessmen.* Washington, D.C., 1980.

U.S. Travel Data Center. *The Importance of Tourism to the U.S. Economy.* Washington, D.C., 1975.

Vavra, Terry G. *Aftermarketing: How to Keep Customers for Life Through Relationship Marketing.* Homewood, Ill.: Business One Irwin, 1992.

Wahab, S., L. J. Crampon, and L. M. Rothfield. *Tourism Marketing.* London: Tourism International Press, 1976.

Willett, George. *A Whack on the Side of the Head: How You Can Be More Creative.* New York: Warner, 1990.

Wilson, Aubrey. *New Directions in Marketing: Business-to-Business Strategies for the 1990's.* Lincolnwood, Ill.: NTC Business Books, 1992.

Index

clubs, 27, 35, 39
department, 25
distribution systems, 33
intermediaries, 25, 33, 39
management, 6, 26
management companies,
26, 34
packages, 27, 39, 191
purchasing systems, 313,
314
Travel Agent, 151
Travel Industry Association of
America, 41
Travel Management Daily, 151
Travel Master, 151
Travel Trade, 151
Travel Weekly, 151
TravelAge East, 151
TravelAge Mid-America, 151
TravelAge Southeast, 151
TravelAge West, 151
Travelers without children, 25
Travelocity, 27, 37
Trend research, 55
Trends in the Hotel Industry,
151
Types of promotions
build, 159, 161
cooperative, 163
ego/recognition, 160
events, 163
introductory, 159, 161
giveaway/sweepstakes,
159, 162
price, 159
refunds/rebates, 161

share, 159
tie-ins, 161, 163
trade allowances, 163
trial, 159

U-V

U. S. Airways, 36
U.S. Census Bureau, 12, 14–15
U.S. flagged carriers, 38
U.S. News, 258
Uniqueness, 260
United Airlines, 6, 36, 43
United Airlines' Mileage Plus,
168
United Airlines' Red Carpet
Club, 213
United Nations, 42
"Up-front signals," 257
USA TODAY, 134
VALS, 17
Value, 7, 19, 165, 170, 198, 236,
324
Variable rates/pricing, 247
Vertical and horizontal
integration, 323, 325
Virtually There, 37
VIP
clubs, 134, 213, 283
needs, 86
reservation request form,
72, 81
Visibility, 204

W

Wall Street Journal, 134, 255
Wal-Mart, 28
Walt Disney World, 194, 196
Weather Channel, 134
Web site, 184, 186, 187
Weekend packages, 194
Wendy's, 18, 28, 318–319, 321
Westin, 133, 321
Westron, 311
Wholesalers, 283
Wholesaling a package, 192
Wilson, Kemmons, 4, 317
"Wizard of Avis,"
World Convention Dates, 151
Worldspan, 36–38
World Tourism Organization,
41–42
Worldwide Lodging Industry,
151
Wyndham Hotels & Resorts,
158

Y-Z

Yankelovich, Clancy, and
Shulman, 17
Yields, 290
Yield management, 246–247
Zero-base
approach, 46
budgeting, 45, 263, 281, 292
method, 263
Zip codes, 14–15
Zone, 11